Forschungen zum Alten Testament
2. Reihe

Edited by

Bernd Janowski (Tübingen) · Mark S. Smith (New York)
Hermann Spieckermann (Göttingen)

31

Fredrik Hägglund

Isaiah 53 in the Light of Homecoming after Exile

Mohr Siebeck

Fredrik Hägglund, born 1967; 1995 ordained in the church of Sweden; 2003–2007 doctoral student at the University of Lund; currently priest in the church of Sweden in Borås Caroli.

ISBN 978-3-16-149773-5
ISSN 1611-4914 (Forschungen zum Alten Testament, 2. Reihe)

The Deutsche Nationalbibliothek lists this publication in the Deutsche Nationalbibliographie; detailed bibliographic data is available in the Internet at *http://dnb.d-nb.de*.

The book was printed by Laupp & Göbel in Nehren on non-aging paper and bound by Buchbinderei Nädele in Nehren.

Printed in Germany.

Preface

Finally to leave this manuscript for printing is filled with both joy and anguish. Now it is no longer possible to make any more adjustments to the text. The book is finished and it is now up to any reader to embrace it or exclude it. However, the struggle to understand Isa 53 will never be finished. Every Eastertide and particularly on Good Friday, a new endeavour begins to understand the poem in the light of the suffering of Jesus. That is however another issue. This thesis is an attempt to understand the historical aim of Isa 53. It is only an attempt, and the questions will probably be even more numerous at the end of the work than they were at the beginning. I am grateful that I have received the financial support to enable me to undertake this adventure and to have had the opportunity to struggle with Isa 53.

I am not only grateful for the financial support, but also for all the support from the people around me, which has been equally important. First, I would like to express my gratitude to my supervisor Professor Fredrik Lindström, and to my assistant supervisor Professor Kirsten Nielsen. With their knowledge and interest in my project, they have been excellent advisors and interlocutors.

My sincere thanks goes also to the members of Old and New Testament seminars at Lund, as well as to the members of OTSEM (A Nordic-German network for Old Testament studies; Epistemologies and Methods). Friends there have given much inspiration and response on parts of my thesis. I am especially grateful to Dr. Göran Eidevall for reading the whole manuscript and for giving me many valuable suggestions, which have improved the outcome of this study.

When the analytical part had been completed, the toughest part began: to produce a readable book. I am obliged to all those who have helped me to improve my manuscript, especially to Kristofer Wollein Waldetoft, Elisabeth Jönsson, and Gerd Swensson. I am also grateful to the editors of the series Forschungen zum Alten Testament, Prof. Dr. Mark S. Smith, Prof. Dr. Bernd Janowski and Prof. Dr. Hermann Spieckermann, for accepting this work for publication. Needless to say, I am responsible for any remaining errors or oddities. My final and deepest gratitude goes to my family, to my wife and to our two children.

Borås 2008
Fredrik Hägglund

Contents

Part One

Introduction

Chapter 1

What is the Aim of This Study?

When I first started my undergraduate study of the Old Testament, I was provoked by the fact that there are so many unsolved puzzles in one of the Old Testament texts, which is most important for the understanding of the New Testament, Isa 53.[1] In order better to understand the problems in the text, I wrote my first minor paper on the subject of a collective or an individual interpretation of Isa 53. While doing so, I encountered the work of Whybray, in which he questions the central issue of the vicarious suffering of the servant.[2] First I thought Whybray was entirely wrong. However, when I reread his study I realised that whether or not the suffering of the servant has the quality of atonement or not, it can actually be questioned. Whybray's work can at least not be as easily dismissed as is sometimes the case.[3]

While working on my first paper on Isa 53, I also discovered that the scholarly discussion of the text is, to quite a significant extent, dominated by the more technical issues: Who is the servant?, How can we translate the difficult language in the text?, and so forth. This focus is natural. The text is complex and translation is the first complicated task of every study thereof. Furthermore, the anonymity of the servant makes us wonder who it is that the text describes. In addition, there are many other issues. Since Duhm, for example, we must also discuss the relationship between the servant songs and the rest of Isa 40–55.[4] Such questions are evoked by the

[1] I will use Isa 53 to signify the whole section Isa 52:13–53:12.

[2] Roger Norman Whybray, *Thanksgiving for a Liberated Prophet: An Interpretation of Isaiah Chapter 53* (JSOTsup vol. 4; Sheffield: JSOT Press, 1978).

[3] See for example the work of John Day, *Yahweh and the Gods and Goddesses of Canaan* (JSOTSup vol. 265; Sheffield: Sheffield Academic Press, 2000), 125. He dismisses Whybray's attempt to question a vicarious suffering in Isa 53 by stating that Whybray has no explanation of the use of the word אשׁם other than to suggest that the text is corrupt. Likewise Bernd Janowski, *Stellvertretung: Alttestamentliche Studien zu einem theologischen Grundbegriff* (SBS vol. 165; Stuttgart: Katholisches Bibelwerk, 1997), 77–78, who studies a similar problem, only refers to and dismisses the work in one footnote. However, the work of Whybray is more important than such treatments indicate.

[4] Bernhard Duhm, *Das Buch Jesaja* (Göttingen: 1922). His theory is forcefully questioned by Tryggve N. D. Mettinger, *A Farewell to the Servant Songs: A Critical Examination of an Exegetical Axiom* (Scripta minora Regiae Societatis humaniorum litterarum Lundensis vol. 3; Lund: Liber/Gleerup, 1983).

text and must be addressed in this study as well. Still, if all the technical issues are allowed to overshadow the aim of the text, we have a real problem.

The main question in this study is therefore: What problem does Isa 53 address and seek to answer? I ask this as a historical question and it is the historical aim of the text that I will search for. There are however many other issues that follow from this basic question, which also have to be attended to. These involve the questions raised above. I also have to ask: Who is addressed by the text? What is the problem or the conflict behind the text? and so forth.

My hypothesis is that the text gives an answer to why the return did not become as glorious as it is described in Isa 40–52. I claim that Isa 53 should be understood from its literary context, first in Isa 52:7–54:17, secondly in Isa 40–55 and thirdly from the horizon of other important parts of the entire book of Isaiah. I also argue that when we read Isa 52:7–54:17 as a unit, it shows a sequence of events. The whole section gives an image of the glorious return (Isa 52:7–12), the astonishment of the kings and the nations (Isa 52:13–15), the embrace of the suffering of those who return as suffering on behalf of the "we" (Isa 53:1–10), and this finally leads to joy for Zion, who has hitherto been barren (Isa 54:1–17). Moreover, the section in Isa 52:7–54:17 functions as a bridge between the glorious return described in Isa 40:1–52:10 and the less glorious reality recorded in Isa 55–66. As a result, I understand the problem behind Isa 53 as a conflict between the people in the land and those who return from the exile. The conflict is based on a reluctance of the people at home to receive the returnees. The solution given in Isa 53 is that the people at home will embrace the suffering of the returnees as a suffering for their guilt. Had this occurred, the situation could have become as glorious as that described in Isa 54, and the mother, Zion, could have rejoiced. However, instead of the joy described in Isa 54, the reality is coloured by the conflicts described in Isa 56–66.

1. The Structure of This Study

The main theme of this study deals with the historical aim of Isa 53. The focus will therefore be on central historical matters of the text, but, before I begin working with the text itself, there are two introductory issues that must be discussed. In chapter two I will discuss some aspects of the methods employed in the present work, and in chapter three I will establish the use of terms about *exclusion* and *embrace* used in this study. This is especially important because Isa 53 is a text of significance for the Christian understanding of the vicarious and atoning suffering of Jesus, and most of the terms used in this study have a range of interpretations in Christian theology. The great and varied symbolic universe associated with terms such as atonement, expiation, reconciliation, vicarious suffering, and so on makes it particularly important to establish the use of these terms in the present investigation. There is also a historical issue that will be discussed in the introduction. In chapter four I will establish my understanding of the identities of the servant and of the "we". The identity of the servant is one of the singularly most discussed exegetical questions in the Old Testament. Despite, or maybe because of, this there is no consensus among scholars, and the arguments in favour of most interpretations are brilliant. This leads to despair about the possibility of finding a final answer to this question. Still, the problem must be addressed, and the conclusion reached in this study is not a new attempt to solve an old problem. Although I argue for a collective interpretation, it is not a total farewell to individual interpretations of the servant songs. I do not rule out the possibility that some of the songs have been open to other interpretations before they were incorporated in this book. I will argue that the image of the suffering servant describes the people in exile who, in Isa 40:1–52:12 had been expected to return, and the "we" are the people in the land who encounter those who return.

When I have established these fundamental issues, I will turn to part two, *Exclusion and Embrace*. The heading is intended to capture the central issue in Isa 53, i.e. both the former and the present understanding of the suffering servant held by the "we". In this section I will first establish the text and the translation of Isa 53 that I will use in this study, and then I will discuss the structure and the form of the text. These topics, which will be further discussed in chapters five and six, are import in order to determine the central issues of the text.

The servant's suffering is a major concern in Isa 53. The encounter with the work of Whybray has made me realise that the meaning of the suffering of the servant must be further defined. Chapter seven is an attempt to establish what notions of exclusion and embrace are expressed in Isa 53. The analysis of Isa 53 shows that it is doubtful that Isa 53 really does illustrate an atoning suffering.[5] In chapter eight I will examine the phrase נשא עון, "to carry iniquity". This is a phrase, which is important for the understanding of the suffering of the servant as an atoning suffering. Since, in the scholarly discussion, the servant's suffering has often been understood as atoning suffering, it is interesting to compare the language in Isa 53

[5] An atoning suffering is a traditional interpretation of Isa 53. Cf. for example Josef Scharbert, *Heilsmittler im Alten Testament und im alten Orient* (QD vol. 23/24; Freiburg im Breisgau: Herder, 1964), 205–212, 296.

with expressions employed in other Old Testament texts that describe atonement, and particularly texts in which atonement is reached through the actions or the suffering of other persons. In chapter nine, I will therefore analyse expressions of exclusion and embrace that are *not* used in Isa 53. I believe that this can also say something about the words and expressions that are used in Isa 53. In chapter ten I turn to the context of Isa 53 in the rest of Isa 40–55. Since the present study questions the understanding of the servant's suffering as an atoning suffering, it is also interesting to examine the rest of Isa 40–55 in order to establish what is said about reconciliation and atonement here. My point is that it is more likely that atonement should be a central issue in Isa 53 if the removal of guilt is a problem in the rest of Isa 40–55 as well. In the second part I will try to show that a central issue in Isa 53 is the "we" group's embrace of the servant's suffering as a suffering caused by their guilt. I believe that this is a more important issue in Isa 53 than the issue of atonement.

In part three, *The Contexts*, I try to show why such an embrace of the suffering of the servant is a central issue. It is in this part that I will try to answer my main question: What problem does Isa 53 address and seek to answer? In order to do this I will analyse three major contexts for Isa 53. First, there is the literary context, both in the book of Isaiah as a whole and especially in Isa 40–55, which I will address in chapter eleven. Closely connected to the literary contexts is the dating of the text, which will also be discussed in this chapter. The second major context is the geographical domicile and the question of which group is addressed by the text, which I will consider in chapter twelve. I will argue that it is the people at home, who are addressed by Isa 53, as well as by significant parts of the rest of Isa 40–55. The third context concerns the social conditions, to which I will turn in chapter thirteen. Here the relationship between those who return and the people at home is of significant interest. The hypothesis advocated in this study is that the problem behind the text is the conflicts between the people in the land and the ones who return from exile. It is therefore essential to explore such conflicts and their impact on texts of the Old Testament. The conflict is examined through modern refugee studies as well as through analyses of texts from various parts of the Old Testament, and finally the conflict reported in Isa 40–55 and 56–66 will be studied.

Finally part four, *Conclusion*, brings the analytical parts of this study to an end and moulds them into a synthesis of the interpretation of the aim of Isa 53.

Chapter 2

Methods and Definitions

As already stated, the main theme of this thesis is a historical question. The methods employed are mainly the historical-critical methods. However, the use of these methods must be defended, since scholars have questioned whether or not it is appropriate to apply these methods to Isa 53, partly because the text is not a carrier of information. This means that it is impossible to talk about the meaning of the text, since the text has multiple meanings.[1] Furthermore, Melugin questions the use of historical-critical methods by arguing that the language of Isa 53 is: "too cryptic to allow for a univocal understanding of textual meaning".[2] I agree that the text of Isa 53 carries multiple meanings, but that is also the case of any simple text of information.[3] Moreover, I fully agree that various methods can highlight important and new aspects of the text, but I also believe that all these methods depend at least to some extent on historical-critical analysis.

The criticism levelled against the traditional methods is important. The historical-critical approach has its limits, both because of the questions asked and the limited possibilities to find any answers, but I do not think that historical-critical methods necessarily stand in total opposition to more literary methods or to any other methods. A text does not only refer to something. It also creates a world, into which the reader is invited to enter.[4] On the other hand, a text is also interpreted by means of its historical background, or rather, by our images of the historical background. Our knowledge of the traditions, conflicts, and not least of the language colours our understanding of every text. The aim of this study is to paint a picture

[1] E.g. David J. A. Clines, *I, He, We and They: A Literary Approach to Isaiah 53* (JSOTSup vol. 1; Sheffield: JSOT Press, 1976), 59–65.

[2] Roy F. Melugin, "On Reading Isaiah 53 as Christina Scripture," in *Jesus and the Suffering Servant: Isaiah 53 and Christian Origins* (ed. William R. Farmer and William H. Bellinger; Harrisburg, Pa.: Trinity Press, 1998), 57.

[3] See Terry Eagleton, *Literary Theory: An Introduction* (Oxford: Blackwell, 1996), 8, for an example to indicate that not even a simple statement is as unambiguous as it might seem at first sight.

[4] Melugin, "On Reading Isaiah 53," 57. Cf. also Paul Ricoeur, *The Rule of Metaphor: The Creation of Meaning in Language* (Routledge Classics London: Routledge, 2003), 377.

of a possible historical background to Isa 53, and to interpret the text against this background. I do not imply that it is the single meaning of the text that will be expressed. Furthermore, it is not only the literary theories that make us aware of the multiple meanings. The redaction-historical approach, which is one of the traditional historical-critical approaches, has also showed how a text can be reused and reinterpreted by rather limited means.[5] These multiple meanings are, however, at another level compared to more modern literary theories. My aim is to answer a historical question. I will use the methods that I find most useful in each part of the study, which means that I will use different methods in the different parts of the thesis, and I will not be restricted to traditional historical-critical methods only.

In the second part I will begin the analysis of the text by mainly applying the tradition-historical approach in order to determine the patterns of thought, which are presupposed by, and incorporated into, the text.[6] The pattern of thought is, however, not a fixed pattern. Metaphorical studies have revealed an openness of the imagery to reinterpretation and reuse. I believe that the traditions have been kept in memory because they can be applied to different situations and still remain meaningful.[7] This is particularly true of Isa 40–55, where we find a fresh reuse of old traditions in a new situation. Unfortunately, form-criticism, which has been very helpful and important for the study of the rest of Isa 40–55, has been of limited value for the study of Isa 53.[8] This is a unique text, which makes it almost impossible to determine its exact form. Even so, I will discuss briefly the character of the text and the forms that have probably influenced Isa 53. This second part could almost be described as a close reading of the text, in both a limited meaning and with a special focus of the terminology. Such reading puts more emphasis on the particular than on the general details, since it pays close attention to individual words, syntax, and the order, in which sentences and ideas unfold to the reader.[9]

---

[5] On Isa 40–55, see among others the work of Reinhard Gregor Kratz, *Kyros im Deuterojesaja-Buch: Redaktionsgeschichtliche Untersuchungen zu Entstehung und Theologie von Jes 40-55* (FAT vol. 1; Tübingen: Mohr Siebeck, 1991). See Odil Hannes Steck, *Old Testament Exegesis: A Guide to the Methodology* (Resources for Biblical Study vol. 39; Atlanta, Ga.: Scholars Press, 1998), for a survey of the traditional historical-critical methods.

[6] See Steck, *Old Testament Exegesis,* 121–142, for a discussion of the method.

[7] Cf. Kirsten Nielsen, "'From Oracles to Canon' – and the Role of Metaphor," *SJOT* 17, no. 1 (2003): 22–33.

[8] There have been many suggestions about the form of Isa 53. I still believe that Roy F. Melugin, *The Formation of Isaiah 40–55* (BZAW vol. 141; Berlin: de Gruyter, 1976), 74, is probably right in suggesting that the structure, as far as we can know, is a new creation.

[9] See further Eagleton, *Literary Theory,* 37–38.

The third part is dominated by an attempt to place the text in its historical settings. The first setting is the texts with which Isa 53 interacts. Therefore the relationship between Isa 53 and the rest of the book of Isaiah will be discussed. During the last decades, there has been a significant discussion about the growth of both Isa 40–55 and of the whole book of Isaiah.[10] The works in this field are helpful, both by separating texts and by bringing them together. However, the identification of literary disunity is a rather uncertain enterprise, since we do not have many witnesses to the growth of the text. Whenever literary disunity is detected, the next uncertain venture is to order the texts chronologically, both in relation to one another and to known historical facts. Both these steps are somewhat speculative, which makes the results even more uncertain. Therefore, it is not surprising that it is hard to find any consensus regarding the details among scholars. On the other hand, the book of Isaiah has grown over several centuries. Since I am searching for a historical interpretation, the dates of the various texts are import. Nevertheless, and because of the ambiguity involved, I will mainly rely on work that has already been done in this field and I will build on the conclusions of previous scholars.[11] This is however not as simple as it sounds. Because of the lack of consensus regarding the details, and the risk of dating texts in accordance with my interpretation, I will seek to avoid any dating of details as far as possible and I will focus instead on the broader patterns. Regarding the relationship between Isa 53 and Isa 1-39, I will mainly focus on some metaphors that are important in both parts. By using specific images, Isa 53 recalls preceding texts, images, and experiences and also reinterprets these images in a new situation.

The historical setting is the next important question. I will search for both the geographical location of the text and for the social conflicts that might have coloured the historical setting and the texts themselves. In this part, I will use some works that study contemporary experiences, especially refugee studies in order to determine further the historical realities related to Isa 53. The intention is to gain greater insight from the experiences of people in similar situations. Hopefully, these experiences can help

---

[10] Klaus Kiesow, *Exodustexte im Jesajabuch: Literarkritische und motivgeschichtliche Analysen* (OBO vol. 24; Fribourg Suisse; Gottingen: Editions Universitaires; Vandenhoeck & Ruprecht, 1979), Kratz, *Kyros im Deuterojesaja-Buch*, Jürgen van Oorschot, , *Von Babel zum Zion: Eine literarkritische und redaktionsgeschichtliche Untersuchung* (BZAW vol. 206; Berlin: de Gruyter, 1993), Hugh Godfrey Maturin Williamson, *The Book Called Isaiah: Deutero-Isaiah's Role in Composition and Redaction* (Oxford: Clarendon Press, 1994), and Zoltán Kustár, *"Durch seine Wunden sind wir geheilt": Eine Untersuchung zur Metaphorik von Israels Krankheit und Heilung im Jesajabuch* (BWANT vol. 154; Stuttgart: Kohlhammer, 2002), among others.

[11] The debate between synchronic and diachronic readings will be further addressed in the third part.

us to understand the historical situation that has coloured our text better. In my search for the geographical domicile, I will for example examine various stages that people in exile might go through and I will then relate these stages to Isa 40–55. In chapter thirteen, entitled *The Conflict*, I will use research on contemporary repatriation in order to understand which conflicts might have emerged between those who returned and those who had stayed at home. The lessons from these conflicts will then be used to seek to understand what possible conflicts might have coloured Isa 40–55 as well as other parts of the Old Testament.

I will mostly refer to the text of Isa 40–55, and not to an unnamed prophet or to any persons behind the text, since a considerable part of Isa 40–55 was already a literary entity at the time when Isa 53 was composed. I will also argue that Isa 53 was probably composed for its present context. Hence, I understand Isa 53 as a literary product that belongs in its present literary context, and I will neither rule out nor take into account any previous possible interpretations.[12] I use the term Deutero-Isaiah as a technical term for the person or the persons behind the text as well as for the meaning employed by various scholars when I refer to their works.

Unless otherwise stated, translations from the Old Testament follow the *New Revised Standard Version*. In a few cases when I propose a different understanding, I offer my own translation, which is then also indicated. I have generally replaced the NRSV term "the LORD" by YHWH. References to biblical passages follow the numbering of the BHS. The abbreviations listed in *The SBL Handbook of Style* have been used. The terms *suffering servant* and *servant song(s)* is used without initial capitals in order not to mix up the historical understanding of the servant described in Isa 53 with later meanings proposed by the New Testament and the church. The *servant song(s)* is used without initial capitals since the theory of Duhm is no longer tenable in its original form.[13] Both terms are however still important in the history of interpretation of Isa 40–55 and in some ways these four poems can be treated as a group.

---

[12] See further the discussion below.

[13] Duhm, *Das Buch Jesaja*, the question will be discussed further below.

Chapter 3

Terminology

There is an ongoing scholarly discussion about the meaning of the suffering of the servant. In order to discuss that subject we must first decide and define an appropriate terminology, which involves some important problems. One is that different languages have different terms by which to describe the relationships between the servant, the "we", the many, and God, in Isa 53. This becomes particularly clear when we compare English and German studies, which use different terms that lack exact synonyms in the other language. Another problem is the entire theological universe, which differs as it is connected to these various terms. It is therefore sometimes difficult to know what is intended when different scholars use a specific term. My interest in this chapter is to define a terminology that is suitable for a characterisation of the description of the servant's suffering. Before I attempt a definition, I will examine the terminology applied by two important and influential studies that seek to define the effect of the servant's suffering. I will do this in order to express the difficulties involved in the choice of any term and also to examine the differences between English and German terminology. Following this survey, I will turn to the terminology applied in this study.

1. Vicarious Suffering or *Stellvertretung*?

The two works, to which I will turn, seek to define the understanding of the suffering of the servant. Since one is in English and one in German, they also highlight the problems caused by the use of different languages. The works are: *Thanksgiving for a Liberated Prophet: An Interpretation of Isaiah Chapter 53* by Whybray and *Stellvertretung: Alttestamentliche Studien zu einem theologischen Grundbegriff* by Janowski. Here my main interest is in the terms used in theses studies and in the difficulties created by the choice of terms. I will also sum up their results regarding the servant's suffering. Their exegetical arguments will however be discussed in other places.

The first study was made by Whybray. His most important term is *vicarious suffering* and he argues that:

[T]he Servant cannot be said to be suffering, or to have suffered, *in place* of the exiles in such a way that they escape the consequences of their sins, since, [...] it cannot be said that these have escaped punishment: they are all actually suffering the consequences of defeat and banishment. The Servant, if, as is here maintained, he is one of them, shares their suffering. Chapter 53 indeed makes it clear that he has suffered more intensely than they, and the "we" who speak there confess that, at any rate compared with themselves, he is innocent; nevertheless this is shared and not vicarious suffering.[1]

The term vicarious suffering is to some extent ambiguous and there is a discussion about what Whybray means with this term. By referring to Whybray, and also to Orlinsky,[2] Hooker argues that:

What we have in Isaiah 53 is much better described as *representative suffering* rather than *vicarious suffering*: as *inclusive* place-taking rather than *exclusive* place-taking.[3]

According to Hooker, the point made by Orlinsky and Whybray is that the servant does not suffer instead of others, but alongside them. Furthermore, he does not suffer as their substitute, but as their representative.[4] The clarification is right to some extent, but it does still not fully recapitulate what is stated by Whybray. He argues, not only that the servant suffered alongside the "we" but he also states that "[W]hat is being repeated is not a statement about vicarious atonement."[5] This is where most scholars have problems about agreeing with Whybray.

To conclude, vicarious suffering is an English term frequently used to describe the suffering of the servant in Isa 53. This term can hold a range of meanings and it must be further defined: Is it inclusive or exclusive suffering? Is it a suffering that expiates guilt, or is it merely caused by someone else?

---

[1] Whybray, *Thanksgiving,* 30. Cf. Yehezkel Kaufmann, *History of the Religion of Israel: From the Babylonian Captivity to the End of Prophecy* (vol. 4; New York: Ktav Publ. house, 1977), 129–131, for a similar understanding of the suffering. He has, however, a different interpretation of the identity of the servant.

[2] Harry M. Orlinsky, "The So-Called Servant of the Lord and Suffering Servant in Second Isaiah," in *Studies on the Second Part of the Book of Isaiah* (ed. Harry M. Orlinsky and Norman H. Snaith; vol. *VTsup*; Leiden: Brill, 1967), 54, argues: "It is our contention that the concept of vicarious suffering and atonement is not to be found either here or anywhere else in the Bible; it is a concept that arose in Jewish and especially Christian circles of post-biblical time."

[3] Morna D. Hooker, "Did the Use of Isaiah 53 to Interpret His Mission Begin with Jesus?" in *Jesus and the Suffering Servant: Isaiah 53 and Christian Origins* (ed. William R. Farmer and William H. Bellinger; Harrisburg, Pa.: Trinity Press, 1998a), 98.

[4] Hooker, "Isaiah 53," 96.

[5] Whybray, *Thanksgiving,* 75.

In the German-speaking context, another path has been chosen, which derives from an extensive discussion in the field of systematic theology about the concept of *Stellvertretung*.[6] This is a useful concept when we seek to define various levels of human interdependence.[7] The discussion also indicates one of the great advantages of this concept, namely that it is closely connected to the specific place that we share with each other. The level and nature of *Stellvertretung* can either enlarge of diminish the place of our common life.

A significant part of the German-speaking discussion about *Stellvertretung* derives from a problem stated by Kant. He remarks that moral guilt is personal and not transferable. It can not be taken over by some other person.[8] This discussion has coloured research on Isa 53. Hence, we will now turn to the second study that seeks to evaluate the understanding of the servant's suffering in Isa 53, a study made by Janowski: *Stellvertretung: Alttestamentliche Studien zu einem theologischen Grundbegriff.*[9] For him also, the problem formulated by Kant is important when he seeks to define the meaning of the servant's suffering. Before Janowski interprets Isa 53, he defines the concept of *Stellvertretung.*[10] In his conclusion, the noetic dimension seems to be of special interest. Isa 53, as Janowski understands it, is about how Israel understands both her guilt and the annihilation of

---

[6] See Christof Gestrich, *Christentum und Stellvertretung: Religionsphilosophische Untersuchungen zum Heilsverständnis und zur Grundlegung der Theologie* (Tübingen: Mohr Siebeck, 2001), for a full view of the discussion.

[7] Svend Bjerg, *Stedfortrædelse: Om Judas og Jesus, Gud og mennesket* (Frederiksberg: Anis, 1991), 43–47, a systematic theologian, defines several different levels of *Stellvertretung*. He begins with the most basic form of representation; as in politics where a few represent the many. And he continues to the most highly esteemed form, in which reciprocity culminates, namely in love.

[8] Immanuel Kant, *Die Religion innerhalb der Grenzen der blossen Vernunft* (Philosophische Bibliothek, 545 Hamburg: Meiner, 2003). The problem is, however, older than Kant. Socianian-criticism is summarized in a similar way by Wolfhart Pannenberg, *Systematic Theology* (vol. 2; Edinburgh; Grand Rapids Mich.: T&T Clark; Eerdmans, 1994), 424. For the discussion see among others, Janowski, *Stellvertretung,* 17, Daniel P. Bailey, "Concepts of *Stellvertretung* in the Interpretation of Isaiah 53," in *Jesus and the Suffering Servant: Isaiah 53 and Christian Origins* (ed. William R. Farmer and William H. Bellinger; Harrisburg, Pa.: Trinity Press, 1998), 223–250, and Gestrich, *Christentum und Stellvertretung,* 9.

[9] Janowski, *Stellvertretung*. Cf. also his article, Bernd Janowski, "Er trug unsere Sünden: Jesaja 53 und die Dramatik der Stellvertretung," in *Der leidende Gottesknecht: Jesaja 53 und seine Wirkungsgeschichte: Mit einer Bibliographie zu Jes 53* (ed. Bernd Janowski and Peter Stuhlmacher; vol. *FAT*; Tübingen: Mohr Siebeck, 1996), 27–48, which is reprinted in English, Bernd Janowski, "He Bore Our Sins: Isaiah 53 and the Drama of Taking Another's place," in *The Suffering Servant: Isaiah 53 in Jewish and Christian sources* (ed. Peter Stuhlmacher and Bernd Janowski; Grand Rapids, Mich.: Eerdmans, 2004), 48–74.

[10] Janowski, *Stellvertretung,* 13–40.

guilt, so that she can be changed and delivered. The suffering is both substitutionary, i.e. something is achieved that the "we" could not achieve for themselves, and representative, i.e. the servant's suffering represents their faith and not his own.[11]

The concept of *Stellvertretung* is important and it has proved useful in the definition of various levels of human interdependence. However, it is more problematic to apply the term to Isa 53. First, because the concept of *Stellvertretung* is closely associated with the problem formulated by Kant, and Kant's distinction creates an important discussion, both in the field of the social science and in that of systematic theology. The dilemma formulated by Kant would also have to be recognised as a problem in Isa 53 before we could analyse the text from such a starting point, and it is very doubtful that such a dilemma is actually a problem in Isa 53. Another significant problem for me with this concept is that it has no exact correspondence in English terminology.

Stellvertretung and atonement, are somewhat ambiguous terms, just like expiation, reconciliation, vicarious suffering, representation, and substitution. They are all closely associated with the Christian tradition and have a long tradition of various theological explanations. Some of these terms are widely used and have a range of definition outside the Christian tradition as well. All the various pre-understandings and definitions that exist, depending on our different traditions, can create a problem when we use these terms in the examination of the sufferings of the servant in Isa 53. This is extra problematic, since the Christian understanding of the vicarious suffering of Jesus is closely connected to the suffering of the servant in Isa 53.[12] Still we have to use some of these terms and I will therefore define

---

[11] Janowski, "Er trug unsere Sünden," 36. Cf. also the critical examination made by Bailey, "Concepts of *Stellvertretung,*" 246–248.

[12] There is a significant scholarly discussion regarding the date when the work of Jesus was interpreted by the use of Isa 53. See for example the discussion between Otto Betz, "Jesus and Isaiah 53," in *Jesus and the Suffering Servant: Isaiah 53 and Christian Origins* (ed. William R. Farmer and William H. Bellinger; Harrisburg, Pa.: Trinity Press, 1998), 70–87, Hooker, "Isaiah 53," Morna D. Hooker, "Response to Mikeal Parsons," in *Jesus and the Suffering Servant: Isaiah 53 and Christian Origins* (ed. William R. Farmer and William H. Bellinger; Harrisburg, Pa.: Trinity Press, 1998b), 120–124, and Mikeal C. Parsons, "Isaiah 53 and Acts 8: A Reply to Professor Morna Hooker," in *Jesus and the Suffering Servant: Isaiah 53 and Christian Origins* (ed. William R. Farmer and William H. Bellinger; Harrisburg, Pa.: Trinity Press, 1998), 104–119. Hooker claims that she finds no convincing evidence to suggest that Isa 53 played any significant role in Jesus' own understanding of his ministry. Parsons, on the other hand, claims that Isa 53 is at least one of the texts, which Luke had in mind when he referred to Christ's suffering. See also Martin Hengel, *The Atonement. The Origins of the Doctrine in the New Testament* (London: SCM Press, 1981), 57–60, and Peter Stuhlmacher, "Isaiah 53 in the Gospels and Acts," in *The Suffering Servant: Isaiah 53 in Jewish and Christian Sources* (ed. Peter

the way in which they are used in this investigation. First I will turn to an alternative pair of terms, namely *exclusion* and *embrace*. These are also shaped by the Christian tradition, but I hope that they are less coloured by various Christian pre-understandings.

2. Exclusion and Embrace

Some years ago the systematic theologian Miroslav Volf presented a study entitled *Exclusion and Embrace: A Theological Exploration of Identity, Otherness, and Reconciliation*. In the preface he tells us about the background for his investigation:

> After I finished my lecture Professor Jürgen Moltmann stood up and asked one of his typical questions, both concrete and penetrating: "But can you embrace a *četnik*?" It was the winter of 1993. For months now the notorious Serbian fighters called "*četnik*" had been sowing desolation in my native country, herding people into concentration camps, raping women, burning down churches, and destroying cities. I had just argued that we ought to embrace our enemies as God has embraced us in Christ. Can I embrace a *četnic* – the ultimate other, so to speak, the evil other? What would justify the embrace? Where would I draw the strength for it? What would it do to my identity as a human being and as a Croat? It took me a while to answer, though I immediately knew what I wanted to say. "No, I cannot – but as a follower of Christ I think I should be able to." In a sense this book is the product of the struggle between the truth of my argument and the force of Moltmann's objection.[13]

This is a book with many implications for contemporary Christianity as well as for contemporary society. Those parts, however, go far beyond the

---

Stuhlmacher and Bernd Janowski; Grand Rapids, Mich.: Eerdmans, 2004), 147–162. Furthermore, there is a discussion about whether Mark 10:45 should be understood against the background of Isa 53 or of Isa 43:3. See for example Rikki E. Watts, "Jesus' Death, Isaiah 53, and Mark 10:45: A Crux Revisited," in *Jesus and the Suffering Servant: Isaiah 53 and Christian Origins* (ed. William R. Farmer and William H. Bellinger; Harrisburg, Pa.: Trinity Press, 1998), and Dieter Vieweger and Annette Böckler, "'Ich gebe Ägypten als Lösegeld für dich': Mk 10,45 und die Jüdische Tradition zu Jes 43b.4," *ZAW* 108 (1996): 494–607, for different opinions. Finally, there is a discussion of both pre-Christian and early Christian interpretations of Isa 53. Cf. Hans Walter Wolff, *Jesaja 53 im Urchristentum* (Berlin: Evangelische Verlagsanstalt, 1952), Martin Hengel, "The Effective History of Isaiah 53 in the Pre-Christian Period," in *The Suffering Servant: Isaiah 53 in Jewish and Christian Sources* (ed. Peter Stuhlmacher and Bernd Janowski; Grand Rapids, Mich.: Eerdmans, 2004), 75–146, and Christopher Markschies, "Jesus Christ as a Man before God: Two Interpretive Models for Isaiah 53 in the Patristic Literature and Theire Development," in *The Suffering Servant: Isaiah 53 in Jewish and Christian Sources* (ed. Peter Stuhlmacher and Bernd Janowski; Grand Rapids, Mich.: Eerdmans, 2004), 225–323.

[13] Miroslav Volf, *Exclusion and Embrace: A Theological Exploration of Identity, Otherness, and Reconciliation* (Nashville: Abingdon Press, 1996), 9.

aim of this study. I nevertheless consider the terms of exclusion and embrace useful for my investigation. Volf maintains that the most basic thought that embrace seeks to express is:

> [T]he will to give ourselves to others and "welcome" them, to readjust our identities to make space for them, is prior to any judgment about others, except that of identifying them in their humanity.[14]

Even if Volf uses these terms in a Christian context, they seem to be somewhat universal. Hopefully, they are not so deeply associated with a Christian context that they can not also be applied to an Old Testament text. Furthermore, in the story about Jacob we see both the fear of conflict and the agonies that are important components in the decision to return after exile.[15] In the same story we also see the embracing brother: "But Esau ran to meet him, and embraced him, and fell on his neck and kissed him, and they wept" (Gen 33:4). The fear of exclusion and the embrace in the Jacob story convinces me that this is a helpful image; at least when we are dealing with exile and homecoming, but probably also when we consider other human relationships and conflicts. I will now sum up the definition of the terms according to Volf, and at the next stage I will recapitulate the parts that can be used in the analysis of Isa 53.

Exclusion

It is not hard to see exclusion as clearly the opposite of embrace. According to Volf, the most powerful current metaphor for exclusion is ethnic cleansing.[16] He defines exclusion by expounding two interrelated aspects of the term. Exclusion is the opposite of *binding*, and also of *separation*. Both binding, or assimilation, and separation can be effective means by which to reduce the other.

With regard to separation, exclusion can entail cutting of the bonds that connect, removing oneself from the pattern of interdependence and placing oneself in a position of sovereign independence. The other then emerges either as an enemy, who must be pushed away from the self and driven out of his or her space, or as a nonentity – as a superfluous being – who can be disregarded and abandoned.

With regard to binding, exclusion can entail the erasure of separation, i.e. the failure to recognise the other as someone who in his or her other-

---

[14] Volf, *Exclusion and Embrace,* 29, his italics.

[15] The name Jacob, and probably also the story, is significant for Isa 40–55. See especially Isa 43:1–7 and 44:1–5. See further Meira Polliack, "Deutero-Isaiah's Typological use of Jacob in the Portrayal of Israel's National Renewal," in *Creation in Jewish and Christian Tradition* (ed. Henning Graf Reventlow and Yair Hoffman; vol. *JSOTsup*; London: Sheffield Academic Press, 2002), 72–110.

[16] Volf, *Exclusion and Embrace,* 67.

ness belongs to the pattern of interdependence. The other will then be assimilated by being made like the self or by being subjugated to the self.[17]

The sociologist Bauman forcefully describes one form of exclusion through separation. The others become like dust that has to be removed when they become:

> the gathering point for the risk and fears which accompany cognitive spacing. They epitomize the chaos which all social spacing aims staunchly yet vainly to replace with order, and the unreliability of the rules in which the hopes of replacement have been invested.[18]

Girard is another explorer of exclusion. He claims that human societies are held together by a powerful desire, known as the mimetic desire, which is also the source of the crises that threaten to destroy them. Harmony is re-established by finding a scapegoat, on which to focus the violence. Since it really works, it re-establishes the basis of society. The scapegoat is invested with sacred attributes and made into a cultic object while still retaining its status of sacrificial victim.[19] Girard has received criticism, not least because he finds this pattern in every, or almost every, subject that he investigates. Even so, Girard seems to have focused on an important drive in society, i.e. on its ability to create scapegoats.

We find the force of exclusion at work in the period of the exile as well as after the exile in the Old Testament. In Ezek 11:15 we meet the people in the land who exclude the exiles by concluding that they have gone far from YHWH. Hence, the land is given to those who remained at home:

> Mortal, your kinsfolk, your own kin, your fellow exiles, the whole house of Israel, all of them, are those of whom the inhabitants of Jerusalem have said, "They have gone far from YHWH; to us this land is given for a possession." (Ezek 11:15)

Smith-Christopher has studied universalism in the messages of Jonah and of Isaiah.[20] He argues that, through this universalism, the evil of the empire that rules the scene can be: "recognised, rejected, repented of and *then* dismissed." Smith-Christopher also argues that the objection to mixed marriages in Ezra and Nehemiah can be understood against this background of the need of the minorities to keep their identity. He argues that this is formed by a strong need to separate their own identity from those around

---

[17] Volf, *Exclusion and Embrace,* 67.

[18] Zygmunt Bauman, *Postmodern Ethics* (Oxford: Blackwell, 1993), 162.

[19] René Girard, *Things Hidden Since the Foundation of the World* (Stanford Calif.: Stanford University Press, 1987). See also a critical discussion of Girard's theory in Johan Asplund, *Rivaler och syndabockar* (Göteborg: Korpen, 1989), and Gianni Vattimo, *Belief* (Stanford, Calif.: Stanford University Press, 1999), 36–38.

[20] Daniel Smith-Christopher, *A Biblical Theology of Exile* (Overtures to Biblical Theology Minneapolis, Minn.: Fortress Press, 2002), 137–162.

them in order to protect their own unique identity.[21] If Smith-Christopher is right, these are also clear examples of exclusion in the Old Testament, both through assimilation and through separation.

Embrace

Now I will turn to the concept of embrace and consider in what way that can function as a term for, and an image of, reconciliation. Volf describes four structural elements in the movement of embrace. These are: the opening of the arms, the waiting, the closing of the arms, and the opening of them again. For an embrace to happen, all four must be there and they must follow one another in an unbroken sequence.

First we have the opening of the arms. This is a gesture of the body reaching out for the other. The open arms are a sign of desire and of discontent with my own self-enclosed identity. This is also a sign that I have created space in myself for the other and that I have made a movement out of myself in order to enter the space created by the other. The open arms suggest an opening within the self, through which the other can come in. Finally, open arms are a gesture of invitation.[22]

For my concern, both the space created and the opening of the self are of special importance. In the return after the exile, the question of space is not only about internal space, but also about physical space, about land to cultivate, about the houses of the ancestors and so on. These two parts are inseparably bound together.

The second element is waiting. The opening of the arms has initiated the move towards the other. This movement is not an invasion. If embrace takes place, it will always be because the other has desired the self, just as the self has desired the other. The other can not be manipulated into an embrace. This distinguishes an embrace from a grasping after the other and holding the other in one's power. Embrace can never reach its goal without reciprocity.[23]

The third element is the closing of the arms. This is the goal of an embrace, a goal which is unthinkable without reciprocity. Each is both holding and being held. For an embrace to happen, a soft touch is necessary. Too tight an embrace is a concealed act of power and signals exclusion through assimilation. It is essential to preserve the alterity of the other in the embrace.

The fourth and final element is the opening of the arms again. Embrace does not transform the boundaries between the bodies into a seam that

[21] Smith-Christopher, *Theology of Exile,* 138.
[22] Volf, *Exclusion and Embrace,* 141–142.
[23] Volf, *Exclusion and Embrace,* 142–143.

holds a body together. For the embrace not to cancel itself, the arms must open again.[24]

As a metaphor, embrace implies that the self and the other belong together in their mutual alterity. Built into the very structure of embrace is a lack of determination of its outcome. Finally, therefore, there is a risk in embrace. When I open my arms to the other I do not know if I will be misunderstood, despised, or even violated or whether the action will be appreciated and reciprocated or rejected.[25]

In my use of the terms embrace and exclusion, I will try not to enter too much into the different movements of the embrace since they belong together in an integrated movement. Still, I regard the first part to be of most interest for our understanding of the relationship between the "we" and the servant. Following the definition made by Volf, I ask, "Who is being embraced in Isa 53?" Are the "we" embraced by YHWH through the suffering of the servant? and "What kind of exclusion does Isa 53 argue against?"

Exclusion and embrace are suitable terms by which to describe various expressions of human relationships and probably also by which to describe the effects of the return after exile, but not for describing all the various aspects of vicarious suffering. I will therefore now define the use of some other terms used in this dissertation.

3. Reconciliation, Atonement and Vicarious Suffering

First, in quotations and summaries of the work of other scholars, I will try to use the terms they employ, with the same meaning as they have in the original text. This is, however, not always easy. As we have seen above, there is a discussion about what Whybray means by the term vicarious suffering. Nor is it always easy to define a meaning of the terms because of the fluidity in its use. Atonement and reconciliation, for example, essentially mean the same thing, but in modern usage, atonement has come to have a restricted meaning.[26] According to the doctrine of atonement, the work of Christ is understood as a substitutionary act, in which he does, before God and on behalf of others, that which they are unable to do themselves. This act is to be distinguished from reconciliation, which, as the restoration of a

---

[24] Volf, *Exclusion and Embrace,* 144–145.

[25] Volf, *Exclusion and Embrace,* 145–147.

[26] E.g. James Atkinson, "Atonement," in *A Dictionary of Christian Theology* (ed. Alan Richardson; London: S.C.M. Press, 1969). See also Gerhard Sauter, "Reconciliation," in *The Encyclopedia of Christianity 4 P-Sh* (ed. Erwin Fahlbusch; Grand Rapids, Mich.; Leiden: Eerdmans; Brill, 2005), 504.

right human relationship to God, is understood to be the purpose of atonement.[27] I will not go into any extensive discussion of the interpretations of atonement, reconciliation, and vicarious suffering, but I will try to define the meaning that I employ for each term in this work.

In this dissertation *reconciliation* will be used with the more general meaning of the resolution of conflicts and the making of peace. Reconciliation can take place between opposing individuals, groups, and peoples. Reconciliation can also take place between God and the world, between God and humans, or between God and individuals.[28]

Atonement will be used for the expiation of sins, which leads to reconciliation between God and humans.[29] Atonement therefore contains two parts: First, a substitutionary act on behalf of others and secondly, the restoration of the relationship between God and humans.

Vicarious suffering will be used with a slightly different meaning than atonement of a suffering that is substitutionary. It is substitutionary because someone suffers instead of another. Contrary to atonement, vicarious suffering does not involve the restoration of a relationship to God. Another difference between vicarious suffering and atonement is that the latter does not necessarily involve suffering. An act of atonement can be an act of intercession, of sacrifice, or of suffering, and so on. It is important to observe that my use of vicarious suffering differs from the use of the term by Whybray and also from the common theological use. When Whybray uses vicarious suffering, he also means suffering that leads to atonement.[30] I have here employed my own definition of the words to his work. I will use the term vicarious suffering with the general meaning of a suffering on behalf of others without any implications for the relationship to God.

4. Conclusion

Exclusion and embrace will be my main terms for the investigation of Isa 53. Hopefully, they are not too charged with Christian preconceptions. They are helpful for a description of both the needs and the effects involved in the return after the exile. *Exclusion* aims at two interrelated aspects: assimilation and separation. Each aspect reduces the other, but

---

[27] E.g. Collin E. Gunton, "Atonement: 3. Systematic Theology," in *The Encyclopedia of Christianity 1 A-D* (ed. Erwin Fahlbusch; Grand Rapids Mich.; Leiden: Eerdmans; Brill, 1999), 156–157.

[28] See further Sauter, "Reconciliation.".

[29] Cf. Sauter, "Reconciliation," 504.

[30] Whybray, *Thanksgiving,* 75.

through different means. *Embrace* aims at the process of reconciliation. It incorporates the risk of opening the arms and the self and the other belong together in their mutual alterity. Built into the very structure of embrace is a lack of determination of the outcome.

Exclusion and embrace cannot grasp all the aspects that I need to define. Therefore, I will also use other terms. *Reconciliation* will be used with the more general meaning of a resolution of a conflict and the making of peace. *Atonement* will be used with a narrow meaning of a substitutionary act of expiation of sins, which leads to reconciliation with God. Finally, *vicarious suffering* will be used as a reference to suffering that is only substitutionary.

Chapter 4

The Identities

1. The Identity of the Servant

One of the more frequently discussed exegetical problems concerns the identity of the servant. We find this question already in the New Testament book of Acts, "About whom, may I ask you, does the prophet say this, about himself or about someone else?" (Acts 8:34). Despite the age of the question and the numerous proposals put forward, it has not reached its final solution. North, in his study of this question, recounts the despair of a commentator of a previous generation who: "is said to have abandoned his projected commentary on Isaiah because this part of his subject overwhelmed him".[1] By 1956, when the second edition of North's work was first published, it could be asserted with some confidence that four identifications of the servant still held the field.

1. The servant is an anonymous contemporary of the Second Isaiah, a man destined to be the Messiah.
2. The servant is the prophet himself.
3. The servant is a group. This is a theory that takes many forms: the empirical Israel, the ideal Israel, the pious remnant of the true Israel, the order of prophets, or some combination of these elements.
4. The excepted Davidic Messiah.[2]

The field of solutions to this old problem has not decreased since North's time. I will therefore draw attention to some of the problems involved in identifying the servant, and I will then present my own position regarding this subject.

The first issue is whether the servant should be identified at all. Westermann regards the veiled manner of speaking as intentional and suggests that we should be conscious of the limits imposed and be careful to call a halt at those places, where the distinctive nature of the songs demands this. He is right that, in principle, exegesis must not be controlled by the question: Who is this servant of God? Westermann argues that this is precisely

[1] Christopher R. North, *The Suffering Servant in Deutero-Isaiah: An Historical and Critical Study* (London: Oxford University Press, 1956), 1.

[2] North, *The Suffering Servant,* 3–4, this is my summary of his survey. Cf. also Clines, *I, He, We and They,* 25–27.

what the songs neither tells nor intends to tell us. The first is certainly true. The second statement is more problematic both to verify and to disprove.[3] Clines appreciates Westermann's refusal of the question of the identification of the servant and considers Westermann to be too fixated by the concept of the text as information.[4] Hence, Clines argues for a literary approach, which describes the poem as open-ended, and which allows for multiple interpretations. A problem with Clines' interpretation is that he draws his conclusion about the poem after his presentation of a great variety of historical-critical interpretations of Isa 53. This makes it somewhat difficult to determine whether he draws a historical-critical conclusion that the poem is open-ended, or a literary conclusion. If the latter is the case, he is right. No text is limited to whatever its author had in mind.[5] However, this does not exclude the possibility that the author may have had a specific servant in mind. A historical-critical openness of the text cannot be proven through a diversity of interpretations. Such diversity could just as well be due to our limited knowledge of the actual historical situation. The reason why the servant is not mentioned by name could also be that his identity was so obvious at the time. Hence, I consider it an open question whether the identity of the servant is intentionally concealed, or whether it is concealed because of our limited historical knowledge, and I will treat the text as if the latter is the case. That makes it is possible to argue for more or less plausible historical solutions to the question of identity.

Another important discussion concerns the question whether the four servant songs present the same servant and the same perspective of the servant. Another issue is related to this discussion: How are the servants inside and outside the songs in Isa 40–55 related to each other? When Duhm separated the servant songs from Isa 40–55, there was no need to discuss the relationship between the servants inside and outside the songs.[6]

---

[3] Claus Westermann, *Isaiah 40–66: A Commentary* (OTL Philadelphia Pa.: Westminster Press, 1969), 93, a similar view has previously been proposed by Lindblom. He argues: "[I]t becomes meaningless to ask *who* is the Servant of Yahweh in the fourth Servant Song. [...] He is a fictitious person, who (from the psychological point of view) is conjured up in the prophet's imagination, and (from the religious point of view) is the subject of divine revelation. Johannes Lindblom, *The Servant Songs in Deutero-Isaiah: A New Attempt to Solve an Old Problem* (Lunds Universitets årsskrift vol. 47/5; Lund: Gleerup, 1951), 46. W. M. Roth, "The Anonymity of the Suffering Servant," *JBL* 83, no. 2 (1964): 171–179, argues that the anonymity of the servant is intentionally concealed even though the identity is known. A problem with Roth's theory is that he finds most arguments in the parallels to the beloved disciple in the Gospel according to John. The parallels are interesting, but this mainly indicates the reason why the disciple is not named rather than the other way round.

[4] Clines, *I, He, We and They,* 59.

[5] Cf. Melugin, "On Reading Isaiah 53," 55–69, for a discussion of this problem.

[6] Duhm, *Das Buch Jesaja,* 311.

Since then, there has been a significant evaluation of the theories, both regarding the composition and the redaction of the book of Isaiah.[7] This makes a discussion about that relationship significant once again. Some scholars argue that the servant songs are a presentation of the prophetic office that incorporates previous experiences. Hence, they are reflection texts describing the prophetic office as it was at that particular moment of the history of the world. It is also argued that the servant inside the songs is inseparably bound up with the servant outside the songs, which is Israel. As an individual, the prophetic servant in the songs represents Israel. The prophetic servant displays the trust in God that Israel still refuses to exercise. The three first songs end with a question hanging in the air: What became of the reward and the success promised to the servant, since he obviously did not receive it during his lifetime? The answer to this question is provided in the fourth servant song. Unlike the three first songs, this fourth song can however not be ascribed to the servant himself.[8] This is one way of both keeping together and separating the various servants described in Isa 40–55.[9]

Blenkinsopp considers the problem of the different descriptions of the servant in another way.[10] He argues that there are different servants in Isa 40–55. The servant in 42:1–4 is identified as Cyrus. The other twelve uses of the word עבד in 40–48 denote Jacob, ancestor and representative of the people of Israel. In the latter three servant songs, we have yet another servant, namely an individual prophetic figure. Blenkinsopp also speaks of the difference between these songs. He argues that the servant that is eulogized in the fourth song is the one who soliloquizes in the second and third songs. Blenkinsopp traces the origin of this description of the servant to the Deuteronomists and he finds it in evidence in Deuteronomy, in the

[7] See Jürgen Werlitz, *Redaktion und Komposition: Zur Rückfrage hinter die Endgestalt von Jesaja 40-55* (BBB vol. 122; Berlin: Philo, 1999), 26–40, for an extensive evaluation of the impact of this discussion of the understanding of the position of the servant songs.

[8] E.g. Hans-Jürgen Hermisson, *Studien zur Prophetie und Weisheit: Gesammelte Aufsätze* (FAT vol. 23; Tubingen: Mohr Siebeck, 1998), 223–225. A similar view is presented by Odil Hannes Steck, *Gottesknecht und Zion: Gesammelte Aufsätze zu Deuterojesaja* (FAT vol. 4; Tübingen: Mohr Siebeck, 1992), 22–23, and Janowski, "He Bore Our Sins," 54–60. They all follow the interpretation by Karl Elliger, *Deuterojesaja in seinem Verhältnis zu Tritojesaja* (BWANT vol. 4; Stuttgart: Kohlhammer, 1933), 6–27, but leave his thesis that the prophet of Trito-Isaiah is the author aside.

[9] Cf. Peter Wilcox and David Paton-Williams, "The Servant Songs in Deutero-Isaiah," *JSOT* 42 (1988): 79–102, who argue that the servant in Isa 40–48 is Israel and in 49–55 is the prophet.

[10] Joseph Blenkinsopp, *Isaiah 40 55: A New Translation with Introduction and Commentary* (AB vol. 19; New York; London: Doubleday, 2002a), 118. Cf. also Blenkinsopp, *Isaiah 40–55,* 356–357.

History, and related writings, including the rewritten book of Jeremiah. The three servant songs in Isa 49–55 provide a kind of rudimentary prophetic biography of a martyr. This is coloured by the Deuteronomic portrait of Moses and the closely related figure of the persecuted Jeremiah. Blenkinsopp also states that the expression "servant" encapsulates the religious significances of the institutions of the monarchy and of prophesy, which were closely related to one another.

There is "also "a" scholarly" discussion about a reinterpretation of the servant, through various redactions, in the book itself. It is argued that Isa 42:5–9 and 49:7–13, for example, belong to an interpretation of the servant in the immediately preceding texts; an interpretation that identifies the individual servant with Israel.[11] Contrary to this, Lindblom understands the servant songs as allegorical pictures. The passages connected to the three first songs suggest the interpretation or application of allegorical pictures.[12] This means that the connected passages are not necessarily a later reinterpretation, but could also be an explanation in line with the servant songs.

Albertz is one of the scholars who argue for a long period of growth of Isa 40–55. He does not understand the servant of the servant songs to be neither a single figure (*eine einheitliche Gestalt*) nor a person, but Israel under various guises seen from the common perspective of their function – different in different situations – in God's plan of salvation.[13] Here it is enough to conclude that it is possible that the servant songs do not present *eine einheitliche Gestalt.* This is a decisive point, since I am most interested in the identity of the servant in the fourth servant song.

This survey has revealed some important problems regarding the identity of the servant. First, we can conclude that the identity of the servant is not finally settled, and probably never will be. It is plausible that the diversity of interpretations is due to our limited knowledge of the historical situation and not to the openness of the text. Therefore, I believe that we can argue for more or less plausible solutions. Secondly, we can not presuppose that the servant has the same identity in all of Isa 40–55 or in all the four songs. Thirdly, the redaction-historical approach has shown that it is possible that the identity of the servant has varied over time, and that it has been changed in the text through the process of redaction.

---

[11] See among others Kratz, *Kyros im Deuterojesaja-Buch,* 206–216 and Oorschot, *Von Babel zum Zion,* 228–239. Cf. also Jürgen Werlitz, "Vom Knecht der Lieder zum Knecht des Buches: Ein versuch über die Ergänzungen zu den Gottesknechtstexten des Deuterojesajabuches," *ZAW* 109 (1997): 30–43, for the understanding of Isa 42:5–9 and 49:7–13 as later interpretations of the preceding sections.

[12] Lindblom, *The Servant Songs,* 102.

[13] Rainer Albertz, *Die Exilszeit: 6. Jahrhundert v. Chr.* (Biblische Enzyklopädie vol. 7; Stuttgart: Kohlhammer, 2001), 303.

The interpretation proposed in this study is that the servant in Isa 53 should be equated with the people in exile. Good arguments have certainly been put forward by most interpretations of the identity of the servant. This indicates that the servant has been coloured by various images, such as the image of the prophet, the king, Moses, and so on. In the fourth servant song in particular there is however some features that go beyond what has previously been stated about any individual. I will therefore argue that there are important aspects of the servant in Isa 53 that suggest that the servant is an image for the people in exile. In Isa 40:1–52:12, the people are referred to as the servant Israel/Jacob.[14] However, the difference between the servant in Isa 53 and the servant Israel/Jacob in Isa 40:1–52:12 is striking. In Isa 42:18–25 we have the most negative description of the servant, who is both deaf and blind. This criticism of the servant cannot to harmonised with the positive description in Isa 53. The description of Jacob/Israel as a servant nevertheless indicates that the servant in Isa 53 might also describe a group of people. We find a similar way of letting an individual represent the people on other occasions at this time.[15]

A significant difficulty with an individual interpretation is that the servant is described as a dead and buried person who comes to life again. This is problematic, since it is questionable whether a belief in the resurrection existed at that time. One way of solving this problem is to argue that the servant was not really dead.[16] This view has, however, been criticised.[17] On the other hand, the individual psalms also use the image of a suffering person who is dead and comes back to life. A clear example can be found in Ps 30. A difference compared to Isa 53 is that in Ps 30, the one who is suffering describes his own situation as if he was dead and has been restored to life. In Isa 53, other people describe the servant as dead. Maybe these differences should not be enforced too much, since both descriptions of the suffering use death and restoration as images to illustrate the consequences of suffering.

---

[14] See Isa 41:8–13; 42:18–25; 43:8–13; 44:1–5; 44:21–22; 48:20–21.

[15] See further Fredrik Lindström, *Suffering and Sin: Interpretations of Illness in the Individual Complaint Psalms* (ConBOT vol. 37; Stockholm: Almquist & Wiksell International, 1994), 271–298, and his analysis of Ps 40. Cf. also his references to Lam 3; Ezek 37; Isa 40–55. For Lam 3 as a collective lament, in which Israel's situation is described as personal suffering, see also Fredrik Lindström, *God and the Origin of Evil: A Contextual Analysis of Alleged Monistic Evidence in the Old Testament* (ConBOT vol. 21; Lund: Liber/Gleerup, 1983), 214–219.

[16] The most extensive argument in this regard has been put forward by Whybray, *Thanksgiving*, 79–106.

[17] See Antti Laato, *The Servant of YHWH and Cyrus: A Reinterpretation of the Exilic Messianic Programme in Isaiah 40–55* (ConBOT vol. 35; Stockholm: Almqvist & Wiksell International, 1992), 138–142, and others.

The description of the servant as someone who is dead but comes alive again is less problematic if the servant represents a collective. We have a parallel in Ezek 37, where the exiled are described as a dead person, who return to life. In both texts, Isa 53:8 and Ezek 37:11, the figures are described as dead by the use of the word גזר, "cut of", in *nipʿal.*[18] Furthermore, in both texts there are references to the "grave" (קבר), Ezek 37:12 and Isa 53:9. The parallel between Isa 53 and Ezek 37 indicates that the servant in Isa 53 could be the people in exile, just as the bones are in Ezek 37.

There are further arguments in favour of a collective interpretation. In my survey below of the metaphor of the tree in the book of Isaiah, I conclude that this metaphor has on several occasions been turned into a source of hope for, or through, the people in exile.[19] The presentation of the servant in Isa 53:2 takes up this feature. Therefore, the use of the tree as a metaphor in Isa 53:2 is a further indication that the servant represents those who were exiled. Furthermore, it is somewhat improbable that a single individual should have such great impact on both the nations and the kings (Isa 52:15) as the servant has.

In Ps 44:11, the experiences of the exile are described in language that comes close to the description of suffering in Isa 53:[20]

You have made us like sheep for slaughter,
 and have scattered us among the nations. (Ps 44:11)

He was oppressed, and he was afflicted,
 yet he did not open his mouth;
like a lamb that is led to the slaughter,
 and like a sheep that before its shearers is silent,
so he did not open his mouth.
 [silence] (Isa 53:7)

This is a further indication that the people in exile is the servant, since the suffering of the exile could be described in language such as that, which we find it in Isa 53.

---

[18] Cf. also Lam 3:54 where the verb גזר, "cut of", in *nipʿal* is also used to describe the situation following 587.

[19] See Isa 6:13; 11:1–16; 27:6.

[20] Ps 44 is probably an exilic complaint psalm even though it is complicated to determine the setting of both its time and its place. Cf. Rainer Albertz, *Religionsgeschichte Israels in alttestamentlicher Zeit: Vom Exil bis zu den Makkabäern* (GAT vol. 8/2; Göttingen: Vandenhoeck & Ruprecht, 1997), 387. See also Hans-Joachim Kraus, *Psalms 1–59* (CC Minneapolis Minn.: Fortress Press, 1993), 445–446 for a survey of the proposals made for its setting.

2. The Identity of the "We"

Regarding the identity of the "we"-group I will argue that they are a part of the people, and further defined as the people left in the land during the Babylonian captivity. This interpretation is controversial, just like many other issues regarding the servant songs. I will begin the investigation with the arguments in favour of another prominent view, according to which the "we" are identified as the nations and the kings. After this I will put forth the arguments in favour of the understanding advocated in this study.

It is often argued that the "we" are the same group as that in Isa 52:15:[21]

so he shall startle many nations;
  kings shall shut their mouths because of him;
for that which had not been told them they shall see,
  and that which they had not heard they shall contemplate.

There are significant arguments in favour of this view. First, there is a smooth transition between Isa 52:15, where the nations shall contemplate what "they have not heard" (לא־שׁמעו) and Isa 53:1, where "we" understand "what we have heard" (לשׁמעתנו).[22] Therefore, the introduction in Isa 53:1 makes a direct link to Isa 52:15 and takes up the final word. Secondly, Isa 53:1 also picks up the conclusion in Isa 52:10:

And to whom has the arm of YHWH been revealed? (Isa 53:1)

YHWH has bared his holy arm
  before the eyes of all the
nations; and all the ends of the earth shall see
  the salvation of our God. (Isa 52:10)

The smooth transition from divine utterance to report, and the parallel between Isa 53:1 and 52:10 are the most important arguments in favour of identifying the "we" with the nations and the kings. Still, we have to ask if the smooth transition and the parallel make such identification necessary.

Skinner claims that the "we" must be the Israelites, or one Israelite speaking in the name of all. He has three arguments that support such a conclusion. First, in Isa 52:15 the nations are surprised by the servant's exaltation, since they have not previously heard of it, whereas in 53:1 "we" have heard of it. Secondly, the nations revise their opinion of the servant because of his ultimate exaltation (Isa 52:14–15) in contrast to the "we" who have already changed "our" view of the servant during his humiliation. Thirdly, the expression עמי, "my people", in Isa 53:8 can only make sense

---

[21] E.g. North, *The Suffering Servant,* 151, and Mettinger, *A Farewell,* 38.

[22] Cf. North, *The Suffering Servant*, 151, and Andrew Wilson, *The Nations in Deutero-Isaiah: A Study on Composition and Structure* (Ancient Near Eastern Texts and Studies vol. 1; Lewiston, N.Y.: Edwin Mellen Press, 1986), 307.

on the lips of an Israelite.[23] The second argument is the most persuasive one. There is a significant difference between the understanding held by the "we" regarding the servant in his humiliation and the nations and kings who see the exaltation of the servant. The smooth transition from divine utterance to report could therefore be due to the embrace of the servant's suffering by the "we". The confession is one step in the exaltation of the servant. This is what the nations and the kings actually see. It is the two events, the embrace of the "we" and the astonishment of the kings and the nations, which are connected. It is not the two groups who are merged into one. Therefore, the "we" should not be identified with the nations and the kings. Two opposite attitudes are expressed regarding their relationship to the servant, one in the divine utterance and another in the report. The attitude held by the "we" to the servant changes from hostility to appreciation because of his humiliation. This is marked in Isa 53:4:

Surely he has borne our infirmities
    and carried our diseases;
yet we accounted him stricken,
    struck down by God, and afflicted.

The relationship between the servant and the nations and the kings is rather different compared to this relationship. The nations and the kings merely look at him and hear about him. Their attitude is altered through the servant's change from humiliation to exaltation. This is what astonishes them and what makes them shut their mouth.[24]

I have so far argued against the understanding that "we" should be identified with the nation and the kings. Now I will argue in favour of the view that "we" are a part of Israel. First, I will examine the similarities with the individual complaint psalms. Secondly, the sheep/shepherd image will be investigated. Thirdly, I will look at the image of a sick man. Fourthly, I will turn to the servant outside the songs in Isa 40–55.

Isa 53 has several similarities to the individual complaint psalms.[25] In Ps 31:12–14 we hear the complaint by the sufferer who is isolated from the community in his suffering:

I am the scorn of all my adversaries,
    a horror to my neighbours,
an object of dread to my acquaintances;
    those who see me in the street flee from me.

---

[23] J. Skinner, *The Book of the Prophet Isaiah: Chapters XL-LXVI* (Cambridge: Cambridge University Press, 1929), 136–137.

[24] Cf. also the analysis of the personae by Clines, *I, He, We and They*, 37–40.

[25] See further Janowski, *Stellvertretung*, 80–83.

I have passed out of mind like one who is dead;
  I have become like a broken vessel.
For I hear the whispering of many–
  terror all around! –
as they scheme together against me,
  as they plot to take my life. (Ps 31:12–14)

Here we see the same contempt that previously characterised the relationship between the "we" and the servant. The difference is the perspective. Here it is the sufferer who speaks, while in Isa 53 all his adversaries confess their guilt. In Ps 41:7–10 we see the social consequences of the suffering. The relationship between the "we" and the servant was like the relationship between the suffering person and his enemies, who understood that the sufferer had been struck by God and who therefore distanced themselves from him:

And when they come to see me, they utter empty words,
  while their hearts gather mischief;
    when they go out, they tell it abroad.
All who hate me whisper together about me;
  they imagine the worst for me.
They think that a deadly thing has fastened on me,
  that I will not rise again from where I lie.
Even my bosom friend in whom I trusted,
  who ate of my bread, has lifted the heel against me. (Ps 41:7–10)

In this psalm, even the bosom friend turns away from the sufferer. There is a parallel between the enemies in the individual complaint psalms and the view previously held by the "we" in Isa 53.

According to Janowski, the "we" can be identified as his fellow Israelites, since the "we" are identified with the enemies in the individual complaint psalms.[26] The identification of the enemy in these psalms is, however, debated and they could also be other people. The use of this familiar language from the psalms would fit better into the mouth of the people than into the mouth of the nations and the kings.

Secondly, there is the image of sheep/shepherd. The arguments regarding this image indicate that the "we" is a reference to the people. Isa 53:6 is a central verse in the composition:

All we like sheep have gone astray;
  we have all turned to our own way.

This is a confession of what "we" have done wrong. The verse is further discussed below. Here it is enough to conclude that the image of sheep and shepherd is an important image for describing the people and their relationship to YHWH. Almost the same formulation is used by the individual

[26] Janowski, *Stellvertretung*, 80–83.

in Ps 119:176: “I have gone astray like a lost sheep; seek out your servant”. The similarity between the descriptions of the servant in Isa 53:6 and the complaint in Ps 44:11 is most astonishing:

You have made us like sheep for slaughter,
and have scattered us among the nations.

It is more likely that such an important image would be used as a metaphor for the people than for the kings and the nations.

Thirdly, I will turn to the image of a sick man. We will see that the description in Isa 53:4 was suitable to describe the situation in the land after the fall of Jerusalem:

Surely he has borne our infirmities (חלינו)
and carried our diseases (ומכאבינו).

In Isa 1:5 חלי, “illness”, is used to describe the conditions in the land following the Assyrian invasion.[27] In Isa 1:5–6 the image of a sick man is used in a way that is distinctly reminiscent of the way in which the servant is described in Isa 53. The “we” in Isa 53, who are now healed and reconciled, are probably identified with the ones who continue to rebel in Isa 1:5. This is not the kings and the nations, but God’s sinful nation, laden with iniquity (Isa 1:4).

Finally, I will turn to the servant outside the servant songs in Isa 40–55. From the analysis of the identity of the servant in Isa 53, I have concluded that it is unlikely that the servant in Isa 53 can be equated with the servant outside the songs in Isa 40–55. This conclusion is based on the observation that the servant outside the songs is described as guilty, and in Isa 42:18–25, the servant is both deaf and blind. This image of the servant cannot easily be harmonised with the positive description in Isa 53. However, there is an urge that the servant outside the songs should turn again to YHWH, and this turn to YHWH takes place when the “we” confess their guilt and admit that the suffering of the servant was unjust. Furthermore, it is not surprising that there are two groups of servants in Isa 40–55, since this division between the people in exile and those who stayed in the land appear already in Isa 40:1–11.

There is one more aspect of the use of an unnamed “we” in the text which must be considered. To identify the “we” is not only a theoretical task. By using such inclusive language, any receiver of the message can identify himself with the “we”. Hence, the receiver is put within the world of the poem, which involves the recognition that things are not quite what they seem to be and that it is possible that a dreadful mistake can have been made about the identity and nature of the true servant of the YHWH. Such identification can occur through inclusive language, and this lays the

[27] See further below regarding the relationship between Isa 1:5–6 and Isa 53.

poem open to new understandings in new situations. At a historical level, the inclusive language makes it more important to determine who the intended receiver of the text was, since that group was probably the first "we". It is unlikely that the receiver was the nations and the kings, but it is most likely that it was some part of the people and probably it was the people who stayed in the land.

3. Conclusion

With regard to the identity of the servant in Isa 53, we can first conclude that it is not necessary to equate, or to harmonise, this text with either the servant outside the songs in Isa 40–55, or with the servant in the first three songs.

The servant in the first three songs was probably originally an individual. An individual interpretation of the servant in the forth song is however problematic. I have therefore argued that the servant of Isa 53 belongs to a later reinterpretation of the servant as an image for the people in exile. Such an interpretation of the identity solves the problem that he is dead and comes back to life. It also explains the image used in the presentation of the servant and some of the images used to describe his suffering.

With regard to the identity of the "we", Isa 53 uses language deeply rooted in the people's piety to formulate this confession. There are similarities with the individual complaint psalms, the description of the nation during the exile and so on. All this makes it likely that the "we" should be identified with a group of the people and probably with the people who stayed at home. They had escaped the suffering of the exile and could therefore identify themselves with such language.

Part Two

Exclusion and Embrace

Chapter 5

Isaiah 53, Text and Translation

In the following part, I will establish the understanding of the text of Isa 53 used in this dissertation. Therefore I will make a translation which incorporates the results of my text-critical and philological analyses. Isa 53 is in many ways a complicated text and the following remarks are not in any way a complete commentary. I will put most emphasis on the parts which are important for the understanding of the servant's suffering.

52:13 See, my servant shall prosper;
he shall be exalted and lifted up, and shall be very high.
14 Just as there were many who were astonished at him (!)
–so marred was his appearance, beyond human semblance,
and his form beyond that of mortals–
15 so he shall startle many nations;
kings shall shut their mouths because of him;
for that which had not been told them they shall see,
and that which they had not heard they shall contemplate.
53:1 Who has believed what we have heard?
And to whom has the arm of YHWH been revealed?
2 For he grew up like a young plant by himself,
and like a root out of dry ground;
he had no form or majesty that we should look at him,
nothing in his appearance that we should desire him.
3 He was despised and rejected by others;
a man of sorrows and acquainted with infirmity;
and as one from whom one hides one's face,
he was despised, and we held him of no account.
4 Surely he has borne our infirmities
and carried our diseases;
yet we accounted him stricken,
struck down by God, and afflicted.
5 But he was wounded because of our transgressions,
crushed because of our iniquities;
the discipline for our wholeness was upon him,
and by his bruises there was healing for us.
6 All we like sheep have gone astray;
we have all turned to our own way,
yet YHWH has laid on him
the iniquity of us all.

7 He was oppressed, and he was afflicted,
yet he did not open his mouth;
like a lamb that is led to the slaughter,
and like a sheep that before its shearers is silent,
he did not open his mouth.
[silence]
8 From protection and justice he was taken away.
Who could have imagined his future?
For he was cut off from the land of the living,
stricken for the transgression of his people. (!)
9 They made his grave with the wicked
and among the rich when he died,
although he had done no violence,
and there was no deceit in his mouth.
10 Yet it was the will of YHWH to bruise him painfully,
if his life is made to guilt. (!)
he shall see his offspring, and shall prolong his days;
through him the will of YHWH shall prosper.
11 Out of his anguish he shall see light; (!)
he shall find satisfaction through his knowledge.
The righteous one, my servant, shall show himself righteous before many
because he bears their iniquities.
12 Therefore I will allot him a portion with the great,
and he shall divide the spoil with the strong;
because he poured out himself to death,
and was numbered with the transgressors;
yet he bore the sin of many,
and he intervened for the transgressors.

VERSE 13: There is a discussion about whether the expression יַשְׂכִּיל, "he shall prosper", refers to the insight of the servant or to his predicted prosperity. The two meanings are, however, closely related. The word occurs rather frequently in the wisdom tradition with the understanding that the one who has the insight will also be prosperous.[1] It is probable that the word has the same connotations here.[2] I therefore believe that the two meanings are combined here. Furthermore, we have the opposite cause and effect in Jer 10:21, where the shepherds are stupid and do not inquire after

[1] See for example Prov 16:20; 17:2.

[2] E.g. Karl Marti, *Das Buch Jesaja* (ed. KHC; vol. 10; Tübingen: J. C. B. Mohr (Paul Siebeck), 1900), 345, Clines, *I, He, We and They*, 14, Jan L. Koole, *Isaiah 49–55* (Historical Commentary on the Old Testament vol. 3/2; Kampen: Kok Pharos, 1997), 264, and Klaus Baltzer, *Deutero-Isaiah: A Commentary on Isaiah 40–55* (Hermeneia Minneapolis, Minn.: Fortress Press, 1999), 394. See also E Lipinski, "שׂכל," in *ThWAT 7* (ed. G. Johannes Botterweck and Helmer Ringgren; Stuttgart: Kohlhammer, 1993), 790–791 for further discussion of the problem.

YHWH, "therefore they have not prospered" (על־כן לא השׂכילו), and this leads to suffering.[3]

It is sometimes argued that the word ישׂכיל indicates that the servant represents Israel. Marti argues in this direction when he claims that ישׂכיל is a corruption of ישׂראל.[4] Against this, Torrey asserts that ישׂכיל might easily be corrupted to ישׂראל, but not the other way round.[5] Duhm on the other hand argues that if we here have a *Schreibfehler* for ישׂראל, this would be the same misinterpretation as we find in Isa 49:3.[6] The scholarly discussion indicates that we can not use ישׂכיל as a decisive argument for the identification of the servant with Israel.

VERSE 14: In this verse we might have the first direct addresses to the servant. Against this BHSapp. suggests that we should read עליו, "at him".[7] It is possible that כ is a writing error for ו. Even though MT has a strong text-critical basis, it is likely that we should read עליו, "at him".[8]

According to BHSapp., we should read מָשְׁחָת, "defect", instead of מִשְׁחַת, "inhumanly disfigured". There has been an extensive discussion about this word; the form in the MT is a *hapax legomenon*. According to Nyberg is מִשְׁחַת a nomen with the prefix *ma-*, it is used as an intensive adjective and does not need to be emended.[9]

Finally, it can be questioned whether the last two cola are in the right place. BHSapp. suggests that they might have been moved to the end of Isa 53:2. However, in the context of the prologue, this assertion, that the servant is below human standards, provides a good introduction to the confession. To move the two cola seems unnecessary.[10]

---

[3] Cf. H. S. Nyberg, "Smärtornas man: En studie till Jes. 52,13-53,12," *SEÅ* 7 (1942): 5–82, 42.

[4] Marti, *Das Buch Jesaja*, 345.

[5] Charles Cutler Torrey, *The Second Isaiah: A New Interpretation* (Edingburgh: T&T Clark, 1928), 415.

[6] Duhm, *Das Buch Jesaja*, 394.

[7] E.g. Westermann, *Isaiah 40–66*, 253, and Baltzer, *Deutero-Isaiah*, 398–399. Contra Torrey, *The Second Isaiah*, 415, and Willem André Maria Beuken, *Jesaja: deel II B* (De Prediking van het Oude Testament Nijkerk: Callenbach, 1983), 189.

[8] Cf. however Eva Strömberg Krantz, "The Commentary of the Hebraist on Isaiah. pp. 142–151," (The National Archives of Sweden: The Swedish Bible Commission's Deposit at the Regional Archives in Uppsala), 143. She argues that this change of person is not unthinkable in the Hebrew. Still, she concludes that we need to use the third person singular when translating into Swedish. Hence, *Bibel 2000* uses the third person singular.

[9] Nyberg, "Smärtornas man," 46. He continues: "to emend such archaisms shows a deplorable lack of philological tactfulness and linguistic insight" (my translation).

[10] E.g. Koole, *Isaiah 49–55*, 271.

VERSE 15: The meaning of the word יזה, "startle", is uncertain.[11] The verb יזה is used for the *spattering* of blood (Lev 6:20) and for *sprinkling* it (Exod 29:21). This has led to interpretations that connect the verb with the purifying power of the sprinkling of blood, but this interpretation has nowadays mostly been abandoned.[12] One objection against such interpretations is that the verb is usually not connected to a direct object. It is more likely that the meaning of the verb should be understood as an expression of some form of astonishment. It is easier to see the parallel to the second half of the verse by such an interpretation.[13] Therefore, a cultic interpretation is less likely.

It is not clearly stated whether עליו, "because of him", belongs to the preceding "many" or to the following "kings". However, the latter appears to be more plausible since we would otherwise lack a reference to the servant in this latter part.[14]

VERSE 2: It has been suggested that the text should be emended to לפנינו, "among us", instead of לפניו, "before him".[15] On the other hand, a possible explanation to the somewhat curious suffix in the Massoretic text could be that לפניו describes a situation in which a plant grows up without good conditions; it grows up on its own.[16] The wordings are complicated. Nevertheless, the last explanation gives a good meaning without the need to correct the text.

VERSE 5: MT has *po ʿlel* participle of חלל II, "wounded", BHSapp. proposes that it should be *pu ʿal* participle of חלל I, "profaned". There is no strong reason to emend the text here.[17] The reading according to the MT

---

[11] See the Swedish Bible Commission, Bibelkommissionen, *Bibelkommissionens komplement: Noter, uppslagsdel, parallellhänvisningar, textkritiska anmärkningar till Bibel 2000* (Stockholm: Verbum, 2001), 335. Cf. also BHSapp. Mettinger, *A Farewell*, 39–40, has a good survey of the different possibilities.

[12] Contra John Goldingay, *The Message of Isaiah 40–55: A Literary-Theological Commentary* (London: T & T Clark, 2005), 492—493, who advocates the translation: "So he will spatter many nations."

[13] E.g. Koole, *Isaiah 49–55*, 272–273, and John N. Oswalt, *The Book of Isaiah: Chapters 40–66* (NICOT Grand Rapids, Mich.: Eerdman, 1998), 374. Strömberg Krantz, "The Commentary of the Hebraist on Isaiah. pp. 142–151," 144, argues that the effort to get a Hebrew נזה II (from the Arabic) is questionable since the Arabic verb means: "to jump". She concludes that it is probably best to assume that יזה has a meaning similar to what we find in, for example, LXX, θαυμασονται, since this is what we expect on the basis of the context. This translation has then been made without looking at the Arabic.

[14] Cf. also Brevard S. Childs, *Isaiah* (OTL Louisville, Ky.: Westminster John Knox Press, 2001), 497.

[15] E.g. Clines, *I, He, We and They*, 16. Contra Baltzer, *Deutero-Isaiah*, 404–405, and Westermann, *Isaiah 40–66*, 253.

[16] E.g. Nyberg, "Smärtornas man," 49, and Janowski, *Stellvertretung*, 71.

[17] Contra Baltzer, *Deutero-Isaiah*, 410.

makes a better parallel to the following statement that he was "crushed because of our iniquities".

The preposition מן is used to state the cause to the servant's suffering.[18] Hence, the preposition is translated "because of". This underlines that it is the cause, and not the effect, which is described. The preposition מן is used in the same way in Ps 107:17:

Some were sick through their sinful ways (מדרך פשעם), (!)
and because of their iniquities (ומעונתיהם) endured affliction[19]

In the Psalm, in contrast to Isa 53, it is the sick person who has sinned himself, and the afflicted is the one who has committed the iniquities.

The word מוסר, "discipline", connected with שלום, "wholeness", belongs to the wisdom tradition, according to which discipline is something essentially good.[20] What is stated here is that the discipline deserved by the "we" has come upon the servant.[21]

VERSE 7: BHSapp. proposes that the phrase "he did not open his mouth" is repeated by mistake in v 7b.[22] It has been argued that it disturbs the rhythm. This line is a brake in the rhythm, but it is probably a deliberate disturbance. The silence is an unusual response to such suffering and the three statements about the servant in v. 7 are built up so that they have an intensifying effect.[23] This last statement is followed by the most effective one, i.e. by real silence. The last line is a full bicolon if there is a pause in the reading. This pause has the function of a forth declaration of the servant's silence. In Isa 5:13, we have a similar disposition with one colon missing. This could also be understood as a pause in silence after the verdict:

Therefore my people go into exile without knowledge;
[silence]
their nobles are dying of hunger,
and their multitude is parched with thirst.

How unusual the silence is as response to suffering is further highlighted by a comparison between this text and Jer 11:19. In Jer 11:19 we find

---

[18] E.g. Janowski, "He Bore Our Sins," 64.

[19] Here I follow the NRSV and make a conjunction, since אולים, "fools", is hardly original. See further Hans-Joachim Kraus, *Psalms 60–150* (CC Minneapolis Minn.: Fortress Press, 1993), 325, and BHSapp.

[20] E.g. Nyberg, "Smärtornas man," 52. Branson, "יסר," in *TDOT 6* (ed. G. Johannes Botterweck and Helmer Ringgren; Grand Rapids, Mich.: Eerdmans, 1990), 133, argues that מוסר, "discipline", is used only twice in the sense of punishment associated with YHWH, Jer 30:12–17 and Hos 5:2. This further supports the suggestion that the term is generally positive.

[21] See also the discussion below.

[22] Cf. Janowski, *Stellvertretung*, 71.

[23] E.g. Baltzer, *Deutero-Isaiah*, 414.

almost the same wording as in Isa 53:7, but Jeremiah certainly does not suffer in silence.

VERSE 8: This is in many ways a problematic verse. The first problem regards the meaning of עצר. Several interpretations are suggested. A common translation of the word עצר is "oppression".[24] This translation is, however, problematic here. Following the rest of the declarations of the "we", it is more probable that we should understand this as a negative statement. Hence, the servant is taken away from something positive and not from oppression. Therefore, I follow Koole and understand עצר as "protection". I believe Koole is right when he argues that it fits the context, because Isa 53 in its entirety emphasises the servant's loneliness. The rendering "protection" also agrees with a probable meaning of the line itself.[25] The parallel word משׁפט often has the positive value of justice in Isa 40–55 and especially in the servant songs.[26] This is what the servant of Isa 53 is deprived of. Following this, the first colon of v. 8 is an expression of a miscarriage of justice.[27]

The suffix in עמי, "my people", should probably be emended עמו, "his people", with 1QIsa[a].[28] It seems unlikely that a singular person, for example the servant or God, speaks in the middle of the confession of the "we".

VERSE 9: The word ויתן, "they made" (lit. "he gave", 3rd per. sg. masc.), is probably used to express an impersonal subject here.[29] 1QIsa[a] has ויתנו, "they gave him". It has also been proposed that we should read וַיֻּתַּן, "and it was given".[30]

The pair רשׁעים, "wicked", and עשׁיר, "rich", are probably parallel with a similar meaning. The word עשׁיר is somewhat problematic, both because it is in singular and because it is more positive than רשׁעים. It has been

---

[24] See Ps 107:39. Cf. also William Lee Holladay, *A Concise Hebrew and Aramaic Lexicon of the Old Testament: Based upon the Lexical Work of Ludwig Koehler and Walter Baumgartner* (Leiden: Brill, 1991). See David P. Wright and Jacob Milgrom, "עצר," in *ThWAT 6* (ed. G. Johannes Botterweck and Helmer Ringgren; Stuttgart: Kohlhammer, 1993), 336, for a survey of the most common translations.

[25] Sigmund Mowinckel, *He that cometh* (Oxford: Blackwell, 1956), 198, suggests this interpretation with the support of 1 Sam 9:17. Koole, *Isaiah 49–55*, 304, regards the appeal to 1 Sam 9:17 as disputable. Still, he regards the exegesis worth considering and he maintains the translation.

[26] Cf. the other occurrences of the term in Isa 40–55: Isa 40:14, 27; 41:1; 42:1, 3, 4; 49:4; 50:8; 51:4; 54:17.

[27] Cf. Aage Bentzen, *Jesaja: Bind II Jes 40-66* (2 vols.; Kopenhagen: Gads forlag, 1944), 105.

[28] See BHSapp. E.g. Westermann, *Isaiah 40–66*, 254, Clines, *I, He, We and They*, 13, and Baltzer, *Deutero-Isaiah*, 393. Contra Mettinger, *A Farewell*, 43.

[29] C. R. North, *Isaiah 40–55* (TBC London: SCM Press, 1964), 137. See also Nyberg, "Smärtornas man," 56, and Koole, *Isaiah 49–55*, 312–313.

[30] See BHSapp.

proposed that we should make a conjunction of עשׁיר to עשׂי רע "evildoers".[31] This is, however, not supported by any versions. That עשׁיר, "rich", is in singular is not necessarily a problem. The word is unusual in plural and the singular could denote a collective.[32] Others have argued that this verse could refer to the wealthy Babylonians in Isa 47 and that, in the Old Testament, rich men are often "wicked". Even so it is questionable whether these two words stand naturally side by side in Hebrew parallelism.[33]

It is somewhat problematic that במתיו, "when he died", is plural. This could be due to the attraction of the opposite בחייו, "during his life", which is constructed in plural.[34] One problem with this solution is that בחייו, "during his life", occurs with במתו, "when he died", in singular in Judg 16:30. Cf. also מותי ירלים תמות, "You shall die the death of the uncircumcised", (Ezek 28:10) where the plural is applied to a violent death.[35] It has also been proposed that this word should be corrected to בָּמָתוֹ, "his high places", cf. 1QIsa[a]: בומתו.[36] Despite the problem with the plural I keep the reading in MT, במתיו, "when he died". It seems to be a probable parallel to קברו, "his grave".

VERSE 10: The meaning of this verse is disputed and complicated. The verse has probably been damaged in some way and I do not believe that we can determine an original reading. Even so, both the translation and the understanding of this verse is decisive for the whole understanding of the servant's suffering, and I will therefore discuss this verse at some length. The first problem concerns the translation of דכאו, "to crush him". Westermann, who follows Elliger, has proposed another translation, which reads "Yet Yahweh took pleasure in him [who was crushed]".[37] The first meaning, that it was the will of YHWH to crush him, is almost outrageous and probably the original.

---

[31] Torrey, *The Second Isaiah*, 420, John L. McKenzie, *Second Isaiah* (The Anchor Bible, 20 Garden City, N.Y.: Doubleday, 1968), 130, and Westermann, *Isaiah 40–66*, 254.

[32] Nyberg, "Smärtornas man," 56–57. Also M Sæbø, "עשׁר," in *ThWAT 6* (ed. G. Johannes Botterweck and Helmer Ringgren; Stuttgart: Kohlhammer, 1989), 452, argues that עשׁיר, "rich", should be understood as a collective parallel, of the unjust rich, to the evildoers.

[33] North, *Isaiah 40–55*, 137.

[34] E.g. Nyberg, "Smärtornas man," 57.

[35] E.g. Franz Delitzsch, *Commentary on the Old Testament: Isaiah* (vol. VII; Grand Rapids, Mich.: 1976), 329.

[36] See Clines, *I, He, We and They*, 20, who understands "high place" as a burial mound. See also Baltzer, *Deutero-Isaiah*, 393, 417, who understands the "high place" as intentionally mysterious.

[37] Westermann, *Isaiah 40–66*, 254. Cf. Elliger, *Deuterojesaja in seinem Verhältnis zu Tritojesaja*.).

The next problem regards the word החלי. The word vocalised as in the MT is explained as *hip ʿil* pf. of חלה with the meaning "he brought sickness to him".[38] According to BHSapp. the reading הֶחלים את־שָׂם, "he healed him who made", has been proposed.[39] This is not quite convincing. It is difficult to understand why such a statement should be changed to a much more complicated statement regarding God's part in the suffering. 1QIsa[a] has ויחללהו, "and he pierced him" or "he profaned him". Delitzsch argues that החלי and דכאו should be understood together in the sense of: "and it pleased Jehovah to bruise Him painfully." Delitzsch further argues that דכאו is an infinitive, dependent on חפץ, cf. Job 32:33.[40] His suggestion seems to be the most probable reading of this complicated verse, even though the word החלי seems superfluous and might be a gloss. His understanding is preferable, since it is an outrageous statement that YHWH took pleasure in causing the pain of the servant. Therefore, it is easier to understand why such a statement could be changed than the other way around.

The second colon also contains several obstacles. The first concerns the translation of the word תשים, 2nd per. sg. m. or 3rd per. sg. f. The ambiguity offers two possibilities for the subject. On the one hand, since נפש is feminine this could be the subject, and the section would then read: "if his life makes a guilt offering". This is, however, a rather odd syntax, since we lack any indication of what is being offered. Another possibility is that the 2nd per. sg. m. is applied to God.[41] However, this does not agree with the 3rd per. form of the context. The least radical suggestion is to repoint the verb to *hop ʿal*.[42] Hence, we have a passive form in agreement with נפש, "if his life is made to אשם, "guilt".[43] This is the understanding advocated here.

The next difficulty regards the translation of אשם. It is generally agreed that, at this time, אשם was not used in the technical sense of the ritual legislation.[44] Still, it is common to translate אשם in that direction. Before we turn to the translation, it is important to determine the syntax of this

---

[38] E.g. Blenkinsopp, *Isaiah 40–55*, 348, but he thinks it might be a gloss.

[39] This was first proposed by Joachim Begrich, *Studien zu Deuterojesaja* (TB vol. 20; München: Kaiser Verlag, 1963), 64.

[40] Delitzsch, *Isaiah*, 330. Cf. also Hans M. Barstad, "The Philological Expert: Jesaja 50–53, " (The National Archives of Sweden: The Swedish Bible Commission's Deposit at the Regional Archives in Uppsala), 7, who argues that החלי should be understood as an instrumental accusative. Hence he reads "JHWH ønsket at slå ham med sykdom".

[41] See Oswalt, *The Book of Isaiah*, 400–403, for a discussion of the alternatives.

[42] This form is attested in Gen 24:33.

[43] For the understanding of שים, "made", cf. for example Exod 4:11.

[44] Already Julius Wellhausen, *Prolegomena to the History of Ancient Israel: With a Reprint of the Article Israel from the Encyclopaedia Britannica* (New York: Meridian, 1957), 64, stated this.

first half of the verse further. In order to do this, I will take Ps 94:17 as my starting point:

If YHWH had not been my help,
  my soul would soon have lived in the land of silence.
    (שכנה דומה נפשי)

Here we have a similar syntax compared to Isa 53:10 even if Ps 94:17 and Isa 53:10 express opposite experiences. The theme of thanksgiving is closely connected to the complaint and the description of suffering. Furthermore, the verses have the same kind of parallelism: the first part is about YHWH's action and the second tells us about what that has done to the individual. The primary interest in the psalm is that, if YHWH had not helped the praying person, he would "have lived in the land of silence". This colon has a similar construction, compared to the colon in Isa 53:10, where YHWH's "will" has caused the servant to be made to **אשׁם**, "guilt". In both these examples we find a verb in 3rd per. sg. fem. at the beginning of the colon. The subject to the verb is the noun for "life" (**נפשׁ**) with a personal suffix, and this is the last word of the colon. Between the verb and the subject, there is a noun that describes the way in which the **נפשׁ** is placed.

In the psalm, the person who prays fears the land of silence. In Isa 53:10 the servant is already in the land of silence. It is stated that he "was cut off from the land of the living" (v. 9). Therefore, a natural interpretation of the "we" is that the servant was forsaken by YHWH. Even though it is an almost offensive statement, the indication is that the servant was not only forsaken by YHWH, but also that it "was the will of YHWH to crush him with pain". This is an interpretation of the "we" in line with a common understanding of cause and effect.

The first colon of v. 10 certainly describes a negative experience. Hence, the second colon should probably also describe a similar, parallel and negative experience. This meaning is reached if we interpret **אשׁם** either in accordance to the meaning it has in Gen 26:10 and Jer 51:5 (guilt) or in accordance to the meaning it has in 1 Sam 6:1–9 (as some form of compensation).[45] In the latter case, the negative side is not as prominent as in the former and therefore it is not such a strong statement as we have in first colon of the bicolon. Hence, I therefore regard the translation "guilt" as more probable. With this interpretation **אם**, "if", is understood to be a conjunction between the two cola of v. 10.[46] The interpretation advocated here has the advantage of making it possible to read the entire verse as an

[45] See further Janowski, *Stellvertretung*, 88–92, and below.
[46] E.g. Janowski, *Stellvertretung*, 72. Contra Koole, *Isaiah 49–55*, 323.

antithetic chiasm, in which the two bicola describe how YHWH's former and future "will" (חפץ), correspond to each other.

Yet it was the will of YHWH to bruise him painfully, if his life is made to guilt.

he shall see his offspring, and shall prolong his days; through him the will of YHWH shall prosper.

This reading, which suggests that the first bicolon of v. 10 is negative and the second positive, finds further support by the fact that v. 10 is preceded by the part that speaks of the former negative things, and followed by two verses, which speak of the future prosperity of the servant.

VERSE 11: This verse could be divided in different ways. One possibility is to read: "Out of his anguish he shall see and be satisfied, through the knowledge of him (or: through his knowledge) my servant, shall make many righteous, and he shall bear their iniquities."[47] However, I regard a division into four cola as preferable, since such a construction connects better to the preceding two verses of four cola.[48]

Both 1 QIsa^{ab} and LXX add אור, "light", as object. This longer reading commends itself because there seems to be a missing object. Still, it is uncertain if the word "light" is the original object or a later insertion to replace the missing object. This is especially so since the expression "to see light" is a rather common expression. Whether or not אור is the original reading, it is our best alternative, and therefore I insert it.

It is possible to read the word יצדיק as an internal causative.[49] The entire poem states that the one who has suffered unjustly is now being restored, and therefore everyone will see that he is righteous.

VERSE 12. Both 1 QIsa^{ab} and LXX read ולפשעם, "for their transgressions", instead of ולפשעים, "for the transgressors". Both readings are possible and equally good. I follow the MT.[50]

Finally we will turn to יפגיע, which is often translated: "he interceded".[51] It has been argued that this does not mean that the servant made prayers of intercession for them, but that he took their place and that he underwent their punishment in their stead.[52] Regarding the translation of the verse it is important to observe that we lack an object for any intercessions.

---

[47] Cf. Nyberg, "Smärtornas man," 60–62.

[48] See further Mowinckel, *He that cometh*, 198–199.

[49] E.g. Mowinckel, *He that cometh*, 199, Westermann, *Isaiah 40–66*, 267, and Clines, *I, He, We and They*, 21–22. Contra McKenzie, *Second Isaiah*, 131, and Oswalt, *The Book of Isaiah*, 399.

[50] Koole, *Isaiah 49–55*, 340. Contra Blenkinsopp, *Isaiah 40–55*, 349.

[51] E.g. Blenkinsopp, *Isaiah 40–55*, 346.

[52] E.g. Westermann, *Isaiah 40–66*, 269.

This would be expected if prayers of intercession were intended. However, the object, which is missing, enforces that intervention is made for the sake of the transgressors. Hence, I prefer the translation *intervene* in favour of *intercede*. Intervene is more open and maybe it has less theological implications.[53]

[53] See further below.

Chapter 6

Isaiah 53, The Structure and Form

1. The Structure

It is of interest to investigate the structure of the poem in order to find out which parts that are highlighted by the text. A reading of this poem shows that it naturally divides into three parts, and in these three parts, three different relationships to the servant emerges. The first and the last parts are speeches by YHWH; the middle part is a speech by the "we" about the servant. The question about the exact division of the poem is debated. It has for example been argued that the poem is composed of five stanzas.[1] This division is, however, questionable, since it depends on an interpretation according to which the whole of Isa 53:10 is a speech by YHWH. This is probably not the case. I will argue for a slightly different division. In my reading, the poem is not divided into equal parts. There are some parts, which are highlighted by the division of the text. This leads to the conclusion that there are some important key formulations and divisions, which will receive attention in the analysis below.

The First Part

The first distinguishable part of the corpus is Isa 52:13–15. This is a speech by YHWH. However, according to Orlinsky, this is a separate part that does not belong to the rest of the text.[2] He has three arguments in favour of such separation. First, he regards the servant as Israel in this part in contrast to an individual in the rest of the poem. His second argument, which is in continuation with the first, is that the expressions "nations" and "kings" point to the servant as Israel and not an individual. Thirdly he argues that in the rest of the text, the treatment is entirely individualistic and nothing is said about the nations and the kings. Orlinsky also remarks that unlike the people, which did not keep silent in the face of destruction and exile, the servant is one that does not complain. Orlinsky is right that there

---

[1] Isa 52:13–15; 53:1–3, 4–6, 7–9, 10–12. E.g. Paul R. Raabe, "The Effect of Repetition in the Suffering Servant Song," *JBL* 103, no. 1 (1984): 77–81, 77–78. He does however agree that the poem has three major sections.

[2] Orlinsky, "The So-Called Servant of the Lord," 17–23. Thus also Roger Norman Whybray, *Isaiah 40–66* (NCB London: Oliphants, 1975), 169.

is diversity in the text. This diversity is, however, understandable since we have significantly different perspectives in the first and the second parts. There are some further important objections against the view of Orlinsky. The most important one is that the first and the last part, taken together, function as a frame, spoken by YHWH. This frame heightens the main part where the servant's suffering is described.[3] Therefore, I understand this first part as essential to the structure of the whole poem. Furthermore, it is an important introduction and presentation of the servant's true identity. If this first section is omitted, the whole poem loses an important element of its structure and balance.

The Second Part

The second part of the poem starts with Isa 53:1. This is a new scene where the "we" are speaking. The focal point in this part is the relationship between the "we" and the servant and the understanding of the servant by the "we". It is clear and generally acknowledged that this part begins with Isa 53:1. Unfortunately it is not equally clear where it ends. It is obvious that there is a new third part when YHWH is speaking again. Furthermore, it is apparent that YHWH is speaking at least in Isa 53:11b. It has been claimed that Isa 53:10a is a question to YHWH which leads over to YHWH's answer.[4] If that is the case, the word תשׂים, "he was put", should be understood as a 2nd per. sg. m. This does however not agree with the 3rd per. form of the context. Hence it is more likely that the verb תשׂים is 3rd per. sg. f. This makes it impossible to read this part as a question.[5]

I regard all of v. 11 as a word from YHWH, since that makes the best sense. It is then YHWH who announces all the good things that will come to the servant.[6] Following from this, v. 10 works as a bridge between the speech by the "we" and the speech by YHWH. The first bicolon, v. 10a, concludes what is stated in vv. 8–9, and the second bicolon, v. 10b, leads over to the positive declaration by YHWH in vv. 11–12. Furthermore vv. 8–9 and vv. 11–12 are connected to each other in a similar way, describing the former fate of the servant and his future prosperity. (See the figure below).

I have now defined this middle part, which consists of Isa 53:1–10. This part can also be divided in some smaller parts. First, v. 1 is an introduction

[3] For further critique, see Laato, *The Servant of YHWH and Cyrus*, 136, and Oswalt, *The Book of Isaiah*, 376.

[4] E.g. Laato, *The Servant of YHWH and Cyrus*, 136. For a critique of such division, see also Ronald L. Bergey, "The Rhetorical Role of Reiteration in the Suffering Servant Poem (Isa 52:13–53:12)," *JETS* 40, no. 2 (1997): 177–188, 177–178.

[5] I have also chosen to make a small emendation of the verb to *hop'al* passive, see further above.

[6] E.g. Baltzer, *Deutero-Isaiah*, 424.

or a headline in the form of a question.[7] This has its counterpart in the summary of the whole poem that is found in v. 12b. The middle section starts in v. 2 with the report of the servant's former life and of his suffering. The first two verses, vv. 2–3, of four bicola tell about the servant's appearance. This part has its counterpart in vv. 8–9, also two verses of four bicola, which describe what the servant's appearance has led to. The middle section moves one step further in vv. 4–5, also two verses of four bicola, where the "we" give a report of their new insight about the true cause behind the suffering of the servant: "Surely he has borne our infirmities". These two verses have their counterpart in v. 6b and 7, also four bicola, which give insight into the contrast between the servant's endurance of his suffering and the "we". This part ends with a colon of silence. From a strictly formal point of view, it can be questioned whether the silence is a colon. However, real silence is probably the most effective way of illustrating the servant's unusual attitude in his suffering.

It is generally acknowledged that v. 4 marks a new start. However, this part is often understood to end with v. 6.[8] Against this view I understand the statement "but YHWH has laid on him" to be a new start. Here there is for the first time an indication about who the actual director behind the whole scene is. Following the confession that the servant has suffered from the sins of the "we", it is explained that YHWH is the active agent.

The colon of silence at the end of v. 7 also indicates that v. 8 marks a new start. The middle section has a key formulation in the confession in v. 6a. See the figure below for a better overview of the way that this confession is highlighted.

The Third Part

As stated above, Isa 53 ends as it started, with a speech by YHWH. These two parts surround and highlight the middle section. Both sections contain a divine proclamation of the final triumph of the servant.

Through the last and final words, v. 12b, there is a summary of the whole poem. Westermann express this in a splendid way:

> The word 'yet' which begins this final line presupposes something left unsaid. Yes, he let himself be numbered with the transgressors; but in reality he was no transgressor, but... Here, as the termination of the whole thing, two brief but weighty statements sum up the meaning of the Servant's work.[9]

Therefore, this is not a summary of the last speech by YHWH, but a summary of the whole poem.

---

[7] Cf. Westermann, *Isaiah 40–66*, 255.

[8] E.g. Clines, *I, He, We and They*, 12.

[9] Westermann, *Isaiah 40–66*, 269.

Conclusion and Figure

To conclude this analysis, the poem is built of three major parts, the two speeches by YHWH, and the confession by the "we". The analysis above and the figure below indicate four key formulations in the poem. The first is the confession in v. 6a, which the surrounding vv. 4–7 helps to explain. The second is v. 10, since it both sums up the previous statements and leads over to the following. The last two key formulations are the presentation in Isa 53:1, which have its counterpart in the summary in 53:12b. These key formulations will therefore be analysed more carefully in the close reading below.

52:13 See, my servant shall prosper;	he shall be exalted and lifted up, and shall be very high.
14 Just as there were many who were astonished at you	– so marred was his appearance, beyond human semblance, and his form beyond that of mortals –
So he shall startle many nations;	kings shall shut their mouths because of him;
for that which had not been told them they shall see,	and that which they had not heard they shall contemplate.
53:1 WHO HAS BELIEVED WHAT WE HAVE HEARD?	AND TO WHOM HAS THE ARM OF *YHWH* BEEN REVEALED?
2 For he grew up like a young plant by himself,	and like a root out of dry ground;
he had no form or majesty that we should look at him,	nothing in his appearance that we should desire him.
3 He was despised and rejected by others;	a man of sorrows and acquainted with infirmity;
and as one from whom one hides one's face,	he was despised, and we held him of no account.
4 Surely he has borne our infirmities	*and carried our diseases;*
yet we accounted him stricken,	*struck down by God, and afflicted.*
5 But he was wounded because our transgressions,	*crushed because our iniquities;*
the discipline for our wholeness was upon him,	*and by his bruises there was healing for us.*
6 All we like sheep have gone astray;	*we have all turned to our own way,*
yet YHWH has laid on him	*the iniquity of us all.*
7 He was oppressed, and was afflicted,	*yet he did not open his mouth;*
like a lamb that is led to slaughter,	*and like a sheep that before its shearers is silent,*
he did not open his mouth.	*[silence]*
8 From protection and justice he was taken away.	Who could have imagined his future?
For he was cut off from the land of the living,	stricken for the transgression of his people.
9 They made his grave with the wicked	and among the rich when he died,
although he had done no violence,	and there was no deceit in his mouth.
10 Yet it was the will of YHWH to bruise him painfully,	if his life is made to guilt.
he shall see his offspring, and shall prolong his days;	through him the will of YHWH shall prosper.
11 Out of his anguish he shall see the light;	he shall find satisfaction through his knowledge,
The righteous one, my servant, shall show himself righteous before many	because he bears their iniquities.
12 Therefore I will allot him a portion with the great,	and he shall divide the spoil with the strong;
because he poured out himself to death,	and was numbered with the transgressors.
YET HE BORE THE SIN OF MANY,	AND HE INTERVENED FOR THE TRANSGRESSORS.

2. The Form

It is hard to classify this pericope from a form-critical point of view.[10] It is usually called a "song" about the suffering servant or the servant of YHWH. I prefer to call it a poem. Still, these are very general terms and they do not give us much information about the character of this "song". Since it is a unique poem, I believe that it is impossible to classify it in a narrow form-critical perspective. Nevertheless, it is possible to discuss the character of the poem.[11] The analysis of the structure shows that it is divided into three parts. A similar structure is also found in the individual complaint psalms. As we have previously seen, and as we will see further on, the language in Isa 53 is influenced by the language in the psalms and especially in the individual complaint psalms.[12] The rest of Isa 40–55 is also highly influenced by the forms and language of the Psalter.

Isa 53 is not an individual complaint psalm. I do however believe that its form is influenced by the individual complaint psalm. One important difference lies in their different subjects. In the psalms, the suffering person is the subject. In Isa 53, the subjects are those to whom the suffering person directs the complaint, or those who are complained about in the psalms.

The individual complaint psalms do not all conform to one fixed structure, but almost all of them begin with an invocation of YHWH. Then the complaint proper and a petition to YHWH often follow. This part often contains a description of the enemies who gather around the suffering person and mock him. Sometimes the psalm includes a protestation of innocence. A fair number of individual complaint psalms conclude on a positive note, expressing confidence in YHWH's deliverance.

Isa 53 has an affinity with this form. The poem starts with YHWH's promise of prosperity for the servant rather than with an invocation of YHWH. In the main part the servant suffered, even though he was innocent. This can be compared to the suffering subject in the individual complaint psalms, who occasionally claims his innocence. It was the "we", the enemies

---

[10] See Koole, *Isaiah 49–55*, 260–262, for a survey of available interpretations.

[11] Cf. Melugin, *The Formation*, 73–74, who concludes that the structure of the poem is the prophet's own creation. Still, he remarks that the poem is influenced by the language of the complaint psalms and their related forms. He also notes that it basically functions as a speech of salvation.

[12] Cf. also Hermann Spieckermann, *Heilsgegenwart: Eine Theologie der Psalmen* (FRLANT vol. 148; Göttingen: Vandenhoeck & Rupricht, 1989), 246–253, who sees the same theological pattern in Isa 52:14; 53:2–3, Ps 8:6 and Ps 22. The background to the suffering figures is probably the theological concept of how YHWH shares his honour (הדר). To lose this honour (הדר) is to lose one's humanity.

of the psalms, which had gone astray like sheep.[13] It was YHWH who let it happen. Finally, YHWH speaks again and promises the servant success. This can be compared to the conclusion of the individual complaint psalms, which express confidence in YHWH's deliverance.

The affinity with the individual complaint psalm highlights the servant's innocence as well as the "we"-group's responsibility. Most of all, it highlights the "we"-group's admittance of their responsibility. A poem that opens one's arms for another person's suffering by confessing one's own guilt is a new form. Even so, both the form and the language have an affinity with well-known traditions. As I have argued above, the identification of the "we" is not only a theoretical issue. By the use of such inclusive language, any receiver of the message can identify himself with the "we". Hence, the receiver is put within the world of the poem. By composing a poem with well known characteristics, even though it is in a new form, the receivers of the message will probably be helped to further enter the world of the poem and to identify themselves with the "we".

[13] Cf. above.

Chapter 7

Isaiah 53, Exclusion and Embrace

The purpose of this chapter is to establish what is actually said about the suffering of the servant in Isa 53. The most prominent view among scholars that the servant's suffering is atoning is questioned. I argue that the emphasis in the text is on the "we"-group's new understanding of the servant's suffering. They have now realised that he has suffered because of their sins, and not because of his own sins. This is a vicarious suffering, but it is not necessarily atoning suffering.

It is important to analyse those parts of Isa 53 that are most important for the scholars who claim that the servant's suffering is atoning. Hence, I will first examine Isa 53:4–6 and then I will turn my attention to other parts of Isa 53 that deal with sin-offering, righteousness, and finally with intercession.

1. Isaiah 53:4–6

This section is essential for scholars who understand the servant's suffering as atoning.[1] It is clear that in these verses we find a deeper and truer understanding of the servant's suffering, which is seen in contrast to the former understanding maintained by the "we".[2] Even so, we must examine whether or not the servant's suffering actually atones for the guilt of the "we". Rather than settling for a too simple answer, it is worth noting that already Mowinckel argued that:

> The thought is rather that of the psychological and moral effect of the Servant's work, bringing about the conversion of the people, and so atoning for their guilt.[3]

In this statement the conversion is at least as essential as the suffering for the achievement of atonement for the guilt. This shifts the focus and turns the centre of attention away from the servant to the "we". Janowski points

---

[1] North, *Isaiah 40–55*, 134, for example, deals with this part under the headline "his vicarious suffering". By this he means what I call an atoning suffering.

[2] E.g. Westermann, *Isaiah 40–66*, 262–264, and Kustár, *"Durch seine Wunden sind wir geheilt"*, 172.

[3] Mowinckel, *He that cometh*, 211.

in a similar direction when he entitles this section: *Israel's Confession of Guilt.*[4] Janowski's heading highlights the confession even more than Mowinckel does.

This brief survey indicates that the report in Isa 53:4–6 needs a thorough interpretation in order to determine more precisely what the "we" declare regarding the suffering of the servant. Is it the servant's suffering that makes YHWH embrace the "we"? This is the most prominent view among scholars. Or is it, as will be argued here, the confession of the "we" group that make them embrace the servant and his suffering as a suffering caused by their guilt? I will first interpret each line separately and then conclude with a summary of the whole section. I will not explore every single aspect in the section but I will focus mainly on the understanding of the servant's suffering.

Isaiah 53:4a "Surely he has borne our infirmities and carried our diseases"

Kaiser expresses a traditional interpretation of this statement. He asserts that these words refer to the servant's suffering as a sacrifice. Most important for such understanding is, according to Kaiser, the verb נשׂא, "to carry". He believes that this verb derives its meaning from the priestly language and that it describes the cause of guilt and how the effect of it is taken over.[5] Two verbs are used in Isa 53 with the meaning "to carry", namely נשׂא and סבל. According to Zimmerli, it is the *Formel* נשׂא עון (which does, however, not occur in Isa 53) that is varied with great independence in all of Isa 53.[6] This so called a *Formel* will be closer examined below. However, the verb נשׂא, "to carry", is a rather common word and it does not in itself refer to a sacrifice, even if it is often used in connection with sacrificial language and issues about guilt. Furthermore, in this verse it is not a form of guilt or transgression that is carried, but "our infirmities" (חלינו) and "our diseases" (מכאבינו). The two words חלי, "infirmity", and מכאב, "disease", are frequently used to describe the condition of the land after the fall of Jerusalem and as a consequence of earlier disasters.[7] The

[4] Janowski, "He Bore Our Sins," 62.

[5] Otto Kaiser, *Der Königliche Knecht: Eine traditionsgeschichtlich-exegetische Studie über die Ebed-Jahwe-Lieder bei Deuterojesaja* (FRLANT vol. 70; Göttingen: Vandenhoeck & Ruprecht, 1959), 101–103.

[6] Walther Zimmerli, "Zur Vorgeschichte von Jes. LIII," in *Congress volume: Rome 1968* (ed. John. A. Emerton; vol. *VTSup*; Leiden: Brill, 1969), 239.

[7] The words are also used to describe other forms of wounds and diseases. This use is the most common use in the books of Isaiah and Jeremiah by which to describe the condition of the land, both after the fall of Jerusalem and after earlier disasters. These texts are most important with regard to the interpretation of Isa 53. The word מכאב, "disease", is also used of Babylon in Jer 51:8. This is understandable, since the figure of Babylon is

word חלי is used, together with other words that describe wounds, in Isa 1:5–6. This text describes the situation in Judah after the Assyrian siege. The book of Jeremiah uses the same word to describe the domestic decline in Israel (Jer 6:7). The word מכאב, "disease", is used three times in the book of Lamentations. There the personified Jerusalem complains about the suffering, with which YHWH has afflicted her through Babylon.[8] Moreover, which is of greater importance, the verb נשא is used in one other example together with the word חלי, "infirmities". In Jer 10:19 we read:

Woe is me because of my hurt!
  My wound is severe.
But I said, "Truly this is my punishment (חלי),
  and I must bear it (ואשאנו)."

Here Zion complains about the suffering, which she has to bear. Like the servant, Zion suffers the consequences of others guilt, she suffers because the shepherds are stupid (Jer 10:21). It is a vicarious suffering, that is, a suffering indirectly caused by someone else. However, it is not an atoning suffering, since it does not expiate any sin. This text is important, since the whole section of Jer 10:19–21 carries several similarities to Isa 53–54. Furthermore, I regard Isa 53–54 as a reinterpretation of the themes in Jer 10:19–21.[9]

To conclude, both these words, חלי, "infirmity", and מכאב, "disease", are used in other examples to describe Israel's suffering during this period.[10] What is stated is that someone else, not the guilty party, carries the consequences, "our infirmities" (חלינו) and "our diseases" (מכאבינו). I do not share the interpretation put forward by Kaiser, namely that the verb describes the cause of guilt and how its effect is transferred, but I do agree with his conclusion:

Was mit dem ersten Halbvers gesagt werden soll, ist eindeutig: Die Krankheiten und die Schmerzen, die eigentlich die Gottlosen verdient hatten, sind auf den Knecht gefallen.[11]

The servant has carried the suffering, which the "we" should have carried, and in which the servant did not have any part himself.

---

opposed to Jerusalem and the two images also carry significant resemblances. Cf. John Hill, *Friend or Foe? The Figure of Babylon in the Book of Jeremiah MT* (Biblical Interpretation series vol. 40; Leiden; Boston, Mass.; Köln: Brill, 1999), 191–192, and his arguments regarding the similarity between Babylon and Judah in Jer 50–51.

[8] Lam 1:12 and twice in Lam 1:18.

[9] See further below.

[10] Cf. also Whybray, *Thanksgiving*, 58–59.

[11] Kaiser, *Der Königliche Knecht*, 103.

Isaiah 53:4b "yet we accounted him stricken, struck down by God, and afflicted"

This part says that the "we" had previously presupposed that the servant's suffering was just. They affirm that the servant "was stricken, struck down by God, and afflicted". Now, the "we" have understood that cause and effect are not quite so simple and straight forward.[12]

The verb נגע, "to strike" (here the participle "stricken"), is rather common. However, seen in its present context it is easy to remember the words of the accuser in Job 1:11: "But stretch out your hand now, and touch (וגע) all that he has, and he will curse you to your face." In Isa 53 we meet the silence of the servant, and this is an apparent contrast to what the accuser suspected of Job. It is also worth observing the similarity between the former understanding ascribed to the "we", about the cause of the suffering of the servant, and the view of Job's friends about his suffering. In Job 4:5 Eliphaz uses the very same expression:

> But now it has come to you, and you are impatient;
> it touches (תגע) you, and you are dismayed.

Now I will turn to the second verb, נכה (here *hopʿal*, "to be struck down"). The expression "to be struck down by God" is probably an analogy with the use of this verb in Deut 28:15–37.[13] There the one who does not obey YHWH is "cursed" and "afflicted" (נכה in *hipʿil*, "to afflict, to strike") by YHWH in different ways. This means that the "we" formerly understood the servant's suffering as a consequence of his own deeds, and therefore they thought that the suffering was justified. In a similar way, the verb ענה (here in *puʿal* participle, "to be humbled/afflicted") is used three times in Ps 119:67, 71, 75. The suffering is understood as something good, which leads the praying person back to YHWH. This psalm is also of interest, since it contains the same confession as Isa 53:6 (Ps 119:176).

All three verbs are often used to describe suffering caused by God as a consequence of guilt. This thought-pattern lies behind Isa 53:4b also. Nothing is said about atoning suffering. Rather the "we" express their former understanding about both the cause and the effect of the servant's suffering: He was afflicted by God. However, this understanding has now changed into a new insight. To claim that someone who is in fact innocent

---

[12] I share the view of Kustár, *"Durch seine Wunden sind wir geheilt"*, 173, when he argues: "Das war innerhalb der damaligen religiösen Denkstruktur eines Tun-Ergehen-Zusammenhanges die rechtgläubige, ja die einzige orthodoxe Folgerung aus dem, was sie gesehen haben: die Leiden galten damals als gerechte Strafe für die Sünden des Betroffenen."

[13] According to Whybray, *Thanksgiving*, 96, אלהים could have the function of a superlative here. However, this is not very likely since it is stated in v. 10 that it pleased YHWH to crush the servant. It is more likely that the "we" wants to emphasise that they regarded him as struck down by אלהים and not by anyone else.

is guilty can be an effective means of exclusion. The "we" now have a new understanding of the cause of the servant's suffering. By expressing this, the "we"-group opens their arms for him.

Isaiah 53:5a "But he was wounded because of our transgressions, crushed because of our iniquities"

Here, we see again that the servant's suffering arose from an alien cause. The preposition מן, "because of", is used to state the reason for the servant's suffering.[14] The servant suffers because of "our transgressions" and not because of his own, which would have been expected. However, the preposition מן is not used to state the way that something is paid, "in exchange for" or "in payment for". The preposition ב could have been used, if this was what the text wanted to state.[15] According to Koole the preposition מן has a causal meaning here, which means that the servant suffers "on account of" the sins of the "we".[16] However, he continues to argue that:

> Just as in the psalms of lament the innocent sufferer is saved and his enemies must be brought down on account of their guilt, so the innocent Servant is now brought down and his opponents are freed of their guilt [.][17]

I share part of Koole's view in this statement. The innocent servant is certainly brought down, but it does not necessarily follow from this that the opponents are freed from their guilt. Rather, they have escaped their own suffering. Nothing is said about atoning suffering in this half verse. That is another issue, which is not touched on here. The "we" understand and confess the consequences of their deeds, but this does not mean that the servant's suffering, atones for their guilt.

Isaiah 53:5b "the discipline for our wholeness was upon him, and by his bruises there was healing for us"

This is perhaps the verse that comes closest to expressing the idea of an atoning suffering. This is also where I regard the arguments put forth by Whybray against vicarious suffering to be at their weakest. Nevertheless, I will start with his arguments, since he has discussed the issue of vicarious suffering at most length. Then I will report on some criticism against this view put forth by Laato, and as the next step I will choose a slightly different

---

[14] Janowski, "He Bore Our Sins," 64. See also Orlinsky, "The So-Called Servant of the Lord," 57–58.

[15] Cf. Whybray, *Thanksgiving*, 61–62. For the use of the preposition ב to describe the price by which something is acquired, see Nyberg, "Smärtornas man," 327, and Isa 52:3.

[16] See Pss 38:19; 107:17; Lam 4:13 for a similar use of the preposition in connection with words for sin. Lam 4:13 is of special interest since there, as well as in Isa 53:5a, those who have sinned are not the prime sufferers of the consequences.

[17] Koole, *Isaiah 49–55*, 294.

starting point. I will argue that even this half verse is in line with both the previous and the following statements, which express the amazement that the servant is punished and suffers while the "we" are being healed.

First I will turn to Whybray, who remarks that the healing activity of YHWH and the bringing of שׁלום, "wholeness", are intimately related to the prophetic message. He notes that it is the prophet who announces שׁלום in Isa 54:10; 55:12, just as it is a prophet who pronounces YHWH's promise to heal in Jer 30:17; 33:6. Whybray asserts that no proof is needed to assert that suffering was intimately connected to the vocation of the Old Testament prophets. I share Whybray's view about a close connection between the prophetic message and שׁלום, but I am not convinced by his argument about the connection between the suffering of the prophets and שׁלום. In the texts, which he gives as examples, it is YHWH who heals and brings about שׁלום. Whybray argues that the servant of this chapter, which he thinks is Deutero-Isaiah, is distinguished by one thing from his prophetic predecessors, namely by the fact that his message was entirely one of hope and promise.[18] Even if the servant was Deutero-Isaiah, it would be questionable whether his message was entirely one of hope and promise.[19] Most importantly, this does not help us to interpret the degree of vicariousness involved in the suffering. Suffering was indeed intimately connected to the vocation of the Old Testament prophets. This does however not mean that their suffering necessarily bringing about peace; it could just as well have been a prefiguration of suffering that was yet to come.[20] Furthermore, I am not certain about how Whybray distinguishes his own interpretation from an atoning suffering. Even Whybray finds his own argument weakest in relation to this text, since he finally concludes:

> Although the phrases under consideration may be capable of bearing a vicarious interpretation, the context, as well as the general considerations urged above concerning the inherent improbability of such a thought in ancient Israel, render this interpretation highly improbable.[21]

Whybray is right that it is unlikely that this half verse would say something radically different than the context. It is more doubtful that "the inherent improbability of such a thought in ancient Israel" does in itself make such an interpretation improbable. Such an argument would imply that it was not possible for the prophets to say anything new – which is after all something that they frequently did.

---

[18] Whybray, *Thanksgiving,* 62–63.

[19] Cf. Blazenka Scheuer, *The Return of YHWH: The Tension between Deliverance and Repentance in Isaiah 40–55* (Lund: Centre for Theology and Religious Studies Lund University, 2005).

[20] Cf. especially Ezek 4:4–8 and the discussion below.

[21] Whybray, *Thanksgiving*, 63.

I will now turn to Laato, who criticises Whybray's argument that a vicarious interpretation of v. 5b is improbable because the context does not contain this idea. Laato states that it: "is – needless to say – not valid".[22] Here I believe Laato has gone a bit too far in his critique. It is most likely that this last part of v. 5 is in line with the rest of vv. 4–5. This is also the view expressed by Laato himself. The difference, compared to Whybray, is that Laato concludes that the rest of the verses convey an atoning suffering. Consequently, Laato argues that this statement does indeed come very close to expressing the idea of an atoning suffering. This is, according to him, clear from the fact that the statement links the suffering of the servant to the redemption of the "we".[23] This is, however, not a proof, but a conclusion. Laato's counter-proof is therefore not much stronger than the proofs put forward by Whybray.

Leaving aside the arguments of both Whybray and Laato, I will take a new starting point in the word מוסר, "discipline". This is a word, which is important in the wisdom tradition. Also the words הבורה, "bruise", and רפא, "to heal", can come from this tradition. In Prov 3:1–12, we see that the person who lets his heart keep the commandments will be granted "length of days and years of life and abundant welfare (שׁלום)" (Prov 3:2). In the same section we also read that to fear YHWH and to turn away from evil will "be a healing (רפאות) for your flesh" (Prov 3:7–8). At the end of the section we are reminded of the importance of receiving the "discipline" (מוסר) of YHWH, since he reproves the ones he loves (Prov 3:11–12). There is further support for the connection of these words (מוסר, רפא, and שׁלום) with the wisdom tradition in Prov 20:30 and Job 5:17–24:

How happy is the one whom God reproves;
therefore do not despise the discipline (ומוסר) of the Almighty.
For he wounds (יכאיב), but he binds up;
he strikes, but his hands heal (תרפינה).
You shall know that your tent is safe (שׁלום),
you shall inspect your fold and miss nothing.
(Job 5:17–18, 24)

Eliphaz, who is speaking in this text, understands suffering according to the wisdom tradition as essentially good and as something that brings שׁלום. YHWH disciplines and even wounds, but he also heals and the pain will eventually lead to שׁלום.

[22] Laato, *The Servant of YHWH and Cyrus*, 148.
[23] Laato, *The Servant of YHWH and Cyrus*, 147–148.

Returning to Isa 53, it is likely that it is in relation to the wisdom tradition that we should understand the confession in Isa 53:5b.[24] If we understand the notion of discipline from this tradition, it is clear that it is something essentially good. However, even if we do find the background to our text in the wisdom tradition, it is still difficult to identify the servant's suffering as a sign that he is blessed. This is just as difficult as it is to sustain such understanding of the suffering of Job, even though his friends try to explain Job's suffering in this way.

The wisdom tradition is, however, not a single homogeneous pattern. There are later uses of this tradition, which must also be considered. For example the prophets of doom transferred the idea in order to adapt it to the dealings of Israel's God with his people. In the prophetic tradition, this idea is connected to the concept that YHWH uses the powers of the world as his "rod of anger" to punish his people for their sins (Isa 10:5).[25] Another use of the same tradition, which is more controversial in the view of current research, but which has been well established by Lindström, is the use in the individual complaint psalms. The idea of YHWH's pedagogical action, which we meet it in for example Ps 6:2, does not assume an interpretation of the divine action as a punishment for sin. The psalmist accepts this pedagogy, but protests against the use of wrath as the instrument.[26]

With the prophets of doom, the punishment has a more fatal effect than in the wisdom tradition, since the accumulation of sins eventually strike back on the people.[27] This is possibly in line with the description of the suffering in Isa 53. What is new is that the "we" have seen their guilt, and they understand that the discipline, which they deserve in order to receive their wholeness, has come upon the servant. Therefore, the text is an expression of the experience that the normal process of cause and effect has been broken. Hence, it becomes a confession of the guilt of the "we" and of the unjust suffering of the servant. This is a vicarious suffering, since the servant suffers instead of the "we". This is, however, not a statement that the suffering of the servant atones for the sins of the "we".

Now I will turn to the last colon of Isa 53:5. Here we meet the statement ובחברתו נרפא־לנו, "and by his bruises there was healing for us". This is the expression, which might come closest to express an atoning suffering in Isa 53:4–6. This statement is sometimes interpreted as if the bruises

---

[24] See Nyberg, "Smärtornas man," 52, for a similar understanding. He refers to Prov 1:3 and 15:33 in his interpretation of מוסר שלומנו.

[25] See also Isa 10:10–11 and Jer 2:19, 30. See further Lindström, *Suffering and Sin*, 138.

[26] E.g. Lindström, *Suffering and Sin*, 137–143.

[27] Cf. Jer 2:1–17; Hos 10:1–15.

were the payment, which brings healing to the "we".[28] With this interpretation, the preposition ב is understood as *beth pretii*. It is right that we have the preposition ב, which was lacking in Isa 53:5a. Still, the statement here is quite differently constructed, compared to Isa 53:5a. It is important to observe that, in other texts where the preposition מן is used together with the verb רפא, it states what someone is healed from, for example the wounds inflicted by someone else.[29] This makes it difficult to use the same preposition, מן, in Isa 53:5a. Moreover, it is not very likely that the preposition ב in ובחברתו indicates a payment. The most common translation is that ב is a reference to the instrument of the healing. If that is right, this part could still be used to indicate an atoning suffering.

To turn to the verb רפא (here *nipʿal*, "to be healed"), already Duhm remarked that the passive form shows that it is not the servant who heals the "we".[30] Moreover, it is neither the servant, nor the bruises, which heal. The verb in *nipʿal* is not normally used with a subject that describes the instrument, by which someone is healed.[31] This makes it less likely that we should understand the phrase ובחברתו as a direct instrument, through which the "we" were healed.[32] The impersonal relation is further emphasised through the use of the preposition ל. A translation which gives more justice to this impersonal relation is reached if we keep the passive form of the verb in ובחברתו נרפא־לנו, "and by his bruises there was healing for us". Hence, this last colon is a statement in line with the previous one, and it expresses the amazement that the servant is being punished and suffers while the "we" are healed. This colon could indicate an atoning suffering. However, read in its context, it is more a confession of the guilt of the "we" than a statement about the atonement achieved by the servant.

In the Psalms, the verb רפא, "to heal", is used by the supplicant, both to urge that God will turn to the suffering person, and in thanksgiving that God has done this.[33] Sometimes it is used in a confession.[34] Isaiah and

---

[28] E.g. Zimmerli, "Zur Vorgeschichte," 238, and Childs, *Isaiah*, 415. Orlinsky, "The So-Called Servant of the Lord," 57–58, argues that if the author had intended vicariousness, he would probably have employed not מן but ב. Then he continues to argue, a single example of ב in our section can hardly be made to prove that this is a matter of vicariousness.

[29] Cf. 2 Kgs 8:29; Jer 30:17.

[30] Duhm, *Das Buch Jesaja*, 399.

[31] See Lev 13:18, 37; 14:3, 48; Deut 28:27, 35; 1 Sam 6:3; 2 Kgs 2:22, Jer 15:18; 17:14; 19:11; 51:8, 9. Cf. however Ezek 47:8; 9, 11, where the stagnant water becomes fresh through the water that flows from the Temple.

[32] E.g. Whybray, *Thanksgiving*, 63, 149.

[33] Pss 6:3; 30:3; 60:4; 147:3.

[34] Pss 41:5; 103:3; 107:20.

Jeremiah both use the word as a means to urge God to turn away from his punishment and to heal his people.[35] In Jer 6:14 we read:

They have treated (וירפאו) the wound of my people
 but only on the surface,[36]
saying, "Peace, peace (שׁלום שׁלום),"
 when there is no peace (שׁלום).

This text is of interest since רפא is used together with שׁלום.[37] In Jer 6:13–15 it is everyone, from prophets to priests, who deals falsely and who treats the wounds על־נקלה, "on the surface". Jer 6:13–15 speaks ironically against a misuse of the wisdom tradition. When the שׁלום is visible on the surface, they have interpreted it as if everything is also שׁלום at a deeper level. It is likely that the "we" have previously spoken in the same manner saying: "Peace, peace" but now they have realised that there was no peace, and that they do have a significant part in the suffering of the servant. That is something, which they had not realised before.

Isaiah 53:6a "All we like sheep have gone astray; we have all turned to our own way"

It is apparent that this bicolon does not express an atoning suffering. It is therefore more important to determine what is actually affirmed through this confession in Isa 53:6, which is probably one of the key verses in the interpretation of the whole section. We have seen this in our analysis of the structure of the text. This is also supported by the fact that this is the first time that the "we" confess something about themselves. In this short text we have two important images. First, we have the image of sheep/shepherd. This is an image deeply rooted in the Old Testament traditions. It is used to describe the relationship between YHWH and his people as well as the responsibility of the leaders to lead the people in the right ways. The image is also used in the surrounding cultures, something which is hinted at in Isa 44:28, where YHWH calls Cyrus "my shepherd". Since the image is so deeply rooted in the people's own traditions, I believe that we should seek to understand this image against the background of the view of the Old Testament. The second image is the image of the way and of going astray.

I will first turn to the second image i.e. to the image of the way and of going astray. The word תעה, "to go astray", is used on one other occasion in Isa 40–55. Then it is all the people, with whom Babylon has laboured, that wander about (Isa 47:15). This indicates that the verb תעה is not a

---

[35] Isa 30:26; 57:18, 19; Jer 3:22; 8:22; 30:17; 33:6.

[36] NRSV has "carelessly", I regard the translation "only on the surface" to be closer to the hebrew על־נקלה.

[37] See Koole, *Isaiah 49–55*, 295.

theological concept. Even so, it is often used with the meaning to turn away from God.[38] See for example Ps 95:10:

For forty years I loathed that generation
and said, "They are a people whose hearts go astray (תעי),
and they do not regard my ways."

Therefore, in this example, in relation to "the sheep" (צאן) and to the context in Isa 53, the verb does have a theological meaning, although it is rather vague, which makes it hard to determine a more specific meaning of the confession. The same is true concerning the phrase לדרכו פנינו, "we have all turned to our own way". The words in the phrase are used rather frequently in various contexts. The word דרך, "way", is often used in Isa 40–55.[39] It is a word, which can describe both a specific and a symbolic way. A symbolic way is also prominent in other texts in Isa 40–55, which do not contain this specific word.[40] This illustrates that it is a prominent image in Isa 40–55.[41]

Since the language of the way is such a prominent theme in Isa 40–55, it is likely that Isa 53:6 is related to other texts with this theme. The complaint in Isa 40:27 is one such important text in relation to Isa 53:6. It is significant that Isa 40:27 is also a statement by the people. It uses the image of sheep to refer to the people, who go their own way. When the "we" in Isa 53:6 confess their previous acts by the use of the image of sheep who go astray, and of people who choose the wrong ways, the statement in Isa 40:27 is reversed. Rather than explaining their present faith by accusing YHWH of not dealing correctly with their chosen way, the "we" confess that their present condition is due to their own choice of the wrong ways.[42]

Even if the description is too vague to help us determine any exact meaning of the confession, it is clear, from its present position in Isa 53:4–6, that it expresses the idea of going astray from YHWH.[43] In Isa 56:11 we meet once more the people who have turned to their own way. This text describes the situation after the exile by using sheep/shepherd images:

---

[38] Cf. Kustár, *"Durch seine Wunden sind wir geheilt"*, 174.

[39] Isa 40:3, 14, 27; 42:16, 24; 43:16, 19; 45:13; 48:15, 17; 49:9, 11; 51:10; 53:6; 55:7, 8, 9.

[40] E.g. Isa 40:9–11; 40:30–31; 43:2; 48:21; 49:10; 52:11–12; 55:12–13.

[41] Cf. Øystein Lund, *"Min vei er skjult for JHWH." veimetaforikk og veitematikk i Jesaja 40–55* (Oslo: Unipub AS, 2004).

[42] E.g. Lund, *"Min vei er skjult for JHWH"*, 267–268.

[43] Kaiser, *Der Königliche Knecht*, 109, argues: "Der eigene Weg steht natürlich im Gegensatz zu dem Wege, auf dem sie nach Jahwes Willen hätten wandeln sollen."

The dogs have a mighty appetite;
they never have enough.
The shepherds also have no understanding;
they have all turned to their own way (לדרכם פנו),
to their own gain, one and all.

This is also a rather general description, but it is still clear that, here too, it is about turning away from YHWH.

There is another important word in relationship to the confession in Isa 53:6. It is the encouragement to "return" (שׁוב) to YHWH. On several occasions this encouragement is connected to their turning away from "the evil way" or to some similar negative expression spoken by the prophets.[44] The encouragement to return also occurs in Isa 40–55; see for example Isa 44:21–22. The people are told to return (שׁוב) because YHWH has swept away their transgressions like a cloud, and their sins like mist. The call to return is not a call to the people to act in such a way that they will thereby repair their relationship with YHWH. This has already been done by YHWH. Even so, as Scheuer puts it:

> [R]epentance can be defined as the people's "positive move" towards YHWH, with a view to reestablishment of the relationship.[45]

Through the confession, in Isa 53:6, the "we" articulate their own responsibility for the suffering and admit that it is the servant who has suffered the consequences. When the "we" confess, that they have gone astray like sheep and that they have all turned to their own way, it is already a return to YHWH. However, the confession is more than a return to YHWH. It is also an embracement of the other sheep, the suffering servant.

We will now turn to the second image, i.e. to that of sheep/shepherd. The image of shepherds who lead the flock astray occurs both in Jeremiah and Ezekiel. Both books express sharp critique against the shepherds.[46] What is special about Isa 53:6 is that the sheep confess that they themselves have gone astray; they have not been led astray. It is also remarkable that the shepherd is totally absent. Instead of discussing shepherds, the confession is followed by a statement about the servant and his suffering. Here we see that the servant is a sheep as well. He is "like a lamb led to slaughter". From the context, in Isa 40–55, we understand that the shepherd is YHWH himself; it is he who will lead the people.[47] The omission of shepherds in

---

[44] Jer 25:5. See also Jer 31:18–22; 35:15; Ezek 33:11.

[45] Scheuer, *The Return of YHWH,* 160.

[46] See Jer 10:21; 12:10; 23:1–4; 25:34–38; 50:6; Ezek 34:1–10. It is not only shepherds who lead the people astray. It can also be false prophets or kings. For the king, see 2 Kgs 21:9 and for prophets, see Jer 23:13, 32; Ezek 14:11, Mic 3:5.

[47] See especially Isa 40:11. Kaiser, *Der Königliche Knecht*, 108, argues: "Gehen wir von diesem Überblick [especially the background in Ezekiel and Jeremiah] zu unserem

Isa 53:6 is, in my view, a key to understanding the confession. It could either be a non-confession: we have all gone astray since the shepherd has led us astray. However, this would be an anticlimax. A more plausible interpretation in line with what has previously been stated by the "we" is that the "we", i.e. the sheep, now see their responsibility for their own predicament. They are not innocent. They might have had bad shepherds, but they have gone astray of their own accord. It is worth noticing that almost the same confession is used as a personal confession in Ps 119:176:

I have gone astray like a lost sheep (תעיתי כשׂה אבד);
seek out your servant,
for I do not forget your commandments.

Hence, what is confessed in Isa 53:6 is that the servant, who is the innocent sheep, suffered and the "we" have escaped.

We have now seen that Isa 53:6 deals with the relationship between the sheep, whose shepherd is YHWH. We have also established that the confession interacts with the complaint in Isa 40:27. I will now turn to Ezekiel 34. It is one of the most prominent Old Testament texts that deal with the relationship between the shepherds of Israel and Israel as God's flock:

Therefore, thus says YHWH God to them: I myself will judge between the fat sheep and the lean sheep. Because you pushed with flank and shoulder, and butted at all the weak animals with your horns until you scattered them far and wide (הפיצעתם אותנה אל־החוצה)[48], I will save my flock, and they shall no longer be ravaged; and I will judge between sheep and sheep. (Ezek 34:20–22)

Ezekiel 34 is a chapter with a long process of gradual expansion.[49] This short passage describes the situation after the exile in which the two groups, the exiled and the people who were left in the land, were pushing each other so that there was not room for all of them.[50] Zimmerli argues about the word הושׁיע, "to deliver, to save", that: "according to the Arabic *wasiʿa* 'to be roomy,' originally meant 'to make room.' 'Deliverance' is 'living space (*Lebensraum*).'"[51] We should probably not put too much emphasis on the etymology of the Arabic. It is more important to observe that we have one text outside Isa 40–55 which uses the images of two groups of

---

Text zurück so wird es sofort klar, dass die Hirtenlosigkeit, die unsere Sprecher irre gehen ließ, nur ihre Gottlosigkeit bzw. ihren Götzendienst meinen kann."

48 Here we have exile terminology. Cf. Walther Zimmerli, *Ezekiel 2: A Commentary on the Book of the Prophet Ezekiel, Chapters 25–48* (Hermeneia Philadelphia Pa.: Fortress Press, 1983), 218.

49 See for example Zimmerli, *Ezekiel 2*, 221–222.

50 For the conflict between these two groups, see further below. Karl-Friedrich Pohlmann, *Der Prophet Hesekiel (Ezechiel) Kapitel 20-48* (ATD vol. 22,2; Göttingen: Vanderhoeck & Ruprecht, 2001), 467, argues that we have the same social situation in the land as Nehemiah encountered in 445 B.C.E.

51 Zimmerli, *Ezekiel 2*, 218.

sheep to describe the conflict after the return from the exile, and it is possible that this conflict is about "living space".

Now I will turn to Isa 40, a chapter where two groups of sheep occur and it is within the section of Isa 40–55. The prologue in Isa 40 was probably still taking shape at the time when Isa 53 was incorporated into Isa 40–55.[52] At this time the text was clearly set in Jerusalem (Isa 40:1).[53] This makes the statement in Isa 40:9–11 rather controversial:

Get you up to a high mountain,
  O Zion, herald of good tidings;
lift up your voice with strength,
  O Jerusalem, herald of good tidings,
    lift it up, do not fear;
say to the cities of Judah,
  "Here is your God!"
See, the Lord YHWH comes with might,
  and his arm rules for him;
his reward is with him,
  and his recompense before him.
He will feed his flock like a shepherd;
  he will gather the lambs in his arms,
and carry them in his bosom,
  and gently lead the mother sheep.

To declare that YHWH comes with the sheep means two things. First, it means that YHWH himself was in the exile, and not in the land. From this follows, secondly, that the people in exile have not gone far from YHWH and the land is therefore not given to those at home.[54] Hence, it is probable that Isa 40:27 is a complaint that God is with the exiled and has forgotten those who are in the land; it is not a complaint regarding the conditions of the exile.[55] Here in Isa 40 we have two distinct groups. We see those who are coming back being carried by YHWH. But we do also have another group, which is addressed through the text.

In Isa 40:3 a voice calls the listeners to prepare a way (פנו דרך) in the wilderness. Maybe it is the confession, in Isa 53:6 itself, which opens such way in the wilderness, or at least in the desert between these two groups.

---

52 For example Isa 40:6–8 was probably incorporated at a late stage. E.g. Kiesow, *Exodustexte im Jesajabuch*, 165, and Kratz, *Kyros im Deuterojesaja-Buch*, 217, among others. I do, however, not believe that 40:9–11 was incorporated as late as Kratz, *Kyros im Deuterojesaja-Buch*, 206–209, 217, suggests. The section is closely connected to 52:7–10 through the use of מבשׂרה, "herald of good tidings", but also to the overall pronouncement in both texts. Cf. also Oorschot, *Von Babel zum Zion*, 157–159, 345.

53 See the discussion of the geographical domicile below.

54 The opposite to what was claimed in Ezek 11:15.

55 See discussion below.

Isaiah 53:6b "yet YHWH has laid on him the iniquity of us all"

The contrast between the "we" and the servant is now enforced once more. In this example it is the phrase הפגיע עון, "has laid on him the iniquity", which might be understood as an atoning suffering. This is a unique use of the verb פגע, "to encounter". It is only used six times in *hip ʿil.*[56] One of these examples is Isa 53:12, but it seems to have a different meaning there since the servant is the subject, while here it is YHWH who is the subject. Isa 53:12 will be closer analysed below. According to Whybray the word is used here in Isa 53:6 with a causative form of the verb, which indicates that it is YHWH who has caused the servant to suffer the punishment, which "we" all deserved to suffer.[57] Whybray finds it interesting to observe that in making the statement that YHWH has afflicted the servant with a punishment, which he did not deserve, but which his compatriots did deserve, the author avoided the use of a language that might have suggested a connection with sacrificial rites. He uses instead a phrase, which is unique and maybe his own invention.[58] Contrary to this view, Koole points out that it is now almost generally accepted that this phrase expresses the vicarious nature of the servant's suffering. In support of this interpretation, he refers to Num 35:19 where the verb (in *qal*) "is used for the avenger of blood who 'comes towards' the guilty man and 'strikes' him to pay off the debt".[59] It is right that the same verb is used in Num 35:19, but it could be questioned whether the debt is paid, since the murderer is killed. It is even more important that the verb is used with its normal meaning about one person (the avenger of blood) who meets another (the murderer). I do not think that Num 35:19 should lead us to interpret Isa 53:6b as an atoning suffering. I believe Koole is right in seeing a parallel to Ps 40:13 "my iniquities have overtaken (השׂגוני) me".[60] Still, this is not an argument for atoning suffering but rather for an unexpected process of cause and effect or, as Hermisson puts it:

> Here, too, the same eerie connection between guilt and its consequences that motivated the observers in verses 2–3 is presupposed.[61]

---

[56] The other occurrences are Isa 53:12; 59:16; Jer 15:11; 36:25; Job 36:32.

[57] Whybray, *Thanksgiving*, 60. Cf. also Isa 53:10a.

[58] Whybray, *Thanksgiving*, 60.

[59] Koole, *Isaiah 49–55*, 298. Cf. also Laato, *The Servant of YHWH and Cyrus*, 145–146, and his criticism of Whybray's interpretation. Still, Laato does not put forward any positive argument in favour of why this verse should hold the notion of a vicarious suffering.

[60] Koole, *Isaiah 49–55*, 298. See also Delitzsch, *Isaiah,* 320–321.

[61] Hans-Jürgen Hermisson, "The Fourth Servant Song in the Context of Second Isaiah," in *The Suffering Servant: Isaiah 53 in Jewish and Christian sources* (ed. Peter Stuhlmacher and Bernd Janowski; Grand Rapids, Mich.: Eerdmans, 2004), 36.

Isa 53:6b is the first time that is clearly stated who caused the suffering of the servant, namely YHWH himself. This is very important, and it is also offensive that YHWH is the cause of the suffering of an innocent servant, of a suffering that the "we" have deserved. This is clearly a vicarious suffering. There is, however, nothing to indicate that this suffering also achieves atonement for the "we".

Conclusion

Isa 53:4–6 is a masterpiece in describing the difference between the "we" and the servant, and also between what the "we" formerly believed and what they have now realised about the servant's suffering and their own guilt. Previously, the "we" had understood the servant's suffering in the same manner as Eliphaz understood Job's suffering. The suffering could then be understood from the wisdom tradition as something essentially good. Even if it is God who disciplines, he also heals, and in the end, the discipline leads to prosperity. Against this background, the sufferer was often seen as responsible for his/her own suffering.

Now the "we" have gained a new understanding of the servant's suffering. The suffering is caused by the "we"-group's guilt and not by his own. This is also what is repeated several times in different ways. The fact that something is stated very clearly at several times, i.e. that the servant has suffered the consequences of the "we" group's guilt, does not in itself imply that something more is meant, such as an atoning suffering.

In the analysis of Isa 53:6a we have observed that the new insight about the relationship between the two groups of sheep has been achieved. The shepherd, which is probably YHWH himself, is only mentioned as the cause of the suffering. The confession in this verse opens the arms of the "we", and thus opens the possibility for reconciliation between these two groups, at least if the servant receives the open arms in an embrace. Therefore, it is not the suffering, which opens the arms, but the "we"-group's confession of their responsibility for the suffering.

2. Isaiah 53 and Sin Offering

There are several problems with establishing the text and the meaning of Isa 53:10a. The understanding of the verse advocated in this study is:

Yet it was the will of the YHWH to crush him with pain,
    if his life is made to guilt.

The interpretation of the second colon of this section is of great significance for the whole understanding of the servant's work, and especially for the meaning of his suffering. I will therefore examine the recent discussion between two scholars, Janowski and Baltzer. Janowski's interpretation is important since it has had a significant impact for the understanding of Isa 53 among scholars. Baltzer's interpretation is important since he discusses and questions the interpretation put forward by Janowski. In this section, I will also discuss some more general aspects of this colon. First, it is of importance to understand what the word אשׁם means in Isa 53:10, and how this meaning is related to the servant's suffering. The translation "guilt", advocated in this study, is not the most common. Therefore, it is necessary to look at some other interpretations of this colon. In NRSV the term אשׁם is translated "offering for sin", and the whole colon reads: "When you make his life an offering for sin." This is a common translation and it is usually based on a supposed connection between אשׁם in Isa 53 and the priestly language in Lev 10:17 and 16:22.[62] Kellermann, who holds a similar view, argues that the term אשׁם has a variety of meanings. In Lev 5:1–7, it is not yet understood as a sacrificial term, but should be seen as a compensatory payment (Lev 5:6). According to him, the first time the term is used as a new description of a sacrifice is in Lev. 5:14–16.[63] In turning to Isa 53, Kellermann nevertheless argues that it is a guilt offering. This interpretation is based on the fact that the servant is like a lamb led to the slaughter (Isa 53:7) and on the fact that the suffering of the righteous is a guilt offering for the many. Therefore, according to Kellermann, the servant's death leads to atonement, to the salvation of the sinner from death, just like a guilt offering.[64] It is important to note that both Zimmerli and Kellermann derive their translations of אשׁם from other parts of Isa 53. They argue that it is doubtful whether the term had this meaning at the time when the text was composed, but since the text is about atoning suffering, the term should be translated in that direction. The language in, for example, Lev 5:14–16 is very different from that in Isa 53:

> YHWH spoke to Moses, saying: When any of you commit a trespass and sin unintentionally in any of the holy things of YHWH, you shall bring, as your guilt offering to YHWH, a ram without blemish from the flock, convertible into silver by the sanctuary shekel; it is a guilt offering. And you shall make restitution for the holy thing in which you were remiss, and shall add one-fifth to it and give it to the priest. The priest shall make atonement on your behalf with the ram of the guilt offering, and you shall be forgiven.
> (Lev 5:14–16)

---

[62] E.g. Zimmerli, "Zur Vorgeschichte," 240, the word אשׁם does, however, not occur in these texts.

[63] Kellermann, "אשׁם," in *TDOT 1* (ed. G. Johannes Botterweck and Helmer Ringgren; Grand Rapids, Mich.: Eerdmans, 1974), 433.

[64] Kellermann, "אשׁם," 435.

In Isa 53 we lack the priest, the ram (even if the servant is described as a lamb), and the statement that it is an offering to YHWH.[65] Another significant problem with the understanding of the servant as a guilt offering is the thought that a human being should be sacrificed for others. This seems very alien to the Old Testament. Whybray argues:

> [T]he idea of acceptance by Yahweh of a human life as an offering for sin is entirely foreign to the Yahwistic tradition, and indeed the idea of human sacrifice was entirely abhorrent to all true Yahwists.[66]

Now we will turn to the arguments of Janowski and Baltzer. The discussion of the understanding of the word אשׁם has been nuanced significantly by Janowski. He argues that Lev 5 is the wrong setting for the translation of the term in Isa 53.[67] Against such a background, he remarks that the servant is not offered as a sacrifice. There is no mentioning of blood and we do not see the slaughter of the servant as a ritual sacrifice. The term דכא, "crush", in v. 10 (cf. also the ptc. in v. 5) is not a sacrificial term. The word טבח, "slaughter", in v. 7 is the term for profane slaughter.[68] Janowski also questions the understanding that Isa 53 should be interpreted with the help of Lev 16:20–22. His argument against such interpretation is – besides the missing term אשׁם in Lev 16 – the difference between a ritual elimination of iniquities, compared to the suffering of the servant. Israel's guilt is not sent away, but carried in Isa 53.[69] Furthermore, Janowski

---

[65] Cf. Heike Henning-Hess, "Bemerkungen zum ASCHAM-begriff in Jes 53,10," *ZAW* 109, no. 4 (1997): 618–626, for a similar critique.

[66] Whybray, *Thanksgiving*, 65. Laato, *The Servant of YHWH and Cyrus*, 148–149, argues against Whybray, stating that there "is a clear difference between the actual practice of the human sacrifice and the use of the sacrificial language in order to explain theologically the innocent suffering of the righteous. Worthy of note is also 2 Macc 7:37 where the Greek word *hileōs* is connected with the Hebrew *kipper*[.]" I agree with this, but I regard this rather as an argument in favour of, rather than against, Whybray's statement. In 2 Macc 7:37 it is one of the seven sons who offers his own life for the laws of the fathers. This shows, as Laato also argues, that sacrificial language could be used in order to explain innocent suffering theologically. To say that the servant's death is a guilt offering, which atones for the guilt of the "we", is something totally different. However, for further critique of Whybray, see also Day, *Yahweh*, 125.

[67] See Janowski, *Stellvertretung*, 88–90. See also Rolf Knierim, "אשׁם," in *TLOT 1* (ed. Ernst Jenni and Claus Westermann; Peabody, Mass.: Hendrickson Publishers, 1997), who determines two foci of the term in the Old Testament. First, a situation of guilt and obligation, in which someone gives something. He incorporates Isa 53:10 to this group. Secondly, a situation in which someone is or becomes obliged to discharge guilt by giving something. The term cannot originally be understood as a sacrifice, even if it later appears alongside sacrificial rites. Furthermore, the old texts that contain the term refer to rehabilitation and restitution. Isa 53:10 is counted among these old texts.

[68] Janowski, *Stellvertretung*, 89.

[69] Janowski, *Stellvertretung*, 89. For a fuller discussion of the relationship between Isa 53 and Lev 16, see above.

argues that the term אשׁם originates, not from the cult, but from the connection to the restitution of damages caused by a misdeed (Gen 26:10; 1 Sam 6:3–4, 8, 17). Here the offender has to give an equivalent.[70] When he applies this meaning to Isa 53:10a, it means that Israel, which is not in a position to take over the obligation that arises from its guilt, must be released from this obligation in order to have any future at all. This liberation comes from an innocent person, who surrenders his life.[71]

Janowski's interpretation gives a more nuanced picture of how a person can be described as an אשׁם. Still, in none of the texts, to which Janowski refers, is a person described as the אשׁם. This is, as previously stated, a thought that is totally foreign to the Old Testament. There are two further significant objections against the interpretation asserted by Janowski. First, he does not discuss the dating of Isa 53. This is problematic, since in recent research, this text is often dated considerably later than the exile. Hence, it could have been influenced by later developments of the אשׁם as a reference to a specific sacrifice. Secondly, and this is an even more important objection, Janowski does not discuss the translation of v. 10 at any length, although this is for him the central statement about the servant's suffering. Janowski only concludes:

> Wenn auch über die ursprüngliche Gestalt dieses Textes keine letzte Sicherheit zu gewinnen ist, so ist doch deutlich, dass das leben (נֶפֶשׁ) des Ebed als אָשָׁם eingesetzt wird.[72]

I am, however, not persuaded by this argument. Before, I return to the alternative translation that is put forth in this dissertation, I will examine Baltzer's argument against Janowski's interpretation.

The interpretation advocated by Baltzer depends on his understanding that the servant is in some way Moses. Referring to Janowski, Baltzer first asserts that a legal interpretation, i.e. that the servant offers his life as a pledge so that the guilt might be paid off, is consistent with the rest of the text. Baltzer argues that it is impossible to overlook the fact that אשׁם is a technical term for a special form of sacrifice. This is, as he says, "at least true for *the postexilic period with which we have to do in DtIsa*" (my italics).[73] Here we see that the interpretations are intimately connected to the dating of the text. If the sacrificial regulations in Lev 7:1–7 alone are taken into account, there could be no greater contrast. As Baltzer puts it, the servant Moses is not a priest. He sacrifices himself, not a ram, and it is not a

---

[70] Janowski, *Stellvertretung*, 89–90. Cf. Henning Graf Reventlow, "Basic Issues in the Interpretation of Isaiah 53," in *Jesus and the Suffering Servant: Isaiah 53 and Christian Origins* (ed. William R. Farmer and William H. Bellinger; Harrisburg, Pa.: Trinity Press, 1998), 29.

[71] Janowski, *Stellvertretung*, 90.

[72] Janowski, *Stellvertretung*, 87.

[73] Baltzer, *Deutero-Isaiah*, 421.

burnt offering. And if YHWH has profaned the servant, he is no longer "holy". He continues:

> This suggests that the present text is arguing against the theory and practice of guilt offerings. It is therefore in line with Isa 43:22–25 and 52:5. In his work DtIsa makes no mention at all of the temple cult and its sacrifices at the restitution of Zion/Jerusalem; and this omission is too striking to be fortuitous. Another point worth considering is how far the polemic against blood sacrifice and burnt offerings was a feature of the discussion during the Persian period. In DtIsa it is only in this one important passage that a sacrificial term is definitely used. But the – true – guilt offering is the Servant Moses.[74]

Baltzer continues to argue that the promise given to Moses, reported in Exod 32:32, where he offers to give his life for the people, renews the promise given to previous generations. Baltzer sees Exod 33:1 as this promise: "To your descendants I will give it [the land]."[75]

I believe Baltzer is right in seeing some form of parallel between the servant and Moses. It is very likely that the Moses-tradition is related to the images of the servant. I am, however, not convinced that the servant is identified with Moses. This is not very persuasive, since the image of the servant is coloured by several different traditions. Baltzer's argument about the lack of sacrificial language in the rest of Isa 40–55 and the use of אשׁם in Isa 53 is important. Nevertheless, I am not convinced that the present text argues against the theory and practice of guilt offerings. It is difficult to find any such argument in Isa 53. Besides, it would be extraordinary if Isa 53:10 actually did describe a servant of YHWH as a guilt offering. This is not only a thought that is totally absent elsewhere in the rest of the Old Testament, but sacrificial language is also remarkably uncommon in Isa 40–55.

As I have concluded above, it is not necessary to translate אשׁם neither as a guilt-offering, nor as a compensatory payment, since it could also mean guilt.[76] This is the understanding advocated here.[77] Against such understanding, Janowski argues that אשׁם is not a term for trespass or transgressions, but a term that always relates to a particular type of consequence of transgression, of which the offender is aware and for which he must take responsibility.[78] However, this understanding seems somewhat complicated when reading Jer 51:5:

---

[74] Baltzer, *Deutero-Isaiah*, 421.

[75] Baltzer, *Deutero-Isaiah*, 421–422.

[76] Gen 26:10; Jer 51:5. See also Koole, *Isaiah 49–55*, 320. Cf. also Kaufmann, *History*, 133, who argues that אשׁם, "in restitution" should be pointed אָשֵׁם, "guilty". He translate this colon "If Thou dost make his soul guilty", with reference to 1 Kgs 19:2; Ps 34:22, 23; Prov 30:10.

[77] See further arguments above.

[78] Janowski, *Stellvertretung*, 90. Contra David J. A. Clines, ed., *The Dictionary of Classical Hebrew* (Sheffield: Sheffield Academic Press, 1993).

Israel and Judah have not been forsaken
by their God, YHWH of hosts,
though their land is full of guilt (אשׁם)
before the Holy One of Israel.

Jer 50–51 are chapters with several parallels to Isa 40–55.[79] In Jer 51:5 the words are directed to those in exile. They are told that land is full of guilt (אשׁם), and they are urged to return and to save their lives, since Babylon will fall. In this case it is probable that the term refers to trespasses or transgressions. In Isa 53:10 the perspective is the opposite. The "we" group, who lives in the land, have previously thought that the servant was full of guilt, since he was taken into exile. Now they have realised their own guilt, and they express their belief that YHWH has made the servant's life to "guilt", since it is God, who has let him suffer. This understanding carries an opposite meaning of אשׁם compared to the more common understanding. Even so, it does sometimes occur in the Old Testament. In Ps 68:22 we have another statement, which carries some similarities to Isa 53:10:

But God will shatter the heads of his enemies,
the hairy crown of those who walk in their guilty ways (מתהלך באשׁמיו).
(Ps 68:22)

Here it is God who will shatter the heads of those who walk in their guilty ways. Given a similar understanding of the cause to the suffering, it would be a natural assumption that the servant in Isa 53 was guilty, since he was actually crushed by YHWH. However, the "we" have realised that this was not the case. Since the servant has suffered the consequences of the guilt of the "we" it must be YHWH who has caused the servant to be אשׁם, with the meaning guilt. Therefore, with the suggested interpretation, Isa 53:10a is not a statement about the servant's true identity, but a statement about the former understanding of his identity. This statement never receives any affirmation. Was it really YHWH's will to crush the servant? Or was that only the assumption of the "we"? The section does not give an answer to such questions. Instead, Isa 53:10a is followed by a promise that indicates the true identity of the servant and the verse continues with the promise of offspring and prolonged days. From this, we understand that it is not the suffering, but the promise of future prosperity, which constitutes the servant's identity in relation to YHWH.

The understanding of this verse as a reference to a specific offer has often been supported by the assumption that Isa 53:4–6 describes the servant's suffering as an atoning suffering.[80] As seen above, it can be questioned

[79] See for example Reinhard Gregor Kratz, "Der Anfang des Zweiten Jesaja in Jes 40,1f. und das Jeremiabuch," *ZAW* 106 (1995): 243–261, for the relationship between Isa 40:1–2 and Jer 50–51.

[80] See Zimmerli, "Zur Vorgeschichte," 238–240.

whether Isa 53:4–6 does describe an atoning suffering. It can be positively affirmed that the central statement of these verses is that the "we" have now realised their guilt for what has taken place. Mowinckel has formulated a somewhat similar view:

The atoning worth of the Servant's action depends on whether his fellow-countrymen appropriate it, so as to see their own guilt and thereby be moved to conversion and penitence.[81]

Following the interpretation suggested here, Isa 53:10a ends with the confession and the description of the former understanding of the servant's suffering. When he was cut off from the land of the living, he was also counted as guilty, at least by the "we".

Conclusion

The term אשׁם in Isa 53:10 should neither be understood against its priestly background in Lev 5, nor should it be seen as a compensatory payment. As Whybray has pointed out, the idea of human life as a sacrifice is "entirely foreign to the Yahwistic tradition".[82] Furthermore, sacrificial language is also remarkably uncommon in Isa 40–55. With the understanding of the word אשׁם as "guilt" we are able to overcome these problems. Even if this translation is abandoned, both arguments against understanding אשׁם as a sacrifice are valid and have to be countered. This is something, which has not been done hitherto.

3. Isaiah 53 and Righteousness

It is possible to translate the phrase יצדיק צדיק עבדי לרבים in Isa 53:11 in at least two ways. It could mean that "the righteous one, my servant, will make many righteous". This is the most common translation and it is supported in many commentaries.[83] The phrase could also mean that: "the righteous one, my servant, will show himself righteous before the many".[84] This is the interpretation which is advocated here.

The translation of צדק, "to be righteous" (*qal*), in *hip'il* is dubious. The verb is rather common, but it is only used twelve times in *hip'il* in the Old

[81] Mowinckel, *He that cometh*, 211.

[82] Whybray, *Thanksgiving*, 65.

[83] E.g. Koole, *Isaiah 49–55*, 332–335, and Walter Brueggemann, *Isaiah 40–66* (Westminster Bible Companion Louisville; London: John Knox Press, 1998), 148.

[84] E.g. Mowinckel, *He that cometh*, 199, Westermann, *Isaiah 40–66*, 267–268, and Beuken, *Jesaja*, 232–233.

Testament.[85] The verb in this form is most frequently used in a juridical sense. Some scholars even want to narrow it down and claim that it is always a forensic term in the Old Testament.[86] This is however questionable, as will be shown below. In order to interpret the use of the verb in Isa 53:11, I will investigate it by two means. First, the other eleven texts will be closer examined in order to clarify how the verb צדק, "to be righteous", can be used in *hip'il*. Secondly, I will narrow down the perspective to Isa 53 to see which interpretation is the most plausible one in this context.

Now it is time to turn to the other eleven occurrences. In three examples, צדק is used in *hip'il* about a judge, whether human or divine, who renders justice, and who does not require the vindication of the guilty party.[87] In 1 Kgs 8:32 we read:

> [T]hen hear in heaven, and act, and judge your servants, condemning the guilty by bringing their conduct on their own head, and vindicating the righteous by rewarding them according to their righteousness (ולהצדיק צדיק לתת לו כצדקתו).

In this, and the other two texts, the innocent is declared innocent and the guilty is condemned. These three sections do not contain the idea of requiring the vindication of the guilty party. This is clear from 1 Kgs 8:32, where it is the righteous who are rewarded "according to their righteousness" (כצדקתו). In two examples, we find texts where a guilty person is acquitted, but these texts are about unjust judges and contain a critique of them:[88]

> [W]ho acquit (מצדיקי) the guilty for a bribe,
> and deprive the innocent of their rights! (Isa 5:23)

In our sixth case, it is God who declares, "I will not acquit the guilty" (כי לא־אצדיק רשע).[89] The verb under discussion also occurs in the third servant song, Isa 50:8, where the servant declares, "[H]e who vindicates (מצדיקי) me is near." This is a similar use, compared to the six previous sections. The servant asserts his willingness to appear before his accusers, because he knows that he is innocent, and that YHWH will vindicate him.

In the other examples, the verb צדק in *hip'il* has a slightly different meaning. It still has some form of juridical sense in these texts, 2 Sam 15:4, Ps 82:3, and Job 27:5 as well. The word expresses or implies an exact apportion of justice. This is clear when we hear Job stating that:

---

[85] Exod 23:7; Deut 25:1; 2 Sam 15:4; 1Kgs 8:32; Isa 5:23; 50:8; 53:11; Ps 82:3; Job 27:5; Prov 17:15; Dan 12:3; 2 Chr 6:23.

[86] E.g. Koole, *Isaiah 49–55*, 232, with the only possible exception in Dan 12:3.

[87] Deut 25:1; 1 Kgs 8:32; 2 Chr 6:23.

[88] Cf. also Prov 17:15.

[89] Cf. Whybray, *Thanksgiving*, 67.

Far be it from me to say that you are right
(חלילה לי אם־אצדיק אתכם);
until I die I will not put away my integrity from me.
(Job 27:5)

The verb is used to show the impossibility for Job to say that he is anything other than right. He will never admit his opponents are right. As we have seen from this survey, צדק in *hip ʿil* is normally used to express justice, which implies that the righteous is vindicated and the guilty is judged. It is not used in a positive way to describe how a guilty person is vindicated.

We have now studied ten of the eleven occurrences; in all of them we have a similar use of the verb in *hip ʿil*. However, the eleventh text, Dan 12:3, falls into its own category and this is particularly interesting, since it is sometimes assumed that this is a reuse of Isa 53.[90] Here we read:

Those who are wise shall shine like the brightness of the sky, and those who lead many to righteousness (ומצדיקי), like the stars forever and ever. (Dan 12:3)

In order to interpret Dan 12:3, it is also important to take a preceding text, Dan 11:33 into account:

The wise (משׂכילים) among the people shall give understanding to many; for some days, however, they shall fall by sword and flame, and suffer captivity and plunder.

It is probable that this section in Daniel alludes to Isa 53. The משׂכילים, "the wise" are probably named after the servant, הנה ישׂכיל עבדי, "see, my servant shall prosper". This allusion is also supported by the statement מצדיקי הרבים, "who lead many to righteousness", in Dan 12:3. It is worth noting that in Dan 11:33, the wise make the people understand, whereas in 12:3 they make them righteous. The two notions are evidently closely related. Some scholars claim that the wise make the many righteous by their death so that their martyrdom is atoning.[91] This suggestion is based on the fact that in Dan 11:33, the wise will be martyred. There is, however, nothing in the text of Daniel to suggest that this martyrdom would be connected to their function of leading the many to righteousness. A simpler and more plausible interpretation is to suppose that the wise make the many righteous by instructing them.[92]

It follows from the discussion above that none of the uses of צדק in *hip ʿil* that are found in other passages of the Old Testament describes an

---

[90] E.g. John Joseph Collins, *Daniel: A Commentary on the Book of Daniel* (Hermeneia Minneapolis, Minn.: Fortress Press, 1993), 385, 393.

[91] E.g. André Lacocque, *The Book of Daniel* (London: SPCK, 1979).:230). Cf. also H. L. Ginsberg, "Oldest Interpretation of the Suffering Servant," *VT* 3 (1953): 400–404, who has advanced the thesis that in Dan 10–12 we have the oldest interpretation of the suffering servant.

[92] E.g. Whybray, *Thanksgiving*, 68–69, and Collins, *Daniel*, 393.

atoning suffering, while in Dan 12:3 it appears that someone vindicates a guilty person. The meanings of this word attested elsewhere in the Old Testament give three possible alternatives for the interpretation of Isa 53. The most common use of the verb צדק in *hip ʿil* is that the innocent is vindicated. This meaning does however seem unlikely in Isa 53:11. The second option is that it should be taken as in Dan 12:3, i.e. to imply that the servant leads many to righteousness through his teaching. The third proposal is more plausible. It is suggested that צדק in *hip ʿil* is an internal causative *hip ʿil*. This means that the servant will show himself to be righteous.[93] According to Whybray, it is not possible to make a decisive choice between these two latter alternatives:

> Between these two interpretations of יצדיק here it is difficult to decide. But whether the Servant brought salvation to the many through his teaching, or acted righteously with regard to the many, his action has nothing to do with vicarious suffering.[94]

The difference between the second and third alternatives are, however, not so slight. Dan 12:3 implies that one person can require the vindication of a guilty party. This is not achieved through suffering, but through teaching. This is a new meaning, compared to the other uses, and it is possible that Dan 12:3 alludes to Isa 53. This opens the possibility that Isa 53:11 is also about vindication of a guilty. Against such an interpretation, it can be argued that Dan 12:3 is a later text and possibly inspired by Isa 53 and not the other way around.

There are further arguments in favour of the interpretation that צדק in *hip ʿil* in Isa 53 is an internal causative *hip ʿil*. This interpretation is supported by the overall description of the servant and his work, and by the statement of the "we". First, the servant is passive throughout the entire poem and does not act. It is YHWH and the "we" who speak. Secondly, the first statement in Isa 52:12 is that something new and unseen shall become visible, namely the prosperity of the servant. The new thing is not the servant's embrace of the "we" but the "we"-group's embrace of the servant. It is the "we" who see and gain a truer understanding of the servant's suffering. He has previously suffered because of the "we", but they now understand and see that the servant is righteous (צדק).[95] This could be equated with the promise in Ps 24:4–5:

---

[93] This is suggested by Sigmund Mowinckel, "Der Knecht Jahwäs," *Norsk Teologisk Tidsskrift* (1921): 1–69, 47–50, Mowinckel, *He that cometh*, 198–199, and followed by Westermann, *Isaiah 40–66*, 267–268. See also Whybray, *Thanksgiving*, 68–69.

[94] Whybray, *Thanksgiving*, 71.

[95] Cf. Ps 36:11; 103:17.

Those who have clean hands and pure hearts,
who do not lift up their souls to what is false,
and do not swear deceitfully.
They will receive blessing from YHWH,
and vindication (וצדקה) from the God of their salvation.

Conclusion

The interpretation that seems most probable is that the many see in him a righteous one, and not that the servant makes the many righteous.[96] The use of the verb צדק in *hip'il* makes Isa 53:11 allude to the words spoken by the servant in Isa 50:8: "[H]e who vindicates (מצדיקי) me is near." This means that the use of צדק in *hip'il* in Isa 53:11 is in line with the more common use of the verb as a juridical term for vindication. The servant, who is righteous, will also be seen as righteous by the many. This is the interpretation, which is closest to the common use of this word, and also closest to the rest of Isa 53.

3. Isaiah 53 and Intercession

In this part I will question the view that Isa 53:12b indicates that the servant made intercession like the prophets. It is sometimes argued that two lines of tradition from the prophetic office come together in the description of the servant in Isa 53.[97] These two lines are the prophet as intercessor and prophetic suffering. Both lines are intertwined in the case of Jeremiah. I agree that prophetic suffering has coloured the image of the servant in the servant songs. This line is most prominent in the third servant song but it also occurs in the fourth. That the tradition of prophetic suffering also colours the description of the suffering in the fourth servant song is especially clear with regard to the affinity between Jer 11:19 and Isa 53:6. It is, however, questionable if we encounter the other line of tradition, the prophet as intercessor, in the fourth servant songs.

Before we go deeper into the critique of understanding Isa 53 in line with the tradition of the prophet as intercessor, we will look at the arguments in favour of this understanding. This view is mainly based on the translation of the last words of the fourth servant song (Isa 53:12b): "and [he] intervened (יפגיע) for the transgressors." Here the translation of the

[96] E.g. Beuken, *Jesaja*, 232.

[97] E.g. Hermann Spieckermann, "The Conception and Prehistory of the Idea of Vicarious Suffering in the Old Testament," in *The Suffering Servant: Isaiah 53 in Jewish and Christian sources* (ed. Bernd Janowski and Peter Stuhlmacher; Grand Rapids, Mich.; Cambridge: Eerdmans, 2004).

word יפגיע (*hip ʿil* 3rd per. sg. m. of פגע, "to encounter") is of great significance. This verb is used with the meaning "to intercede" in Jer 7:16 and "to urge strongly" in Jer 36:25. In Jer 36:25 the urging is directed to the king. The text in Jer 7:16 is more important with regard to the interpretation of Isa 53:12b since it refers to intercession:

As for you, do not pray (תתפלל) for this people, do not raise a cry or prayer (ותפלה) on their behalf, and do not intercede (תפגע) with me, for I will not hear you. (Jer 7:16)

In this verse it is probable that the verb פגע, "to encounter", means to intercede since it is paralleled with both פלל in *hitpa ʿel*, "to pray", and תפלה, "prayer". The affinities between the servant and Jeremiah have led to the assumption that also Isa 53:12 describes the servant as interceding. Such an understanding is uncertain. The verb פגע is rather unusual in *hip ʿil.* Of a total of five occurrences, three are in the book of Isaiah and two of these are in the fourth servant song.[98] In order to understand Isa 53:12, we must ask: What could be expected as a last statement summing up all of Isa 53? Is it a new thought that the servant made intercession? In order to answer these questions I will return to the structure of the fourth servant song and to the description of the servant. Then as a second stage of the analysis, I will try to translate יפגיע and the last bicolon of Isa 53:12.

As we saw in the analysis of the structure of Isa 53, the last bicolon is a summary of the whole text and also a parallel to the first bicolon in Isa 53:1:

Who has believed what we have heard?
And to whom has the arm of the YHWH been revealed?

This is the question asked, and the answer is given between this text and the summary of the answer in the last bicolon in Isa 53:12. What is striking with the answer is the total passivity of the servant. He does not speak, he does not act, he does not intercede, and he does not even complain. The only thing that the servant does is to suffer. This is, however, not an activity in the song. The activity, if we can talk about any activity at all, is performed by the "we"-group. They see, they speak, and they confess their new understanding of the servant's suffering. Following this, the new understanding of the servant's suffering is also what we could expect to find summarised in Isa 53:12. This last bicolon also states that "yet he bore the sins of many". This is a clear summary of the new understanding of the servant's suffering expressed by the "we"-group. If the last colon means that the servant made intercession, we encounter a new feature, which we have not previously met in the text. The servant, who is so undoubtedly described as silent, is now supposed to have made intercession. It is not very likely that a summary gives such a new, important, and different

[98] Isa 53:6, 12; 59:16.

statement compared to the rest of Isa 53. Furthermore, if the summary actually wants to make a new and different statement at the end, it could have been expressed with greater clarity. There are two problems with the common translation of the summary, namely that it is odd to find a new feature in a summary, which is contrary to the rest of the text, and the word יפגיע is open to other understandings. Therefore I will now turn to another possible translation of the verb פגע, "to encounter".

The verb פגע in *qal* does mean "to encounter". It can be used in both a positive and a negative way and it can also mean "to attack". More interesting for our concern is that it is used in the sense "to put pressure on someone".[99] In relation to the verb, the preposition ל indicates on whose behalf the urging is made (cf. Gen 23:8), and the preposition ב indicates who that is encountered or urged (cf. Jer 7:16). The verb in *hip ʿil* conveys at least two distinct meanings. In Isa 53:6 פגע is used with a causative sense "to cause to strike", the preposition ב indicates who is stricken. In Jer 36:25 the same word means to urge or to plead with words, and this is probably also the meaning in Jer 15:11. With regard to Isa 59:16, some scholars argue, with reference to the context, that the ptc. מפגיע refers to the intervention with deeds rather than words.[100] This brief survey indicates that the verb does not always refer to intercession. It can also describe other forms of interventions.

To turn to Isa 53:12, the first thing that strikes us is that the text lacks any direct object for the verb. The preposition ל in ולפשׂעים, "for the transgressors", indicates on whose behalf the verb is used. It is also most probable that והוא, "he" is the subject of the verb. Here the *hip ʿil* form is probably not used in a causative sense, since we lack both the direct and the indirect object. The text is, however, not fully established here, 1QIsa[a] uses the verb יפגע in *qal* and LXX has a passive form παρεδοθη, "he was given". Neither of these texts declares that the servant interceded. It has been suggested that this verse should be translated in the sense that he let himself be hit on behalf of the unfaithful.[101] This proposal seems probable, since we do not have any object for an intercession and since the servant is not said to have intervened previously. Furthermore, this translation is a better parallel, both to the preceding colon and to Isa 53:6. The parallel to Isa 53:6 is important, since it seems rather improbable that the text would use the same unusual form of this word twice, and with two very different meanings.

---

[99] Cf. Maiberger, "פגע," in *TDOT 11* (ed. G. Johannes Botterweck and Helmer Ringgren; Grand Rapids, Mich.: Eerdmans, 2001), 470–476.

[100] E.g. Maiberger, "פגע," 474, and Whybray, *Thanksgiving*, 72–73.

[101] Cf. Beuken, *Jesaja*, 236–237.

However, the most common interpretation of Isa 53:12b is that the servant made intercession for the transgressors. This translation is partly based on the understanding that the text refers to the prophet as intercessor.[102] If this is the intention of the text, it might have been more natural to use the more common and specific word פלל, "to intercede". We could at least expect there to be a direct object to פגע. A greater clarity could be expected, since intercession is not spoken of earlier in the text.

However, the verb פגע is probably used with a special intention. It makes us look back at the confession in Isa 53:6 where it is declared that God has caused this suffering of the servant on behalf of the "we" group, who had sinned. Now, in the summary, we are also reminded that the servant let it all happen to him, since he quietly let himself be led to the slaughter. Westermann concludes with regard to Isa 53:12:

> This does not mean, as some editors imagine, that he made prayers of intercession for them, but that with his life, his suffering and death, he took their place and underwent their punishment in their stead.[103]

With regard to the translation of this verse, we must take into account the fact that an object for intercession is missing. This omission enforces that what is done is done for the sake of the transgressors. I therefore prefer the translation "to intervene" in favour of "to intercede". To intervene is more open and has less theological implications. Hopefully, the understanding "to intervene" can enforce the conclusion that the servant suffered on behalf of the transgressors. I translate the last bicolon:

> yet he bore the sin of many,
> and intervened for the transgressors.

If we return to the connection between prophetic suffering and intercession, we can see that Jer 15:10–11 shows a significant resemblance to Isa 53. Like Jeremiah, the servant has suffered the consequences of the actions of others, in spite of what both the servant and Jeremiah have done for these others. It is not the intercession that should be enforced, but the difference between what the servant (like Jeremiah) has done, and what the others have done.

Conclusion

There are three important arguments against understanding this last colon of Isa 53 as a declaration about the servant's intercession. First, in the whole of Isa 53, the servant is silent and obedient. The silence of the servant is enforced in several ways. Moreover, he does not perform any active action. Therefore, it seems peculiar that the last statement and the summary of the whole poem would contain a totally new feature, namely that the

---

[102] See among others Whybray, *Thanksgiving*, 72–74.
[103] Westermann, *Isaiah 40–66*, 269.

servant intercedes. Secondly, the verb is unusual as a term for intercession in the Old Testament. Thirdly, the syntax of the verse lacks the important object for an intercession. What is enforced by the text is on whose behalf the servant intervenes, not to whom this is directed.

Chapter 8

The Phrase נשׂא עון in the Old Testament

In Isa 53 it is stated about the servant that: ועונתם הוא יסבל, "he bears their iniquities" (v. 11), and והוא חטא־רבים נשׂא, "yet he bore the sin of many" (v. 12). These phrases are important for scholars who understand the servant's suffering as an atoning suffering, a view, which will be questioned here. One of the most influential studies regarding these expressions in Isa 53 was undertaken by Zimmerli. According to him, there is no doubt that these phrases should be understood in connection to "[d]ie Formel נשׂא עון die in Jes. liii in grosse Freiheit variiert ist".[1] He concludes:

Kehren wir von diesen Wahrnehmungen her zu Jes. liii zurück, so kann kein Zweifel daran bestehen, dass wir uns trotz des freien Sprachgebrauches auf der Linie der priesterlichen Verwendung des נשׂא עון befinden. Hier ist mit dem „Schuld tragen“ nicht auf das Schuld-Tragen Gottes gedeutet, sondern im Sinne von Lev. xvi 22 und x 17 auf das stellvertretende Schuld/Strafe-Tragen eines Menschen, des Knechtes Jahwes. Die Nähe zu priesterlicher Rede verrät sich auch in der Verwendung des Begriffes אשׁם. Ein Vergleich von Lev. v 1 mit 2–4 zeigt, dass verbales אָשֵׁם geradezu synonym zu נשׂא עון verwendet werden kann. Der Knecht, der sich zum אשׁם macht, trägt in der Zerschlagenheit, die an ihm sichtbar wird, die Schuld- und Straflast der Vielen.[2]

However, some objections must be raised against Zimmerli's interpretation. First, the connection between נשׂא עון and the term אשׁם is not that uncomplicated. We have seen that the translation of Isa 53:10, where the term אשׁם occurs, is problematic because of both text-critical and linguistic problems. I have a different understanding of this verse compared to Zimmerli.[3] It is doubtful if the term אשׁם, in Isa 53:10, should be interpreted in connection to Lev 5:1.[4] Hence, we should not take as a starting point in the interpretation of Isa 53:11–12 the supposition that נשׂא עון and אשׁם are synonymous. Secondly, it can be questioned whether the phrase נשׂא עון, "to carry iniquity", is a *Formel* since the meaning of this phrase varies in different texts. Furthermore, even if the phrase נשׂא עון is a *Formel* this does not necessarily help us to interpret the meaning of Isa 53:11–12, since this exact expression does not occur in Isa 53. These ob-

[1] Zimmerli, "Zur Vorgeschichte," 239–240.

[2] Zimmerli, "Zur Vorgeschichte," 240.

[3] See further above.

[4] See further above.

jections make it important to undertake a close analysis of the interpretation of both Isa 53:11–12 and of the phrase נשׂא עון.

I will first turn to Isa 53:11b. The words סבל, "to carry", and עון, "iniquities", that are used here are only used together in one other example in the Old Testament. This is in Lam 5:7, where we hear the children in the land complaining:

Our ancestors sinned; they are no more,
and we bear their iniquities (עונתיהם סבלנו).

The children do not complain that they suffer an atoning suffering, but rather a vicarious suffering. It is a complaint over what they see as a corrupt cause and effect.[5] Therefore, it seems natural to interpret Isa 53:11b with a similar meaning. However, before we decide in favour of such an interpretation I will deal with some objections raised by Laato against translating Isa 53:11b in the same direction as Lam 5:7.[6] First, Laato argues that the suffering in Lam 5:7 is ongoing in contrast to Isa 53, where it belongs to the past. Secondly, in Lam 5:7, the people lament that they have to bear the consequences of the sins of their ancestors. In Isa 53 the "we" confess that it was their own guilt that the servant had to bear. Thirdly, the fundamental error in seeing a parallel between Lam 5:7 and 53:11b is, according to Laato, the lack of attention to the distinctive features of respective contexts. For that reason he believes that a parallel is based only on linguistic comparison of phrases. Against the third point, it can be maintained that in both examples, the suffering described is probably the consequences of the exile, and the suffering is associated with the exile. Therefore, both sections have similar references. Consequently, there is more than a linguistic comparison, even if the texts do not contain exactly the same idea. The second objection, that there is a confession in Isa 53 and a complaint in Lam 5:7, is important. This indicates that there is a new understanding of the cause and effect of the suffering. This is something to which I will return in the interpretation of the whole passage of Isa 53. This does, however, not indicate that the suffering is atoning. The first point does not in any way show why the meanings in the two texts should be different. Furthermore, the main point in the critique by Laato is that these texts can not be interpreted as parallels to each other. His critique does not give any arguments to convince us why Isa 53:11b should describe an atoning suffering in contrast to Lam 5:7. However, there are two important arguments in favour of seeing a parallel between these two texts. First, they are the only two occurrences of this combination of words. Secondly,

---

[5] See also Whybray, *Thanksgiving*, 30. He compares this to Exod 20:5, where the iniquity of the parents is visited to the third and the fourth generation.

[6] E.g. Laato, *The Servant of YHWH and Cyrus*, 143.

both texts describe the consequences of the exile. Therefore, it can be argued that the obligation to prove one's case must rest with those who understand the texts to have fundamentally different meanings. To conclude, there is problem with the cause and effect of the suffering in both texts. Still, this is not an argument in favour of an atoning suffering.

Now I will turn to Isa 53:12b. The phrase נשׂא חטא, "to bear sin", occurs, apart from here, in eight passages in the Old Testament.[7] In all of these examples, the phrase describes a situation where a person bears the consequences of his/her own sin. A suffering on behalf of others is never present.[8] In Ezekiel we have a situation where this is described in the case of the exile:

> They shall repay you for your lewdness, and you shall bear the penalty for your sinful idolatry (וחטאי גלוליכן תשׂאינה); and you shall know that I am YHWH God. (Ezek 23:49)

This is neither vicarious nor atoning suffering. Isa 53:12b is the only example in the Old Testament where the phrase is used to describe a person who bears the sin of others. However, I agree with Whybray who states that:

> It may however be said that the similarity of והוא חטא־רבים נשׂא here to ועונתם הוא יסבל in verse 11 can hardly be accidental, and it is extremely improbable that any difference of meaning between the two should have been intended by the author, especially since נשׂא in the sense used here is exactly equivalent to סבל, and חטא and עון are used interchangeably in the priestly writings.[9]

Regarding the exact words in Isa 53:11b and 12b, it seems probable that these verses describe a situation where the servant suffers the consequences of the sin and iniquity of others. This, however, is a vicarious suffering, but not necessarily an atoning suffering.

We have seen that the exact expressions used in our text do not normally have the meaning of an atoning suffering. To complete the analysis, I will turn to the phrase נשׂא עון. Zimmerli, among others argues that the tradition behind this phrase also helps us to understand Isa 53:11b, 12b. However, as been stated above, this specific phrase does not occur in Isa 53. It can also be noted that it is never applied to the servant of YHWH in Isa 40–55. It occurs, however, in some passages which have frequently been used to support the theory of atoning suffering in Isa 53. To interpret Isa 53 with the help of this phrase is not unreasonable since it has almost the same meaning and sometimes occurs in similar texts as the phrases discussed above. I am, however, not convinced that this also means that the servant suffers an atoning suffering.

---

[7] Lev 19:17; 20:20; 22:9; 24:15; Num 9:13; 18:22, 32; Ezek 23:49. See also Whybray, *Thanksgiving*, 30, and Zimmerli, "Zur Vorgeschichte," 239.

[8] Cf. Whybray, *Thanksgiving*, 30–31.

[9] Whybray, *Thanksgiving*, 31.

The verb נשא, "to carry", in *qal* together with עון, "iniquity", as direct object occurs 29 times in the Old Testament.[10] There are two further texts where a similar relationship is implied.[11] We have one similar text where the verb is used in *hip῾il* (Lev 22:16). Three other texts have the similar form: נשא בעון.[12] In seven cases, God is the subject and takes away the sins, which means that he forgives. These passages are positioned outside the priestly writings of P and Ezekiel.[13] Zimmerli divides the other texts into three categories.[14] First, in the sphere of sacral law, the phrase is used in concluding formulations for the purpose of establishing a condition of guilt. Secondly, in a weaker usage, the expression can take on the meaning "to be responsible for something" (such as the sanctuary, Num 18:1). Thirdly, with reference to substitutionary acts, it can express the "guilt-bearing" of the substitute. Thus the scapegoat takes the guilt of the people on itself and bears it into the desert (Lev 16:22). The scapegoat in Lev 10:17 is ordained by YHWH so "that you may remove the guilt of the congregation, to make atonement on their behalf". Zimmerli asks if the fact that Aaron bears on his gold headband "any guilt incurred in the holy offering" (Exod 28:38) makes the text belong to this category. He states that Ezek 4:4 should clearly be understood against the background of this third circle. Zimmerli also argues that we can scarcely deny that ideas are set in motion here, which were to be more fully worked out in Isa 53, again probably in a prophetic figure.

---

[10] Exod 28:38, 43; 34:7; Lev 5:1, 17; 7:18; 10:17; 16:22; 17:16; 19:8; 20:17, 19; Num 5:31; 14:18, 34; 18:1 (twice), 23; 30:16; Ezek 4:4, 5, 6; 14:10; 44:10, 12; Hos 14:3; Mic 7:18; Pss 32:5; 85:3.

[11] Gen 4:13 and Isa 33:24.

[12] Ezek 18:19, 20 (twice).

[13] Exod 34:7; Num 14:18; Isa 33:24; Hos 14:3; Mic 7:18; Pss 32:5; 85:3.

[14] Walther Zimmerli, *Ezekiel 1: A Commentary on the Book of the Prophet Ezekiel, Chapters 1–24* (Hermeneia Philadelphia Pa.: Fortress Press, 1979), 164–165. Cf. Also Kelvin G. Friebel, *Jeremiah's and Ezekiel's Sign-acts: Rhetorical Nonverbal Communication* (JSOTsup vol. 283; Sheffield: Sheffield Academic Press, 1999), 219. He makes a different division. First, he states that עון can have both the meaning of (a) sin/guilt and (b) the resulting punishment for sin. Then he argues: "When the phrase נשא + עון is used biblically, it functions with both senses of עון: (1a) culpability for sin (cf. Lev 5.1, 17; 7.18; 22.16) for which provision was given for the atoning of the guilt incurred; (1b) bearing responsibility as a substitute or representative in incurring the guilt of others (cf. Aaron and the priests with respect to the Temple and people: Num 18.1, 23; Exod 28.38; husband for his wife: Num 30.16); (2a) receiving the punishment for the sin […] (2b) The punishment was borne by a representative or substitute (scapegoat; Lev. 10.17; 16.22)." See also Baruch J. Schwartz, "The Bearing of Sin in the Priestly Literature," in *Pomegranates and Golden Bells: Studies in Biblical, Jewish, and Near Eastern Ritual, Law and Literature in Honor of Jacob Milgrom* (ed. David P. Wright, et al.; Winona Lake Ind.: Eisenbrauns, 1995), 3–21. None of these scholars are, however, dealing with the examination of the phrase made by Whybray, *Thanksgiving*, 31–57.

For our concern, the third group is of most interest. If these texts hold what Zimmerli calls substitutionary acts, that is acts which could be equated to atonement, it is more likely that Isa 53:11b and 12b should also be interpreted in that direction. The texts belonging to this group are: Exod 28:38; Lev 10:17; 16:22; Num 14:34; Ezek 4:4, 5, and 6, and sometimes Num 18:1, 23 have also been included in this group. The texts from Leviticus and Ezekiel have most often been seen as parallels to Isa 53. Consequently, I will start with those texts and then proceed with the others. Ezek 18 does not involve an act of substitution but will be discussed here since it might be related to Isa 53.

1. Leviticus 10:17

Lev 10:17 is the first text, which contains the phrase נשׂא עון that I will examine:

> Why did you not eat the sin offering (החטאת) in the sacred area? For it is most holy, and God has given it to you that you may remove the guilt (לשׂאת את־עון) of the congregation, to make atonement (לכפר) on their behalf before YHWH.

Lev 10:17 belongs to a narrative about an apparent and inadvertent breach of the commandments (Lev 10:16–20). Moses has made enquiries about the disposal of the victim and discovers that it has been entirely burnt, whereas Eleazar and Ithamar should have eaten it. It is not necessary to go into detail about the commandment and the purpose of Lev 10:16–20. It is, however, important to observe that the phrase לשׂאת את־עון, "to remove the guilt", does not refer to the actual eating. The statements in Lev 10:17 are all statements about the "sin offering" (חטאת). And it is the חטאת that "makes atonement" (לכפר).[15] However, this does not indicate that the guilt is transferred to the victim. It is so far from being contaminated by sin that it is called קדשׁים קדשׁ, "most holy". It is for that very reason that it is to be eaten by the priests alone (Lev 6:22).[16]

We may conclude that the expression לשׂאת עון does signify that the guilt is removed. Aaron's sons are the principal agents in the rite that removes the people's sin. This does, however, not mean that they themselves carry the guilt in any vicarious way, since it is the חטאת, "the sin offering", which removes the guilt. This also means that the action described in

---

[15] Cf. Rolf Rendtorff, *Leviticus 1,1–10,20* (BKAT vol. 3/1; Neukirchen-Vluyn: Neukirchener Verlag, 2004), 319. However contra Jacob Milgrom, *Leviticus 1–16: A New Translation with Introduction and Commentary* (AB vol. 3; New York: Doubleday, 1991), 622–625.

[16] Cf. Whybray, *Thanksgiving*, 45–46.

Lev 10:17 is so different compared to Isa 53 that it can hardly help us with the interpretation of that text.

2. Leviticus 16:22

The second text to which I will turn is from the Day of Atonement:

The goat shall bear on itself all their iniquities to a barren region (ונשׂא השׂעיר עליו את־כל־עונתם אל־ארץ גזרה); and the goat shall be set free in the wilderness. (Lev 16:22)

The concept of the scapegoat is often understood to have a decisive role for the theological deep structure of Isa 53.[17] There are important parallels between these two texts. One parallel is obviously that the goat carries the iniquities of the people. Another similarity is that the root גזר is used both in Lev 16:22 (אל־ארץ גזרה, "to a barren region") and Isa 53:8 (where it is used in *nip ʿal*: "to be cut of" from life). On the other hand, the same root is also used in Ezek 37:11. There the bones describe the suffering of the exiles, which are "cut off" (נגזרנו) completely. Ezek 37:11 is possibly a closer parallel to Isa 53:8 than Lev 16:22. The verb גזר is probably used in both Isa 53:8 and Ezek 37:11 as a reference to the exiles, who are cut off from the land. In this way the verb could be used in connection to the same root in Lev 16:22, not as an expression of real death, but of social death.

There are also significant differences between Isa 53 and Lev 16, which warn us against seeing too close a connection between these texts. Janowski even argues that the ritual of the scapegoat used for the elimination of disaster and the servant's vicarious surrender of life are incomparable.[18] Even though I believe Janowski's statement is a little too strong, it is true that Isa 53 is not a ritual about the scapegoat. Still, there are similarities at a literal level, which indicate that the texts can have exerted an influence on one another. Therefore, Lev 16 can have significance for the theological deep structure of Isa 53 even though the two events described are rather different.

Lev 16 is the only text in the Old Testament where the expression נשׂא עון is used with an animal as the subject to the verb. It is not necessary here to discuss the many controversial issues concerning the origin of the ritual and the composition of the text. Our concern is mainly with the meaning of the statement: ונשׂא השׂעיר עליו את־כל־עונתם, "The goat shall bear on itself all their iniquities". I will argue that the verb נשׂא means "to carry away" rather than "to bear" with the sense "to suffer".

[17] E.g. Zimmerli, "Zur Vorgeschichte," 239–240, and Mettinger, *A Farewell*, 41.

[18] Janowski, "He Bore Our Sins," 67–68.

There are two important arguments for this. The first is the adverbial clause אל־ארץ גזרה, "to a barren region", which gives the verb the character of motion.[19] The second is that nothing is said about the suffering of the second goat.[20] There are objection against this view. One such objection is put forth by Laato, who argues that:

The expression *nāśā ʾ ʿawōn* in Lev 16:22 emphasizes the idea that the sins of the people were removed by sending an animal to the desert, a place which symbolizes chaos and destruction. Even though we cannot say that a precise equivalent of modern concept "vicarious punishment" is emphasized in Lev 16's description of the fate of the animal, it is clear that this idea is present. It is the animal and not society which is banished and through its removal the sins of the society were believed to be erased.[21]

In order better to understand the meaning of the sending away of the scapegoat, I will turn to the discussion of עצאזל, to which the goat is sent. There are, according to Rudman, four main interpretations of the term: first, that it is the name of a demon, secondly, that it refers to a place, thirdly, that it is an abstract noun (with the meaning "destruction" or "entire removal"), and fourthly that it is a corruption of the words עז עזל, "the goat that got away".[22] I regard the first solution as the most probable. However, the goat is not sent there as a sacrifice, rather it is a symbolic act of carrying Israel's sins into the wilderness. In doing so, the chaos in all its forms is removed from Israel.[23] Rudman also argues that we have a similar idea expressed in Zech 5, where, through YHWH's intervention, wickedness is removed to Babylon, the land of chaos.

Therefore, even if Isa 53 is interpreted with the help of Lev 16:22, it is not the suffering of the animal that removes the sins of society, even though it is sent "to a barren region". Although it is possible that the animal suffered, this is not any main concern in the text. What is stated is that the iniquities are removed from the society to a region where they no longer have a negative effect on that society. In line with this, Whybray argues that the ritual of the scapegoat reflects a concept of sin as something menacingly close to the sinner, which terrifies or threatens to destroy him by weighing on him (cf. Ps 51:5). This state can only be relieved if the sin is taken away and removed to a distance. That can be achieved, either

---

[19] E.g. Whybray, *Thanksgiving*, 49, see also Janowski, *Stellvertretung*, 36.

[20] E.g. Whybray, *Thanksgiving*, 49.

[21] Laato, *The Servant of YHWH and Cyrus*, 144.

[22] Dominic Rudman, "A Note on the Azazel-goat Ritual," *ZAW* 116, no. 3 (2004): 396–401, 396.

[23] E.g. David P. Wright, *The Disposal of Impurity: Elimination Rites in the Bible and in Hittite and Mesopotamian Literature* (SBLDS vol. 101; Atlanta: Scholars Press, 1987), 24, and Rudman, "Azazel-goat Ritual." To make a sacrifice to goat-demons is also forbidden according to Lev 17:7.

through repentance and turning away from one's sin (cf. Job 11:14) or by God's removal of the sin:[24]

as far as the east is from the west,
  so far he removes (הרחיק) our transgressions from us.
(Ps 103:12)

To sum up, it seems probable that the central function of the rite described in Lev 16:22, is to transport the iniquities to the "barren region", rather than the suffering of the animal in this "barren region". It is possible to observe parallels to Isa 53 in this transportation. If the servant is the people who live in exile, which I am arguing, Isa 53 expresses the former view held by the "we", that they were cut off from the land because of their own guilt. This is also in line with Zech 5. What is new in Isa 53 is the recognition that those in exile, have not carried away their own sins, but rather, as the scapegoat, they have carried away the sins of the "we".

3. Ezekiel 4:4–8

According to Zimmerli, the tradition that lies behind Ezek 4:4–8 appears to have made its contribution to the formation of the picture of the servant who bears the guilt of the many. In this, I agree with Zimmerli. The question is however if this also implies that the suffering in Isa 53 is an atoning suffering. In Ezek 4:4–8 we read:

Then lie on your left side, and place the punishment of the house of Israel upon it; you shall bear their punishment for the number of the days that you lie there. For I assign to you a number of days, three hundred ninety days, equal to the number of the years of their punishment; and so you shall bear the punishment of the house of Israel. When you have completed these, you shall lie down a second time, but on your right side, and bear the punishment of the house of Judah; forty days I assign you, one day for each year. You shall set your face toward the siege of Jerusalem, and with your arm bared you shall prophesy against it. See, I am putting cords on you so that you cannot turn from one side to the other until you have completed the days of your siege.

This passage is a part of a larger section, Ezek 3:16–5:17, which contains a number of sign-acts. The corpus raises several difficulties. This longer section has undergone considerable expansion and editing.[25] The nature and function of the prophetic acts have also been widely discussed.[26] I will not discuss the questions at length here, but I believe Friebel's conclusion

[24] Whybray, *Thanksgiving*, 49.

[25] Cf. Zimmerli, *Ezekiel 1*, 142–178.

[26] For an extensive discussion of the theoretical basis for the understanding of the sign act, see Friebel, *Sign-acts*, 11–78.

about the sign-acts of Jeremiah and Ezekiel is well argued and relevant to our passage:

Their intent in employing the nonverbal channel did not stem from any inherently 'efficacious' nature of the actions, but from the ability of the nonverbal behaviors to communicate graphically specifiable message-contents. Since the intent of the prophetic messages was also suasive (interactive), the sign-acts served the two prophets effectively as rhetorical vehicles in addressing the perceived exigencies of the people's theological presuppositions.[27]

Ezekiel's symbolic action in Ezek 4:4–8 is undertaken at YHWH's bidding. Ezekiel suffers the consequences and he "bears the punishment" (נשׂא עון). In this way he represents Israel and his suffering prefigures the suffering that the people have deserved and will experience. Ezekiel does not bear it instead of the people, and his suffering does not take away, nor reduce the people's future suffering.[28]

According to Zimmerli, the Ezekiel-tradition has contributed to the formation of the picture of the servant of YHWH, who bears the guilt of the many.[29] Even so, in his article about the traditions behind Isa 53, he argues that:

Vor allem aber geht Jes. liii darin über Ez. iv hinaus, als hier nun ganz voll die Erwirkung von Heil und Heilung durch das Tun des Knechtes ausgesagt wird: „Die Strafe, die uns zum *Heil* wurde, lag auf ihm und durch seine Wunden ist uns *Heilung* zuteil geworden."[30]

The line of argument here is important. Zimmerli specifies that it is not actually the phrase נשׂא עון, which indicates that the servant's suffering makes YHWH embrace the "we", but rather what is stated previously in Isa 53:4–6. Hence, if we follow Zimmerli, the phrase נשׂא עון does not in itself go beyond the meaning of Ezek 4:4–8.

However, I believe that we can draw more conclusions from the similarities between Ezek 4:4–8 and Isa 53. In Ezek 4:4–8, the prophet bears the iniquity of the people and thereby prefigures their future suffering. The purpose is to show the people what is coming because of their sin, and maybe to evoke in them a turn of heart.[31] A similar turn of heart is what the "we" confess in Isa 53:4–6, and this is further confirmed in Isa 53:11b, 12b.

---

[27] Friebel, *Sign-acts*, 466–467.

[28] Friebel, *Sign-acts*, 221, concludes: "But in his action Ezekiel did not expiate the sin, rather only provided a figurative, nonverbal demonstration of the people's responsibility for their sin which would result in divine punishment, that is, the siege."

[29] Zimmerli, *Ezekiel 1*, 165.

[30] Zimmerli, "Zur Vorgeschichte," 243.

[31] Cf. Zimmerli, *Ezekiel 1*, 164–165, he argues: "Ezekiel's lying bound is regarded as an event of substitutionary sin-bearing." Then he continues: "Ezekiel, by lying bound, became a revealer of guilt, an accuser, as he had been previously in threatening punishment (4:1–2[3]). We must add a further consideration to this. In the prophet's עון guilt-bearing there occurs at the same time an act of public identification. His own life is

4. Ezekiel 18

This passage does not contain any notion of an atoning suffering. It even argues against vicarious suffering. My interest in this text depends partly on the fact that it has been associated with Isa 53. Spieckermann turns to this text in search of the root of the *Stellvertretungsgedanke.* He argues that Ezek 18 is formed by the conviction that it is only the individual "justice" (צדיק) that can save the person's own life. In Ezekiel, the individual responsibility is so radical that the prophet can only show by a symbolic act what will happen to the people (Ezek 4:4–8). Spieckermann claims that the *Stellvertretungsgedanke* in Isa 53 is a response to such a thought, and that it also overcomes the radically heightened doctrine of individual responsibility in Ezekiel.[32] I agree that Isa 53 can be a response to individual responsibility. There are also other similarities between Isa 53 and Ezek 18, similarities where both passages argue in a similar direction.

The first dilemma countered by the prophet in Ezek 18 is the proverb:

> The word of YHWH came to me: What do you mean by repeating this proverb concerning the land of Israel, "The parents have eaten sour grapes, and the children's teeth are set on edge"? (Ezek 18:1–2)

The people express the view that their fate is determined by the actions of their fathers, and from this it follows that their own moral choices are irrelevant. This is forcefully countered by a statement, which contains the thought of individual responsibility:

> As I live, says YHWH God, this proverb shall no more be used by you in Israel. Know that all lives are mine; the life of the parent as well as the life of the child is mine: it is only the person who sins that shall die. (Ezek 18:3–4)

The thesis of individual responsibility is concluded in Ezek 18:20,[33] which denies that the generations are bound together. Furthermore, a clear personal responsibility with regard to righteousness is expressed.[34] However,

---

brought into the עון (guilt-punishment) of the people. He brings together in his symbolic bondage the guilt of Israel as a burden in his own life."

[32] Spieckermann, "Vicarious Suffering," 13–15. Cf. Fredrik Lindström, "'Han bar de mångas skuld' Profetia och uppfyllelse utifrån Jes 53," *STK* 75, no. 3 (1999): 98–109, 105, for a similar view.

[33] It has been argued that Ezek 18 has undergone redactions and expansions over a long time. The oldest parts are then found in 18:1–20 and the youngest parts in 18:21–32, and there are also several stages in between. See Karl-Friedrich Pohlmann, *Ezechielstudien: Zur Redaktionsgeschichte des Buches und zur Frage nach den ältesten Texten* (BZAW vol. 202; Berlin: de Gruyter, 1992), 219–244, for an extensive discussion. This is possible and even probable. I will anyhow treat the chapter in its final shape, this since it in its present form is an important line of argument where the later part depends on the earlier.

[34] E.g. Zimmerli, *Ezekiel 1*, 385.

neither the section, nor the theological argumentation, ends there. In case this should sound too much like the assertion that the righteous will be saved by righteous deeds in the past and the wicked doomed by their wickedness in the past, Ezekiel clarifies the matter further. The wicked person, who turns away from his wickedness, will be delivered. Similarly, the righteous, who backslides into wickedness, will be doomed (Ezek 18:21–24). In Ezek 18:25, 29 we have two almost identical verses, which both react to the accusation that YHWH might be "unfair" (תכן). The prophet's reaction to this accusation is that instead of charging YHWH, Israel should look in the mirror, since their behaviour is unscrupulous. After this comes the divine judgement for each individual in Ezek 18:30a, but this divine judgement is not the end.[35] The discourse ends instead with a vigorous exhortation to turn away from the transgressions that the people have committed. A call to repentance appears three times in this short section. From the complaint of the people in v. 2, the chapter has now turned into an urgent call to repentance. This indicates that the appeal to turn away from their sins is more important in Ezek 18 than the statement about individual retribution. It seems likely that the latter is used with the aim to make the people recognise their own guilt, i.e. with the same aim as we saw in Ezek 4:4–8.

There is however one new and important aspect, which distinguishes Ezek 18 from Ezek 4:4–8. In Ezek 18, the appeal is connected to the command: "make yourselves a new heart and a new spirit!" (Ezek 18:31). In Ezek 11:19; 36:26 the change of heart and spirit is promised as a divine act and as a gift of God. I propose that Ezek 18:31 should be understood in the same direction, as a divine act and as a gift of God, since all three texts deal with "a new heart and a new spirit" together with the problem of the people's guilt. Hence, I believe Block is right when he argues:

> The use of the imperative mood does not mean that Ezekiel believes his audience capable of moral and spiritual self-transformation. The command *create a new heart and a new spirit for yourselves* is a rhetorical device, highlighting the responsibility of the nation for their present crisis and pointing the way to the future. The prerequisites for positive divine intervention are a wholesale reorientation of life *and* an internal change in disposition. The former will not happen without the latter.[36]

---

[35] Daniel Isaac Block, *The Book of Ezekiel: Chapters 1–24* (NICOT Grand Rapids, Mich.; Cambridge: Eerdmans, 1997), 587, argues: "In a typical judgment oracle, the form of v. 30a would probably have signaled the end of the prophecy and sealed the hearers' fate."

[36] Block, *The Book of Ezekiel*, 588. Contra Jacqueline E. Lapsley, *Can These Bones Live? The Problem of the Moral Self in the book of Ezekiel* (BZAW vol. 301; Berlin: de Gruyter, 2000), 76–77. Cf. also Zimmerli, *Ezekiel 1*, 386, who states: "When we find commended in the imperative here what is promised in indicative in 11:19, it is made clear in this doubling of clauses, with their logical tensions, that in the divine salvation

Ezek 18 starts with the complaint of the people's unjust suffering and ends with an exhortation to turn away from their transgressions. Here it is the people who suffer who should see their own responsibility for their suffering. In Isa 53 it is the "we" who are led to see their responsibility for the suffering of the servant. An important centre in both texts is to achieve a right insight about ones own guilt, and hence to embrace the salvation that is given by YHWH. In Ezekiel it is "a new heart and a new spirit", in Isaiah it is the promise that "I, I am He who blots out your transgressions for my own sake" (Isa 43:25).

5. Exodus 28:38; Numbers 14:34; 18:1, 23

I will now take a brief look at the other passages, which have sometimes been understood to contain the thought of a vicarious suffering.

Whybray makes a long and convincing analysis of Exod 28:38. He concludes that Aaron carries (נשׂא) into the sanctuary an object which symbolizes the sin (עון) of the people. Aaron does not bear the guilt or punishment of others. He is the instrument, since only he is permitted to approach YHWH, but he is not more than an instrument.[37]

In Num 14:34 we see the children, here together with their parents, suffering the consequences of their parents' sins. They are forced to remain in the wilderness for forty years. This is partly a vicarious suffering, since the children share the punishment justly meted out to the parents. This is not an atoning suffering, since the parents are not saved from their guilt.[38]

To turn to Num 18:1, it is not just any sin that is carried, but את־עון המקדשׁ, "offences connected with the sanctuary", and את־עון כהנתכם, "offences connected with the priesthood". Hence, the "offences" (עון) is not those of the people, but those of Aaron and his sons. As agent, they perform their duties, and in doing so, they save the people. If the duties are not properly performed, it will be they who commit sin. They do not bear the sins or punishment of others.

Our last text is Num 18:23. The most important issue here concerns the translation of the suffix ם, "their", in עונם. It could refer to the עון of the people, which the Levites bear, or it could be their own עון. The grammatical form provides no answer, but the second suggestion seems to be the more probable, since the situation is similar to that of the priests in

man never appears simply as a vague object, but always as the purposeful subject of grace for a new beginning."

[37] Whybray, *Thanksgiving*, 46–48.

[38] Cf. Whybray, *Thanksgiving*, 46–48.

Num 18:1.[39] If this is right, the text is dealing with the עון, which the Levites have to bear for themselves, and not one transferred to them from the people.

6. Conclusion

First, we can conclude that the phrase נשא עון is not a *Formel* with one specific meaning. Furthermore, this exact formulation does not occur in Isa 53. In my survey, I have not found that any texts that contain the phrase נשא עון hold the notion of an atoning suffering. However, in Exod 28:38, Lev 10:17, and 16:22 we have different agents, who bring about the removal of guilt. Still, they are only agents in this; they are not the subjects of a vicarious suffering. Exod 28:38 and Lev 10:17 are very different compared to Isa 53. There is nothing to suggest a connection between these texts and Isa 53. Regarding Lev 16:22, the situation is somewhat different since we have both differences and similarities. The most significant similarity is that Isa 53 describes the people in exile as a sheep that transports the sins from the land, just as the scapegoat in Lev 16:22, who bears away the sins of the people. Isa 53 is however not a scapegoat ritual. The similarity lies in the removal of guilt from the community and not in a vicarious or atoning suffering.

Ezek 4:4–8 is a text, which expresses a vicarious suffering. This is also the text, which is closest to Isa 53. In Ezek 4:4–8, the prophet suffers the consequences of the people's עון, but it is not an atoning suffering. It prefigures the future suffering of the people and, therefore, it does neither remove their suffering, nor their guilt. Maybe the people could have been healed and saved if they had turned away from their sins. This is an open question. Still, the prophet bears the sin, so that the people will see their own guilt. The urge for the people to recognise their own sin is also an important component in Ezek 18. This text starts with the complaint that the people have to bear the consequences of the sins of their fathers, but the chapter ends with an exhortation to repent and to make for themselves "a new heart and a new spirit!"

The prophetic texts in Ezek 4:4–8 and 18 are the most helpful in our interpretation of Isa 53:11b; 12b. The "we" in Isa 53 do now confess what Ezekiel wanted his audience to see and to confess. By this insight, the "we" have been healed.

---

[39] E.g. Whybray, *Thanksgiving*, 44.

Chapter 9

Isaiah 53, The Terms of Embrace That Are Not Used

It is possible to take one step further in the interpretation of the suffering of the servant through the recognition of some important concepts for describing the removal of guilt or impurity, which are in other texts of the Old Testament but not in Isa 53. This part could be considered an argument from silence, although my argument is rather the opposite. I do not suggest that the person behind Isa 53 was ignorant of these concepts, but I want to demonstrate that there are some common concepts of importance in the Old Testament that could have been used if the intention in Isa 53 had been to describe an atoning suffering. If the poem actually intended to describe a person's suffering as an atoning suffering, it would have been natural to use the most common concepts in order to express this unusual thought as clearly as possible. The first concept, which will receive my attention is the word כפר, "to atone". Then I will briefly look at some expressions regarding sacrificial language, and finally I will turn my attention to words connected to intercession; namely to פלל, "to intercede", and חלה, "to appease".

1. The Term כפר

The word כפר, "to atone", is the most important Old Testament word for describing the expiation of sin. The word is frequently used to describe how guilt is removed through a cultic action. It is most frequently used in the priestly work and in Ezek 40–48.[1] The word כפר is also used to describe reconciliation between people,[2] forgiveness or non-forgiveness from YHWH,[3] and what is of special interest here, it is used to describe how a

[1] The root כפר is used 149 times in the OT. A majority of the occurrences (119 times) are within texts from a priestly tradition. Cf. Janowski for a more detailed analysis. Bernd Janowski, *Sühne als Heilsgeschehen: Traditions- und religionsgeschichtliche Studien zur Sühnetheologie der Priesterschrift* (WMANT vol. 55; Neukirchen-Vluyn: Neukirchener Verlag, 2000), 105–107.

[2] See especially Gen 32:21 but also 2 Sam 21:3; Prov 16:14.

[3] See Deut 32:43; Isa 22:14; Jer 18:23; Ezek 16:63; Pss 65:4; 78:38; 79:9; 2 Chr 30:18. We have a special case in Isa 6:7.

person's non-cultic action removes the guilt of someone else. This occurs in the story about Phinehas (Num 25:6–15) and once about Moses (Exod 32:30–34).[4] The non-cultic action of a person is of interest, since Isa 53 also describes a non-cultic event, even if it is not an action.

Phinehas

The story about Phinehas, as we have it in Num 25:1–18, is a rather brutal story. When Israel stayed at Shittim, the people began to have sexual relations with the women of Moab and to sacrifice to their gods, and the people ate and bowed to them. Thus YHWH's anger was kindled against them. One Israelite brought his Midianite woman into the sight of Moses and the whole congregation. Phinehas then took a spear in his hand and pierced the two of them. So the plague was stopped.

> And YHWH spoke to Moses, saying: "Phinehas son of Eleazar, son of Aaron the priest, has turned back my wrath from the Israelites by manifesting such zeal among them on my behalf that in my jealousy I did not consume the Israelites. Therefore say, 'I hereby grant him my covenant of peace. It shall be for him and for his descendants after him a covenant of perpetual priesthood, because he was zealous for his God, and made atonement (ויכפר) for the Israelites.' " (Num 25:10–13)

The section in Num 25:1–18 is rather inconsistent. Many scholars understand the discrepancies in the story to be caused by editorial combinations of more than one source. One indication of the different sources, which strikes the reader, is that in Num 25:1–5 is the problem due to sexual relations with women of Moab. In Num 25:6–15, we encounter instead a Midianite woman. There is also further evidence which makes it most probable that different sources have been combined, but it is more important here to discuss the atoning work of Phinehas.[5] It has been argued that the making of atonement implies the mediatory work of a priest. The priest normally averts God's wrath by some sort of offering, and here the sacrifice is supposed to be the Israelite man and Midianite woman.[6] This understanding can, however, be questioned. It is most important that God himself says that it was Phinehas' "zeal" (קנא) which has turned away God's wrath (Num 25:11, 13).[7] This is a unique story in the Old Testament, suggesting as it does that a person's, non-cultic, action has actually "made atonement"

---

[4] We also have one story about Aaron which could belong to this group (Num 17:6–15).

[5] Timothy R. Ashley, *The Book of Numbers* (NICOT Grand Rapids, Mich.: Eerdmans, 1993), 514–515. See also Ludwig Schmidt, *Numeri 10,11-36,13* (ATD vol. 7/2; Göttingen: Vandenhoeck & Ruprecht, 2004), 144–148, and Horst Seebass, *Numeri 22,2-26,65* (BKAT vol. 4/3 2; Neukirchen: Neukirchener Verlag, 2005), 124–130, for a more detailed discussion.

[6] E.g. Ashley, *The Book of Numbers*, 523.

[7] Cf. Janowski, *Sühne als Heilsgeschehen*, 146–147, and Seebass, *Numeri 22,2-26,65*, 120.

(ויכפר) for other persons. For this reason, it is not surprising that Phinehas has a significant posthumous reputation. The story reappears in Ps 106:28–31, where Phinehas' action is described as an intercession.[8] Here it is enough to conclude that we have an important tradition about a person who actually makes atonement for others through his non-cultic actions. This is described by the help of the term כפר, a word which is absent from Isa 53.

Moses

In the story of the golden calf, Moses says that he will go up to YHWH. Moses thinks that: "perhaps I can make atonement (אכפרה) for your sins" (Exod 32:30). Previously, in Exod 32, Moses has successfully intervened on behalf of his people.[9] As Exod 32 now stands, this attempt to make atonement presuppose the previous intercession. The hope for כפר, "atonement", does, however, not imply a vicarious suffering, which is sometimes argued on the basis of Moses' statement in Exod 32:31–32:

> So Moses returned to YHWH and said, "Alas, this people has sinned a great sin; they have made for themselves gods of gold. But now, if you will only forgive their sin – but if not, blot me out of the book that you have written."

It is sometimes argued that this statement means that Moses offers to die and vicariously seeks atonement for his people.[10] However, what Moses says is that he is prepared and willing to suffer *with* his people. He does not offer to suffer himself *instead* of the people.[11] Therefore, it is probable that we should understand Moses' words "blot me out" as a powerful statement intended to add force to his intercession. The only means, by which Moses can try to achieve atonement, is by his intercession to YHWH for forgiveness.[12]

---

[8] This translation has been questioned, since LXX has the verb εξιλασχεσθαι, "to atone". See Bernd Janowski, "Psalm CVI 28-31 und die Interzession des Pinchas," *VT* 33 (1983): 237–248, for an extensive and well argued article about the interpretation of ויפלל as intercession.

[9] Exod 32:7–14. See further below.

[10] E.g. Martin Noth, *Exodus: A Commentary* (OTL London: SCM Press, 1966), 251, and Brevard S. Childs, *Exodus: A Commentary* (OTL London: SCM Press, 1974), 573–574. See also Henning Graf Reventlow, *Gebet im Alten Testament* (Stuttgart: Kohlhammer, 1986), 236, who argues: "Dass Mose sich selbst als Sühneopfer für das Volk anbietet, ist nicht ausdrücklich gesagt. [...] Doch verknüpft Mose ausdrücklich sein Leben mit dem des Volkes."

[11] Cf. Scharbert, *Heilsmittler*, 84–85, Umberto Cassuto, *A Commentary on the Book of Exodus* (Jerusalem: The Magnes Press, the Hebrew University, 1974), 423, and Erik Aurelius, *Der Fürbitter Israels: Eine Studie zum Mosebild im Alten Testament* (ConBOT vol. 27; Stockholm: Almqvist & Wiksell International, 1988), 89.

[12] Cf. Janowski, *Sühne als Heilsgeschehen*, 143–144, and Cornelis Houtman, *Exodus 20–40* (Historical Commentary on the Old Testamen vol. 3; Kampen: Kok Pharos, 2000), 672–673.

However, in this section, not even the intercession of Moses can achieve atonement. The story nevertheless demonstrates yet again that the term כפר could be used also of a person's non-cultic action intended to bring atonement.

2. Sacrificial Language

It is sometimes argued that the suffering of the servant is described by using sacrificial language.[13] This is correct to some extent, but it is not as prominent as is sometimes assumed. According to Kaiser, the word נשׂא, "carry", describes the servant's suffering as a sacrifice.[14] However, as we have seen above, Isa 53 does not describe a cultic action. The closest parallel to the use of this verb is found in Ezek 4:4–8 and Lam 5:7, and none of these texts describe a cultic carrying of sin. A term closer connected to the cult is the word אשׁם, "guilt" or "guilt offering", which is used in Isa 53:10. As I have argued above, not even this term belongs as straightforwardly to sacrificial language as is sometimes claimed. My interest in this section is focused on the sacrificial and cultic terms that appropriately express atonement, but which are not used in Isa 53. However, the reference to slaughter, which is used in the text, is closely related to this issue.

About Slaughter

The suffering servant is described as a lamb led to the slaughter. The image of a lamb has led scholars to conclude that the suffering is a sacrifice.[15] As we have seen previously the most important priestly term for describing atonement, כפר, is not used, neither with cultic nor non-cultic references. Furthermore, when the suffering is described as a slaughter, the term used is one for profane slaughter, טבח, and not one used for sacrifice. In the Old Testament, there is a distinction between general slaughter, when the verb טבח is used, and the slaughter of a sacrificial animal, when verbs like זבח and שׁחט are used.[16]

---

[13] See for example Lars G. Rignell, "Isa. LII 13-LIII 12," *VT* 3 (1953): 87–92, 89, who argues that the mission of the servant is influenced by the Pentateuchal description of sacrifice.

[14] E.g. Kaiser, *Der Königliche Knecht*, 101–103. Already Christoph Starke, *Synopsis bibliothecae exegeticae in Vetus Testamentum Kurzgefasster Auszug der grundlichsten nutzbarsten Auslegungen uber alle Bucher Altes Testamentes* (vol. 5; Leipzig: 1766), 866, concluded that the carrying of sin in Isa 53 should be read in the light of the Levitical sacrifice. Such interpretation is also made by Zimmerli, "Zur Vorgeschichte," and others.

[15] Cf. Wolff, *Jesaja 53*, 28, and Koole, *Isaiah 49–55*, 301.

[16] Hamp, "טבח," in *TDOT 5* (ed. G. Johannes Botterweck and Helmer Ringgren; Grand Rapids, Mich.: Eerdmans, 1986), 284.

However, the root טבח is not only used for profane slaughter. It is also used as an image by which to describe the judgement of YHWH against the nations[17] and also of the judgment of YHWH against Israel.[18] The root טבח is even most frequently used with this transferred meaning, to refer to some form of judgement. We have one clear example of the use of the root טבח as a description of the suffering of the people in Ps 44:23:

Because of you we are being killed all day long,
and accounted as sheep for the slaughter (טבחה).

The image of sheep that are led to "the slaughter" (טבח) is more likely to give a picture of the suffering of the exile than of a cultic sacrifice. The wording of Ps 44:23 come close to Isa 53:6:

He was oppressed, and he was afflicted,
yet he did not open his mouth;
like a lamb that is led to the slaughter (לטבח),
and like a sheep that before its shearers is silent,
he did not open his mouth.
[silence]

What is unexpected in Isa 53 is not the image of slaughter; it is the quietness of the sufferer and the confession of the "we", who are not suffering. The silence could be compared to the complaint in Ps 44, where they try to wake YHWH by their complaint (Ps 44:24–25).

To conclude, the term used to describe the image of a slaughter in Isa 53:6 is none of the terms used for sacrificial slaughter. Furthermore the most prominent priestly term by which to describe atonement, כפר, is, as I have previously shown, absent from Isa 53.

3. Terms for Intercession

It is frequently maintained that the servant made intercession or intervened in a way which led to the removal of guilt.[19] This is argued on the basis of the last colon of Isa 53: "and he intervened (יפגיע) for the transgressors." The verb יפגיע, "and he intervened", has been analysed above. It is, however, important to observe two words, which are not used in Isa 53. The first is פלל, "to intercede", in *hitpaʿel*, and the second is חלה II, "to appease". Both of these words are used in other examples where the consequences of sins are averted through intercessions.

[17] Isa 34:2, 6; Jer 48:15; 51:40.

[18] Lam 2:21; Ezek 21:15, 20 and in v. 33 it is used against Ammon. Cf. also Isa 65:12 and Jer 12:3 where it is used as a more general description for the judgement of YHWH.

[19] Cf. North, *Isaiah 40–55*, 141.

The verb פלל in *hitpa'el* is the Old Testament term most frequently used with the meaning to intercede for another person.[20] An overview of the passages reveals that Abraham, Moses, Samuel, Job, and Jeremiah among others all fulfilled the role of intercessor. There are some texts where the intercession by one person actually makes YHWH embrace another person. However, before turning to those examples I will consider Jer 7:16, where the prophet is forbidden to intercede:

As for you, do not pray (אל־תתפלל) for this people, do not raise a cry or prayer on their behalf (אל־תשׂא בעדם רנה ותפלה), and do not intercede (ואל־תפגע) with me, for I will not hear you. (Jer 7:16)

This verse contains several words that describe a forbidden intercession. The first word, which is thereafter further defined by other terms, is פלל in *hitpa'el.* The prohibition against intercession conveys the thought that prayers from the prophet could make YHWH change his mind and embrace the people again.[21]

We have two texts where Moses' intercession actually changes the thought of YHWH from exclusion to embrace. These are Num 21:7–8 and Deut 9:19–20:

The people came to Moses and said, "We have sinned by speaking against YHWH and against you; pray (התפלל) to YHWH to take away the serpents from us." So Moses prayed (ויתפלל) for the people. And YHWH said to Moses, "Make a poisonous serpent, and set it on a pole; and everyone who is bitten shall look at it and live." (Num 21:7–8)

For I was afraid that the anger that YHWH bore against you was so fierce that he would destroy you. But YHWH listened to me that time also. YHWH was so angry with Aaron that he was ready to destroy him, but I interceded (ואתפלל) also on behalf of Aaron at that same time. (Deut 9:19–20)

In both these passages, the action of Moses is needed in order to avert the wrath of YHWH and to make him embrace the person or persons who have done wrong.

There is another remarkable text in the final chapter of Job. YHWH is full of wrath against the friends of Job, since they have not spoken rightly about YHWH, as Job has (Job 42:7). The wrong they have spoken about YHWH is the understanding that Job was suffering because of his own sins. This is similar to the former understanding of the "we" with regard to the suffering of the servant in Isa 53. What is also interesting is that the need

---

[20] Followed by the preposition בעד, "on behalf of", in Gen 20:7; Num 21:7; Deut 9:20; 1 Sam 7:5; 12:19, 23; 1 Kgs 13:6; Jer 7:16; 11:14; 14:11; 29:7; 37:3; 42:2, 20; Ps 72:15; Job 42:10 and followed by the preposition על, the term conveys the same general nuance of "praying for", in Job 42:8; Neh 1:6; 2 Chr 30:18. See further Samuel E. Balentine, "The Prophet as Intercessor: A Reassessment," *JBL* 103, no. 2 (1984): 161–173, 162–164.

[21] The same thought occurs also in Jer 11:14; 14:11.

for Job's friends to offer a burnt offering and for Job to pray for them, in order that YHWH may not deal with them according to their folly. In Job 42:9–10 we read:

So Eliphaz the Temanite and Bildad the Shuhite and Zophar the Naamathite went and did what YHWH had told them; and YHWH accepted Job's prayer. And YHWH restored the fortunes of Job when he had prayed (בהתפללו) for his friends; and YHWH gave Job twice as much as he had before.

It is clear that the intercession of Job is an indispensable part in making YHWH embrace the friends again. It is also through this prayer that the fortune of Job is restored.

Now I will turn to the second intercessory word, חלה II, "to appease", which is not used in Isa 53. This word occurs in the story about the golden calf in Exod 32. In contrast to כפר, which also occurs in this section, this word occurs at the beginning of the story, where Moses successfully intervenes on behalf of his people:

But Moses implored (ויחל) YHWH his God, and said, "O YHWH, why does your wrath burn hot against your people, whom you brought out of the land of Egypt with great power and with a mighty hand? [...]" And YHWH changed his mind about the disaster that he planned to bring on his people. (Exod 32:11, 14)

Once more we see that it is possible, at least sometimes, to remove the wrath of YHWH with a non-cultic action.

Before leaving this survey, I will turn to Amos 7:1–8 where Amos twice succeeds in averting YHWH's anger. Scholars have seen this story as one of the main sources behind the tradition of prophetic intercession.[22] However, there is a significant scholarly discussion about how much, if any part, of this story can have any claim of authenticity.[23] This is not the place to discuss the growth of the text. Furthermore, Becker has convincingly argued that when we examine the structure and construction of the story, it stands as a literary entity and should be read as such. He further argues that it can no longer be known if there are parts of the vision that originally belonged to Amos. The final story, as we have it, represents a dramatic stage and a theological reflection. Following on from this, the two first visions, where Amos averts the judgment, cannot be read separately. They are rhetorical means by which to achieve the whole purpose of the text. The text contrasts the people's unwillingness to repent to the patience of YHWH.[24] This brief discussion shows that the main interest is not in showing that Amos

[22] Nils Johansson, *Parakletoi: Vorstellungen von Fürsprechern für die Menschen vor Gott in der alttestamentlichen Religion, im Spätjudentum und Urchristentum* (Lund: Gleerups, 1940), 44. Cf. also Reventlow, *Gebet im Alten Testament*, 246–249.

[23] See further Spieckermann, "Vicarious Suffering," 8–13.

[24] See further Uwe Becker, "Der Prophet als Fürbitter: Zum Literarhistorischen Ort der Amos-Visionen," *VT* 51, no. 2 (2001): 141–165.

succeeded twice in averting the judgement, but rather in emphasising the patience of God. Still, we can observe that neither of the two successful petitions made by Amos, סלח־נא, "forgive, please", and חדל־נא, "cease, please", are used in Isa 53.

4. Conclusion

The survey has shown that there are important Old Testament concepts by which to describe how acts performed by various persons can avert the wrath or the judgement of YHWH and make him embrace the person or the people again. Nevertheless, none of these concepts appear in Isa 53. We find neither the cultic nor the non-cultic use of the word כפר, "to atone", in Isa 53. Scholars frequently refer to the servant as an intercessor, although none of the most important terms for intercession are used in Isa 53. Neither פלל, "to intercede" in *hitpa'el*, nor חלה II, "to appease" occur in Isa 53. Isa 53 also lacks terms used in intercessions, such as the phrase סלח־נא, "please forgive", and the phrase חדל־נא, "please cease". Instead of these, the rather dubious verb יפגיע, "and he intervened", occur in Isa 53:12.

None of these common terms, by which to describe how various acts can avert the wrath or the judgement of YHWH, are used in Isa 53. This makes it doubtful whether Isa 53 actually intends to show a totally new and unprecedented thought, namely that the suffering of an innocent person makes YHWH embrace another, guilty person. It would have been natural to build on the concepts, which are closest to expressing such a thought. However, the most important of these concepts are absent from Isa 53. Furthermore, as will be shown in the next part, there is no need for atonement in Isa 40–55. God has already blotted out all their sins.

Chapter 10

Reconciliation in Isaiah 40–55

If Isa 53 actually does describe an atoning suffering, we could expect the removal of guilt to be a significant problem in the rest of Isa 40–55. In this part I will argue that the opposite is the case. Consequently, I will examine texts in Isa 40–55 that describe in different ways the penalty paid, the blotting out of the sins, and so on. This has a twofold purpose. First, I want to understand in what way reconciliation is linked to the suffering of exile in Isa 40–55, since it is sometimes argued that earlier sins are vindicated by the suffering of the exile.[1] To put it as a question: Is it the exilic suffering that atones for the guilt and that makes YHWH embrace his people once again? The suffering which the receivers of the message have experienced is frequently mentioned and of significance in Isa 40–55.[2] Still, it can be questioned whether the suffering makes God open his arms to embrace his people again. The issue is important, because if it is the suffering that makes God embrace his people in Isa 40–55, it makes it more likely that atonement is a theme in Isa 53. Secondly, I want to understand why God talks about the sins of Jacob/Israel in Isa 40–55. Is it because the sins have been atoned for? Does Isa 40–55 expect a specific response, or are there other reasons for this?

In the analysis, I will first turn to two passages, which could be interpreted to suggest that reconciliation will in some way be achieved through suffering. Then I will interpret some texts that assert that it is YHWH who blots out the sins in order to understand the cause of this blotting out and the reason why God still talks about their sins and not only about liberation from exile or about hope for Zion.

[1] N. K. Gottwald, "Social Class and Ideology in Isaiah 40–55: An Eagletonian Reading.," *Semeia* 59 (1992): 43–57, 55, states: "To be sure, it is not as though the author of Isaiah 40–55 rebuts the older prophetic social critique, or even quibbles with it. It is rather that he assumes it to have been vindicated and decisively transcended by the sufferings of exile."

[2] Cf. Isa 41:12 and 42:21–24.

1. Isaiah 40:2

The first text I will turn to is the frequently discussed Isa 40:2:

Speak tenderly to Jerusalem,
  and cry to her
that she has served her term,
  that her penalty is paid (כי נרצה עונה),
that she has received from YHWH's hand double (כפלים)
  for all her sins (חטאתיה).

There are a number of interpretations that explain what it means that Zion has received "double" (כפלים) for all her sins. I will argue that the term should be understood rather literally with the meaning that Zion has suffered twofold by being both widowed and childless. Before I turn to this understanding, I will look at some other influential interpretations. The word is not problematic in itself, but the use of כפלים in this specific way is unique in the Old Testament. We have only one other example where כפלים is used together with a word that refers to guilt, namely in Job 11:5–6. (In Job עון, "iniquity", is used instead of חטאת, "sin", which is used here, but both words have a similar meaning.)

But O that God would speak,
  and open his lips to you,
and that he would tell you the secrets of wisdom!
  For wisdom is double (כפלים)
Know then that God exacts of you less than your guilt (מעונך) deserves.
(Job 11:5–6)

The background, in Job 11, is Zophar's verdict that Job is wrong, because Job believes that he is clean in the sight of God. According to Zophar, the reason for Job's suffering is his own iniquity. This understanding is based on the belief that "God exacts of you less than your guilt deserves". The word כפלים is connected to תושיה, "wisdom", and not to the suffering. Furthermore, the reading of כפלים is also uncertain here.[3] Therefore, Job 11:6 does unfortunately not help us much in interpreting Isa 40:2. Still, it is interesting to notice that Zophar declares that God exacts less than the guilt deserves. According to Zophar, suffering is caused by guilt, but there is not an exact calculation of the penalty on God's part.

To return to Isa 40:2, it has been suggested that the use of כפלים means that the suffering corresponds to, or is equivalent to, the guilt. With such an understanding, the text describes that the guilt is paid. This interpretation is reached by a legal interpretation, according to which כפלים is understood as a parallel to שׁנים, "twofold". In the law of obligation, a claim

[3] Cf. BHSapp.

should be met by correspondence; debt and payment are equal in value.[4] It has also been proposed that the word should be given more force by reference to Jer 16:18:

And I will doubly (משׁנה) repay their iniquity and their sin, because they have polluted my land with the carcasses of their detestable idols, and have filled my inheritance with their abominations. (!)[5]

Following this, the meaning of כפלים is the full amount, which is twice the debt. First the debt itself, and secondly the usual legal compensation is given.[6] According to both these interpretations, the point is that the debt has been settled.[7] However, both interpretations also rule out the possibility stated by Zophar: "that God exacts of you less than your guilt deserves."

Before continuing with the interpretation of כפלים, it is necessary to interpret the phrase כי נרצה עונה, "that her penalty is paid". The verb is probably רצה II in *nip ͑al*, "to be paid of". Hence, the form leaves open whether Jerusalem herself has paid, or whether the debt has been settled by someone else.[8] As Elliger puts it: "Der Grundtenor in 2a bleibt: die Schuld und ihre Folgen sind erledigt."[9] Still, if an exact form of compensation for guilt as we find in the laws were intended, it would have been more suitable to use the *qal* form of the verb. When the *nip ͑al* form is used, it rather enforces the end of the suffering. Westermann understands the parallelism in the two parts of Isa 40:2b as an impressive example, both in Deutero-Isaiah and in the whole of the Old Testament, of how closely deliverance and forgiveness are bound together. It is, according to Westermann, the fact that God turns once again to his people in forgiveness, which puts everything right.[10] Westermann continues:

---

[4] See von Gerhard von Rad, "כפלים in jes 40:2 = Äquivalent," *ZAW* 79, no. 1 (1967): 80–82. He refers, among other texts, to Deut 15:18 and Jer 16:18.

[5] ראשׁונה is removed in accordance with LXX. Cf. BHSapp.

[6] E.g. Karl Elliger, *Deuterojesaja 40,1-45,7* (BKAT vol. 11/1; Neukirchen-Vluyn: Neukirchener Verlag, 1978), 15–17.

[7] Karl Budde, "The So-Called 'Ebed-Yahweh Songs,' and the Meaning of the Term "Servant of Yahweh" in Isaiah, Chaps. 40–55," *AJT* 3, no. 3 (1899): 499–540, 509–510, argues that this means that only half of the punishment is deserved. Therefore, already here the prophet has a reference to the suffering, which was indispensable to the fulfilment of the mission, in order to bring true religion to the heathen; this is what we encounter in Isa 53. Anthony Phillips, "'Double for all her Sins'," *ZAW* 94 (1982): 130–132, argues in a similar way when he claims that כפלים should be interpreted literary as an indication that the suffering has been twice as long and that a second, innocent generation is suffering. And it is through their vicarious suffering that the glorious future will be realised.

[8] E.g. Elliger, *Deuterojesaja 40,1-45,7*, 14–15, and Baltzer, *Deutero-Isaiah*, 52.

[9] Elliger, *Deuterojesaja 40,1-45,7*, 15, (his expansion).

[10] Westermann, *Isaiah 40–66*, 36.

Israel's having received from Yahweh's hand double – double punishment, that is – for all her sins is not to be taken as implying calculation. Deutero-Isaiah is thinking of the actual condition of the victims of the punishment. The people he addresses are no longer able to sustain the burden of their grievous fate. The prophet says to them, "now is enough, now it is over and done with". But his words make them once more aware that what is now over and done with was the consequence of Israel's iniquities. And only recognition of this fact made any continuance of her history possible.[11]

Two things are important in this argumentation. First, the iniquity is mentioned, because it is only recognition of this fact, which made any continuance of Zion's history possible. Secondly, I believe Westermann is right when he argues that כפלים should not be taken to imply calculation. Such calculation in regard to guilt does not fit the overall description of God's turning towards his people in Isa 40–55. Besides, no extra comfort is needed or possible, if one always receives what one deserves. What is more, it is not the exiled who are addressed, at least not directly, but Zion. There is a great fluctuation of the images in Isa 40–55. Isa 40:2 is directed to Zion, and this makes it possible that כפלים has a more concrete reference to the specific suffering, which Zion has experienced, that is to widowhood and childlessness. This would also underline further that כפלים does not describe such an exact form of compensation for guilt as we find in the laws. Furthermore, the word שׁנים does not only occur in the laws. If כפלים is a parallel to שׁנים, which is likely, it does have a concrete reference in Isa 40–55. In Isa 47:8–9 we read:

Now therefore hear this, you lover of pleasures,
  who sit securely,
who say in your heart,
  "I am, and there is no one besides me;
I shall not sit as a widow
  or know the loss of children" –
both (שׁתי) these things shall come upon you
  in a moment, in one day:
the loss of children and widowhood
  shall come upon you in full measure,
in spite of your many sorceries
  and the great power of your enchantments.

Babylon is a counter image to Jerusalem in Isa 40–55. In Isa 47:8–9 Babylon is about to experience the suffering, which Jerusalem has already received. Childlessness and widowhood are the double fate that Jerusalem herself has experienced (Cf. Isa 54:1, 4 where this comes over for her). In Isa 51:17 we read that Jerusalem has received the cup of YHWH's wrath. There too, the loss of children is mentioned (Isa 51:18, 20). In Isa 51:19 it is stated that "These two things (שׁתים) have befallen you". It is not clearly

[11] Westermann, *Isaiah 40–66*, 36.

stated that שׁחים refers to childlessness and widowhood in Isa 51:19. However, it is settled that the children have gone and there is no one "to take her by the hand" (Isa 51:18). Following this assertion, a question is asked: who "will comfort you?" (Isa 51:19).[12] It is probable that both these latter statements refer to the absence of YHWH, her husband.[13]

To return to Isa 40:2, it is possible and even probable, that כפלים refers to these two concrete things, which Jerusalem has suffered, widowhood and childlessness. This understanding has the advantage of finding the meaning of כפלים in Isa 40–55. Hence, such an interpretation seems more probable than to search for the meaning in the law of obligation.

Against this understanding, it could be countered that these two things, widowhood and childlessness, are not explicitly mentioned in Isa 40:2. On the other hand, it is now mostly accepted that the prologue in Isa 40 has its origin in the land.[14] With such a domicile, there are rhetorical arguments in favour of not being too specific in the opening word. By using the expression כפלים the listeners could agree that the suffering had been great, and by referring to the guilt, the listeners could start to see their own responsibility for what had happened. If the opening words had explicitly mentioned that Jerusalem was childless and a widow, it is likely that the listeners would have stopped listening already at that point. The people at home could say about the exiled: "They have gone far from YHWH; to us this land is given for a possession" (Ezek 11:15). Isa 40–55 states the opposite. YHWH is coming home together with his children, the exiled.

To conclude, it seems plausible that כפלים refers to Zion's specific experience of childlessness and widowhood. In focus stands the fact that God once again turns to his people with words of comfort. The guilt is mentioned in order to show that the suffering has its own cause. This cause lies not in God's weakness, but in their sins. In order to receive the open arms of YHWH in an embrace, the people have to open their own arms by recognising their guilt. To recognise such guilt is one thing that Isa 40:2 is, by very subtle means, trying to prepare the listener to do. It is through the acceptance of the guilt that the listener can embrace those who return from the exile and also be embraced by God's forgiveness.

[12] I follow the reading suggested in BHS.

[13] Both expressions are used to refer to YHWH in Isa 40–55. In Isa 42:6 it is YHWH who says: "I have taken you by the hand". And in Isa 51:3 it is YHWH who "will comfort Zion".

[14] See further below.

2. Isaiah 43:3b–4

The second passage I turn to, Isa 43:3b–4, is of special interest, since this is the only text in Isa 40–55 where the root כפר (here the noun, "ransom") is used.[15] This root is often used to state that atonement has been accomplished.[16] Hence, it is import to find out if the word is used with such a meaning here:

I give Egypt as your ransom (כפרך),
  Cush and Seba in exchange for you (תחתיך).
Because you are precious in my sight,
  and honored, and I love you,
I give people[17] in return for you (תחתיך),
  nations in exchange (תחת) for your life.

The dating of this section is debated.[18] One issue which is important for the dating is how closely connected this passage is to the preceding Isa 43:1–3a. The following section (Isa 43:5–7) is rather generally seen as a later expansion. This is probable, since Isa 43:5–7 seems to refer to a period when the people are scattered in diaspora. Even though it is possible that Isa 43:3b–4 is also a later expansion, I will treat it as a continuation of the preceding text and, which is more important for this discussion, as a text preceding Isa 53 in terms of origin. There are no decisive arguments for a late dating.[19]

The area of land that is stated as the exchange is the Northeast Africa. There is no need to conclude that the prophet had heard about Cyrus' plans for Africa, which has sometimes been argued. A closer motivation for bringing in the three countries and their peoples (these also occur in Isa 45:14) is that the כפר can simply not be made with something which already belongs to the other.[20] To be a ransom, it has to be an object outside Cyrus' dominion. In the bicolon Isa 43:4a we understand why YHWH gives such a

---

[15] This text is of special interest since it might be to this text that Mark 10:45 alludes. Cf. Thomas Knöppler, *Sühne im Neuen Testament: Studien zum urchristlichen Verständnis der Heilsbedeutung des Todes Jesu* (WMANT vol. 88; Neukirchen-Vluyn: Neukirchener Verlag, 2001), 284–288.

[16] See for example Lev 5:6, 10, 13, 16, 18, 26.

[17] Some amend this to איים, "islands", which gives a better parallelism. E.g. Elliger, *Deuterojesaja 40,1-45,7*, 274, and Baltzer, *Deutero-Isaiah*, 155, 159.

[18] According to Kratz, *Kyros im Deuterojesaja-Buch*, 148, Isa 43:1–4 belongs to *Die Grundschrift des Dtjes-Buches*. Oorschot, *Von Babel zum Zion*, 243, 291, on the other hand separates Isa 43:3b–4 from the rest and dates this part to his *Die sekundäre Zionsschicht*, which he dates to around the middle of the fifth-century B.C.E.

[19] Contra Oorschot, *Von Babel zum Zion*, 243.

[20] Elliger, *Deuterojesaja 40,1-45,7*, 298.

great כפר. This bicolon takes up the inner line of this oracle of salvation, where the listeners are assured of God's love to them. The ransom is given: "Because you are precious in my sight".[21] Israel has its value, not in itself, but in the eyes of YHWH.[22] A similar understanding of the כפר is also expressed by Janowski. He argues that it is not the specific political circumstances, which are at stake, but rather the incomparable greatness of the divine salvation. Isa 43:3b, 4b is, hence, put as an inclusive bracket around the reflection about the cause for this, which is the love of YHWH. Janowski also states that:

> An der Lösegeldaussage v. 3b ist bedeutsam, dass hier, im Unterschied zu Ex 21, 30 und zu Ex 30, 12, nicht der Urheber der Verschuldung, sondern der Geschädigte (Jahwe) das כֹּפֶר zur Auslösung des Schuldigen (des aufgrund eigener Verschuldung ins Exil geratenen Volkes Israel) gibt.[23]

Still, even though Isa 43:4a is the inner line of the text, and even though it is YHWH who gives the כפר and not the guilty party, the כפר is given on behalf of someone to someone else. This is what makes it most doubtful that it could refer to any form of guilt. The כפר is most likely given to Cyrus, and certainly not to YHWH, since he gives it.[24] This makes it an impossible statement, if it is in any way a reference to the guilt that was paid off. The guilt of Israel is understandably not referred to at all in Isa 43:1–7. When the transgressions are referred to in the preceding section, Isa 43:25–28, it is in order to state that it is YHWH who blots them out for his own sake. To conclude, the כפר that is given is, therefore, probably intended as a ransom for the liberation of Israel from exile and not as atonement for their sins. Furthermore, the ransom is not the core of the text. The core is found in the way that this text points to God's love for his people.

In connection with this text, we must also pay attention to two other texts, which are closely related to Isa 43:3b–4. These are Isa 45:13b and 52:3:

> [H]e shall build my city
> and set my exiles free,
> not for price or reward (במחיר),
> says YHWH Sabaoth. (Isa 45:13b)

> For thus says YHWH: You were sold for nothing, and you shall be redeemed without money (בכסף תגאלו). (Isa 52:3)

[21] Cf. Isa 43:1b, 3a.

[22] E.g. Elliger, *Deuterojesaja 40,1-45,7*, 298. Cf. also Westermann, *Isaiah 40–66*, 118, for a similar view.

[23] Janowski, *Sühne als Heilsgeschehen*, 169–170.

[24] Cf. Isa 45:14.

Both these texts appear at first sight to be countering the message in Isa 43:3b–4. However, Hermisson argues convincingly regarding Isa 45:13b that:

> [Das] Lösegeld [in Isa 43:3] sind dort ein Zeichen der übergroßen Liebe Jahwes zu Israel, und an unserer Stelle wäre die scheinbar widersprechende Aussage (da der Empfänger des Lösegelds in 43,3 doch nur Kyros sein könnte) ein Ausdruck der Souveränität Jahwes – der Prophet entwirft keine Detailprogramme für Jahwes Verfahren, und als Argument für Unechtheit ist der »Widerspruch« nicht zu gebrauchen.[25]

Hermisson does, however, regard Isa 45:13b to be a later addition.[26] Our interest at this point is not in the dating of these verses. Here it is more significant to see that all these three texts emphasise God's love for his people by their liberation. The tension that emerges, at a quick glance, must not be enforced. The core of the passages, the way in which all three texts direct our attention to God's love for his people, should be emphasised instead.

3. Isaiah 43:22–28

I will now turn my attention to texts which testify that it is YHWH who blots out the sins, this in order to understand the cause of this blotting out and the reason why the sins and transgression are mentioned. The first of these texts is Isa 43:22–28:

Yet you did not call upon me, O Jacob;
  but you have been weary of me, O Israel!
You have not brought me your sheep for burnt offerings,
  or honoured me with your sacrifices. (!)[27]
I have not burdened you with offerings,
  or wearied you with frankincense.
You have not bought me sweet cane with money,
  or satisfied me with the fat of your sacrifices.
But you have burdened me with your sins;
  you have wearied me with your iniquities.
I, I am He who blots out your transgressions for my own sake,
  and I will not remember your sins.
Accuse me, let us go to trial;
  set forth your case, so that you may be proved right.
Your first ancestor sinned,
  and your interpreters transgressed against me.
Therefore I profaned the princes of the sanctuary,
  I delivered Jacob to utter destruction,
    and Israel to reviling.

---

[25] Hans-Jürgen Hermisson, *Deuterojesaja 45,8-49,13* (BKAT vol. 11/2; Neukirchen-Vluyn: Neukirchener Verlag, 2003), 26.

[26] Hermisson, *Deuterojesaja 45,8-49,13*, 26.

[27] Following 1QIsa^{a}: ובזבחיכה. E.g. Baltzer, *Deutero-Isaiah*, 176.

This passage presents the picture of a trial speech used in legal procedures. The formal trial speech is modified in at least two ways to suit the purpose in Isa 40–55. The first modification is in v. 25. Instead of the expected summon, this verse changes into a proclamation of salvation.[28] The second modification is in v. 28. This verse indeed bears the remembrance of a judgement. But the pronouncement of a sentence is changed into a statement about the judgement that has already been accomplished.[29] Before I return to these two modifications, I will turn to another feature of this section.

In this text we meet a sacrificial language, which is rather unusual in Isa 40–55. Several of the words occur only here in Isa 40–55. The rest of the corpus has little interest in the cult. Despite the unusual language, the text is generally understood to belong to the early parts of Isa 40–55.[30] According to North, two interpretations have been suggested for the complaint by YHWH that his people have not brought him sacrificial offerings. First, it has been suggested that he is only stating the fact that, with the conditions of the exile, sacrificial worship was impossible. Secondly, it has been suggested that it refers to the sacrifices of pre-exilic times, and the attitude to sacrifice in Isa 40–55 was just as unfavourable as that of the great pre-exilic prophets.[31] It seems rather unlikely that Isa 43:22–28 only indicates that worship was impossible in exile. The real question is whether the cult actually served YHWH or whether it served the people themselves, who tried to make their God serve them.[32] However, the reference to the cult is a minor problem, since I understand the text to belong in the land. Even when the temple was in ruin, there was probably some cult going on in the land. Hence, we could understand Isa 43:22–28 as a reference to a complaint made by the community. Such complaints are then countered by the prophet, who states that they have only served YHWH by their sins and iniquities.

Now we will leave the sacrificial language, which is somewhat foreign to Isa 40–55. There are two other images, which are important in Isa 40–55. The first is the image of the servant. Westermann argues:

---

[28] Cf. Melugin, *The Formation*, 48–50.

[29] E.g. Antoon Schoors, *I am God your Saviour: A Form-Critical Study of the main Genres in Is. XL-LV* (VTsup vol. 24; Leiden: Brill, 1973), 189–197.

[30] E.g. Kratz, *Kyros im Deuterojesaja-Buch*, 217, and Rainer Albertz, *Israel in Exile: The History and Literature of the Sixth Century B.C.E* (Studies in Biblical Literature vol. 3; Atlanta: Society of Biblical Literature, 2003b), 398. However, contra Oorschot, *Von Babel zum Zion*, 347.

[31] North, *Isaiah 40–55*, 76.

[32] Cf. Elliger, *Deuterojesaja 40,1-45,7*, 372–373, Th. Booij, "Negation in Isaiah 43:22–24," *ZAW* 92 (1982): 390–400, 394–395, and John Goldingay, "Isaiah 43,22–28," *ZAW* 110 (1998): 191–203.

> If God is made into a *'ebed*, if he is made to serve, he has his divinity taken from him.
>
> Here in 43.24, this reversal of the natural relationship between God and man, in which God is lord and man God's servant, flashes out for just a moment. [...] However, what here is the momentary sounding of a note, is to be taken up again in the poems about the *'ebed*, the servant of God: there is to be a servant who, at God's behest, is to take the sins of the others upon himself. This connection between 43.22–28 and the poems about the *'ebed* is, in my view, the clearest proof that the latter come from Deutero-Isaiah.[33]

Like the first image, the second one, i.e. the image of the sheep, also has a special connection to Isa 53. The precise word שׂה, "sheep", occurs only here and in Isa 53:7. In Isa 53:7 we encounter the servant who was led to "slaughter" (טבח, in this text it is a profane slaughter in contrast to Isa 43:22–28, where we have the ritual slaughter). The people who are addressed in Isa 43:22–28 have made God their servant through their iniquities. The servant in Isa 53 has suffered on behalf of other persons' sins, which they also confess in Isa 53:6. The image of sheep/shepherd is also prominent in other parts of Isa 40–55. In Isa 43:22–28 the images of both the sheep and the servant are used to make the receivers of the message aware of their own responsibility. Later in Isa 53, we see the contrast to the servant who suffered because of "our iniquities". The first verses, Isa 43:22–24, do show that the people are guilty of not serving YHWH. The natural verdict after such a trial would be that the accused is guilty. Instead of a summons to trial, the outcome is a promise that YHWH "blots out" (מחה) the transgressions. The only motivation for this is that YHWH will do this for his own sake. In this section we have no reference to vicarious suffering, neither by the people nor by anyone else. On the contrary, it is when YHWH has met the complaint and when he has proven the people guilty that he gives the promise of forgiveness. Therefore, Isa 43:22–25 is actually not a trial speech, but a dismissal of a plea.[34]

The appeal for a trial, properly speaking, follows in Isa 43:26. The basis of the whole trial is probably given in Isa 43:28, where the charge is brought against God by Israel. This text has often been read from the perspective of exile. Contrary to this, I interpret the text from the perspective of the people in the land at the end of the exile. The accusation is therefore not that YHWH has driven them into exile, but there is a question why YHWH has allowed the whole situation to change again for the people in the land.

Now it is time to turn to the name of Jacob. It has been suggested that this name takes a stand on a tradition about Jacob, which is also presupposed in Hos 12:3–4:

---

[33] Westermann, *Isaiah 40–66*, 131–132.

[34] Cf. Westermann, *Isaiah 40–66*, 131, and Claus Westermann, *Sprache und Struktur der Prophetie Deuterojesajas* (Stuttgart: Calwer, 1981), 59.

YHWH has an indictment against Judah,
and will punish Jacob according to his ways,
  and repay him according to his deeds.
In the womb he tried to supplant his brother,
  and in his manhood he strove with God.

In this tradition, the Jacob-stories are tried and found wanting.[35] Therefore, it is a possible that the people had already associated their present situation with this understanding of the Jacob-stories. If this is the case, they saw the people in exile as the punished Jacob (Hos 12:3) and hence as someone whom they did not want to receive back home. Again, this is in contrast to Esau, who embraced Jacob when he returned. By referring to Jacob in Isa 43:22, the prophet turns the whole picture around and claims that the people at home are guilty (Isa 43:22–24, 27) and the only way to embrace those exiled is by recognition of their own guilt.

4. Isaiah 44:21–22

Remember these things (אלה), O Jacob,
  and Israel, for you are my servant;
I formed you, you are my servant;
  O Israel, you will not be forgotten by me.
I have swept away your transgressions like a cloud,
  and your sins like mist;
return to me, for I have redeemed you.

It is crucial, and widely discussed what it is that should be remembered. Does the word אלה, "these things", refer to the preceding verses[36] or the coming ones?[37] The picture is even more complicated, since there is also a discussion about what would be the preceding part. The immediately preceding verses are Isa 44:9–20 with their polemics against idols. However, these verses have often been understood as a later addition.[38] One argument for a late dating of Isa 44:9–20 is that these polemics against idols are theologically inferior to the other texts in Isa 40–55. Maybe this view

[35] E.g. Westermann, *Isaiah 40–66*, 133. Cf. also Baltzer, *Deutero-Isaiah*, 179–182. Contra Else Kragelund Holt, *Prophesying the Past: The Use of Israel's History in the Book of Hosea* (JSOTSup vol. 194; Sheffield: Sheffield Academic Press, 1995), 30–46.

[36] Here there are also various suggestions. According to Westermann, *Isaiah 40–66*, 139–144, אלה refers to Isa 44:6–8, since he regards the rest as a secondary insertion. Baltzer, *Deutero-Isaiah*, 205, and Knut Holter, *Second Isaiah's Idol Fabrication Passages* (BBET vol. 28; Frankfurt am Main: Peter Lang, 1995), 199–202, regard אלה as referring to Isa 44:9–20.

[37] E.g. Elliger, *Deuterojesaja 40,1-45,7*, 445.

[38] E.g. Kratz, *Kyros im Deuterojesaja-Buch*, 217.

was persuasive as long as Deutero-Isaiah was pictured as a distinct person, who wrote the book himself.[39] Albertz, following Werlitz, argues that RE[1] is responsible for 44:10–11, 12–17.[40] Seen in this context, there is a close parallel to the preceding section, Isa 44:9–20, which describes those who have formed idols and their relationship to the idols, and also to Isa 44:20–21, where God has formed his servant.[41] The order is as follows: YHWH has formed Jacob/Israel and hence the people also form their idols. The idols are totally worthless. As small as Jacob/Israel is in relation to YHWH, so small are the idols compared to those who make them.

There is a close parallel between Isa 44:21–22 and the preceding 44:9–20. Still the word אלה, "these things", probably refers to the following verses. It is used in both ways in other examples in Isa 40–55.[42] The most important argument for assuming that the word refers to the following verses is that the particle כי, "for", in both verse 21 and 22 give the reason for the preceding statement: "for (כי) you are my servant" and "for (כי) I have redeemed you".[43]

The exhortation: "Remember these things" is an urge to return to YHWH, not as a condition for forgiveness, but because he has swept away the transgressions like a cloud. It is YHWH who blots out the sins. This he does without any clearly stated reason or cause, except that it is YHWH who has formed his servant. Atonement, or other means to remove sins, is not in any way needed. Still, Isa 44:21–22 contains an explicit urge to return to YHWH. Hence, this text also contains an urge to recognise ones own guilt.

5. Isaiah 48:8–11

Now I will turn to the last verses of the section Isa 48:1–11. Having proclaimed that the people are guilty and undeserving of salvation, the verses give an explanation for the fact that YHWH comes back with salvation. There is no explanation in any action of atonement. The only thing that prevents YHWH from a final judgment is his own glory:

---

[39] E.g. Albertz, *Israel in Exile*, 396.

[40] See Albertz, *Israel in Exile*, 396, and Werlitz, *Redaktion und Komposition*, 221–235.

[41] Cf. Holter, *Idol Fabrication Passages*, 200.

[42] In Isa 42:16 and 45:7 it refers to the preceding. In Isa 48:14 it refers to the coming.

[43] Cf. Elliger, *Deuterojesaja 40,1-45,7*, 445–446.

You have never heard, you have never known,
  from of old your ear has not been opened.
For I knew that you would deal very treacherously,
  and that from birth you were called a rebel.
For my name's sake I defer my anger,
  for the sake of my praise I restrain it for you, so that I may not cut you off.
See, I have refined you, but not for silver;[44]
  I have tested you in the furnace of adversity.[45]
For my own sake, for my own sake, I do it,
  for why should my name be profaned?[46]
My glory I will not give to another. (Isa 48:8–11)

The whole section of Isa 48:1–11 is often understood to have a rather complex growth. However, in recent years it has more often been understood as a unit.[47] Whether or not the whole section has a long growth is not particularly decisive for the interpretation of the three verses that are of interest here. They are probably postexilic. The whole of Isa 48:1–11 probably depends on some texts in Ezekiel.[48] In Ezek 20:9 we read:

But I acted for the sake of my name, that it should not be profaned in the sight of the nations among whom they lived, in whose sight I made myself known to them in bringing them out of the land of Egypt.

The section of Isa 48:8–11 also bears a resemblance to the words about refinement in Jer 6:27–30 (cf. also Ezek 22:17–20). Our text has, however, another meaning compared to Jeremiah's words of doom. That the text in Isaiah might depend on texts in Ezekiel and Jeremiah is not the only argument for a later origin. There are other more decisive arguments. One is that the ingress in Isa 48:1 is rather foreign to Isa 40–55. This argument also holds for the description of Jerusalem as a holy city in Isa 48:2 (a similar description occurs in Isa 52:1 but it played a greater role in post

---

[44] The meaning is probably that no silver has appeared through the refinement. E.g. Hermisson, *Deuterojesaja 45,8-49,13*, 246.

[45] I read with 1QIsa^a: בחנתיכה, "I have tested you", instead of בחרתיך, "I have chosen you". It is, however, possible that בחר is used in the sense of "test". Cf. Baltzer, *Deutero-Isaiah*, 281. In Jeremiah the refinement is followed by rejection. This makes it possible that בחר should also remind us of the election of the people, Hermisson, *Deuterojesaja 45,8-49,13*, 207.

[46] Here a number of different readings have been suggested. See BHS. The word יחל, "it be profaned", refers to "my name" in Isa 48:9. With BHS I insert שְׁמִי, "my name", even if this might be a later gloss. Cf. also Hermisson, *Deuterojesaja 45,8-49,13*, 207. He has a similar understanding, even if he does not insert שְׁמִי.

[47] E.g. Hermisson, *Deuterojesaja 45,8-49,13*, 207–212. Cf. also Chris Franke, *Isaiah 46, 47, and 48: A New Literary-Critical Reading* (Biblical and Judaic studies from the University of California, San Diego vol. 3; Winona Lake, Ind.: Eisenbrauns, 1994), 164–261, for a different way of seeking the unity within the text.

[48] Cf. Ezek 20:9, 14, 22; 36:22.

exilic time). We also have a deuteronomistic language in Isa 48:4.[49] Taken together, all these arguments point to a post-exilic origin for Isa 48:1–11.

The statement in Isa 48:8b, "from birth you were called a rebel", is rather similar to Isa 43:27. Still there is a difference between these two texts. In Isa 43:25–28, the words serve to give the reason for the punishment, which God had been forced to bring upon Israel. But that is not the final word. God has blotted out the sins and this has changed the whole situation. Here in Isa 48:8–10, Israel's sinfulness seems to be of a more permanent state.[50] The double למעני, "for my own sake", in Isa 48:11 puts the text in relation to the double אנכי, "I", in Isa 43:25. Even if the text in Isa 48 emphasises the sinfulness of Israel further, the text is still in line with Isa 43:25. Everything in a new beginning depends exclusively on God. There is no need for atonement or expiation of sins, even though the people are guilty and undeserving of salvation.

6. Conclusion

The first text to which I turned was Isa 40:2. I did so because the word כפלים, "double", has often been interpreted as if the debt has been settled through the suffering. This interpretation is based on the similarities with שׁנים, "twofold", and its use in the laws of obligation. The same word שׁנים does, however, occur within Isa 40–55, where it refers to the twofold suffering of being both childless and a widow. Since this is what has actually happened to Jerusalem (Isa 54:1), it is probable that Isa 40:2, which is directed to Zion, should be interpreted in line with the rest of Isa 40–55. Therefore כפלים in Isa 40:2 should be understood as a specific reference to Jerusalem's double suffering of being both childless and a widow. With the exception of Isa 53, Isa 40:2 is the single text in Isa 40–55 in which the reconciliation has most often been understood as dependent on the suffering. As we have seen, this is not the point made in the text. The core of the text lies in the comforting words to Jerusalem, that she will no longer be a widow and childless.

In turning to the other texts, we saw that it is "because you are precious in my sight" (Isa 43:4) that God turns again to his people. There is no cause outside God himself, which gives any reason for this new forgiveness. Even if the forgiveness is without a cause, the suffering, which is now over and done with, does have a cause. The suffering was caused by the ancestors, who had sinned, and because "you have burdened me with your sins; you have wearied me with your iniquities" (Isa 43:24). In Isa

---

[49] For a fuller discussion, see Hermisson, *Deuterojesaja 45,8-49,13*, 213–215.

[50] E.g. Westermann, *Isaiah 40–66*, 198.

40–55, the sins and the iniquities are frequently mentioned in order to make the listeners recognise their own part in what has happened, and in order to make them receive God, who turns to them again. This is also the case in Isa 44:21–22 and Isa 48:8–11. None of the sections mention any need for expiation or atonement, even though the people are guilty and absolutely undeserving of salvation. These passages emphasise that YHWH opens his arms to embrace his people again, and there is no cause for this outside YHWH himself. The open arms hold an expectation of a response, a response from the people that they might return to YHWH and recognise their own guilt.

We have to ask why a suffering subject, such as we encounter in Isa 53, should turn up in this context. Is it really in order to illustrate a suffering, which has atoned for the sins of the listeners? If God has already forgiven their sins, why is there a need for an atoning suffering? As we have previously seen, it is problematic to defend an atoning suffering on the basis of the text of Isa 53. Now we have also seen that there is no need for atonement in the rest of Isa 40–55.

Part Three

The Contexts

Chapter 11

Isaiah 53 in the Book of Isaiah

Regarding the interpretation of Isa 53 it is decisive to determine how this section is related to the rest of the book of Isaiah. Starting with Duhm, it has been almost a scholarly consensus, both to read Isa 40–55 as a separate unit and to interpret Isa 53, as well as the other three servant songs, as rather loosely connected to the rest of Isa 40–55.[1] This view still influences studies on the book of Isaiah and especially those on the servant songs, even though the theory of Duhm has been questioned and modified in several ways.[2]

I will try to show that Isa 53 has been incorporated by different means into its present position in Isa 40–55 and that the section is related to important chapters in the book of Isaiah as a whole. The way in which it has been integrated indicates that Isa 53 might have been composed for its present position in this book. This will be shown through the links between Isa 53 and significant texts in Isa 1–39, 40–55, and 56–66. At the compositional level, Isa 53 is rather loosely integrated into Isa 40–55 and probably does not belong to an earlier edition of this part.[3] This makes it probable that Isa 53 has been incorporated in the book at a rather late stage. I will therefore argue that the section functions as a reflection on what has previously been stated, first in Isa 40:1–52:12, and also to some extent in Isa 1–39, and that it leads over to the situation described in Isa 56–66.

Before turning to the analysis, I must position myself briefly with regard to some of the methodological questions in the scholarly works on the book of Isaiah. In recent years, an immense discussion about the book of Isaiah has taken place, both with regard to its redaction, composition, and various synchronic readings. The synchronic readings have the advantage of bringing all the parts together into a greater whole, and of disclosing the overall composition of the book. The most important advantage is that they

---

[1] Duhm, *Das Buch Jesaja*. There has, however, never been a total consensus. For an early critique of the separation of the servant songs, see Budde, "The So-Called 'Ebed-Yahweh Songs'," and Kaiser, *Der Königliche Knecht*.

[2] The most elaborated critique of the theory of the servant songs has been put forward by Mettinger, *A Farewell*. Richard. J. Coggins, "Do We Still Need Deutero-Isaiah," *JSOT* 81 (1998): 77–92, has even questioned whether we still need Deutero-Isaiah.

[3] Kratz, *Kyros im Deuterojesaja-Buch*, 217, and Albertz, *Die Exilszeit*, 297, among others.

work with the object that we actually have, namely the final text.[4] Still, there are problems with a synchronic reading of the book of Isaiah, especially if we want to relate a text to its historical situation. We know that we probably have texts from at least three centuries in this book and the final text has a long and complicated history of growth. This gives the diachronic readings significant value.

Many prominent scholars have shown the importance of diachronic readings in all parts of the book of Isaiah. Those who deal with Isa 40–55 are of course of special interest to the present work.[5] Regarding Isa 40–55, the diachronic reading has a clear starting point in the text as it is presented to us. First, there are significant differences between Isa 40–48 and 49–55. Even if Isa 40–55 is a compositional unity, it is not a coherent text, but rather a collection of shorter and longer texts. Furthermore, important themes of the first part are withdrawn in the second part. One of the more important indications of different conceptions in Isa 40–48 and 49–55 is that in the first part, the exiled are called Jacob and Israel, while in 49–55 they are called the children of Zion, the wife and the bride of God. This is not simply different perspectives, but fundamentally different concepts.[6] Hence, one clearly legitimate question concerns the diachronic question of how these different themes and perspectives have come together as one book. The diachronic reading has also shown the importance of studying the whole book of Isaiah, although in another way. There are themes that run through the whole book and there are late redactions in all parts of the book. This brings the book of Isaiah into a compositional unit. A significant problem with the diachronic readings is that we only have rather late editions of the whole book. We do not have access to the earlier stages of the growth of this book. This makes the theories regarding various literary layers rather speculative.

---

[4] In recent years, some scholars have made literary readings of the entire book of Isaiah. Antti Laato, *"About Zion I will not be Silent": The Book of Isaiah as an Ideological Unity* (ConBOT vol. 44; Stockholm: Almqvist & Wiksell International, 1998), and Robert H. O'Connell, *Concentricity and Continuity: The Literary Structures of Isaiah* (JSOTsup vol. 188; Sheffield: Sheffield Academic Press, 1994), present such works.

[5] See among others the works of Kiesow, *Exodustexte im Jesajabuch*, Kratz, *Kyros im Deuterojesaja-Buch*, Oorschot, *Von Babel zum Zion*, Werlitz, *Redaktion und Komposition*, and Albertz, *Die Exilszeit*, 283–332. For a summary and a critical examination of the major ones of these works, see Charles Conroy, "The Four 'Four Servant Poems' in Second Isaiah in the Light of Recent Redaction-Historical Studies," in *Biblical and Near Eastern Essays: Studies in Honour of Kevin J. Cathcart* (ed. Carmel McCarthy and John F. Healey; vol. *JSOTSup*; London: T&T Clark, 2003). See Hendrik Leene, "Auf der Suche nach einem redaktionskritischen Modell für Jesaja 40-55," *TLZ* 121 (1996): 803–818, for a critique of the search for a *Grundschicht*, of among others Kratz and Oorschot, in Isa 40–55.

[6] This is clearly expressed by Kratz, *Kyros im Deuterojesaja-Buch,* 1–3.

If some of the divergence between synchronic and diachronic readings could be overcome, there would be advantages. Werlitz proposes a combination of the insights gained by synchronic study of the book's composition and by the use of redaction-criticism. He concludes that both synchronic and diachronic modes of study are justified. What is important is an attitude of self-questioning on the part of scholars, who practise either mode of study.[7] I will not propose any new methods or theories regarding the growth of the book, but I will try to use some insights derived from various parts of research.

I will start my investigation by using the old division of the book into three parts, Isa 1–39, 40–55, and 56–66. This is not totally satisfactory.[8] Still, it is a division that to some extent exists, both at a literary and a historical level of the book.[9] Furthermore, it is helpful since Isa 53 is, at least to some extent, differently related to the three parts. First, I intend to show how Isa 53 is both connected to, and separated from, the text of Isa 40–55. Secondly, I will turn to Isa 1–39. In this part I will mainly look at some important images in Isa 53 and consider how they are used in Isa 1–39. Furthermore, in this part of the book there are some important sections that are generally acknowledged to have a special relation to Isa 40–55. These are chapters: 1, 6, and 35.[10] I will argue that Isa 11 and 36–39 are also related to Isa 53. Thirdly, when turning to Isa 56–66, there is a less obvious impact and I will primarily show that Isa 57:17–21 and 59:16 are associated with Isa 53.

---

[7] Werlitz, *Redaktion und Komposition*, 1–14, 359–363. Cf. also Ulrich Berges, *Das Buch Jesaja: Komposition und Endgestalt* (Herders Biblische Studien vol. 16; Freiburg: Herder, 1998), 535–546, for an attempt to combine the syncronic and diacronic perspectives.

[8] Hermisson, *Studien zur Prophetie und Weisheit*, 144, argues for example regarding the relationship between Isaiah and Deutero-Isaiah that: "[D]er deuterojesajanische Grundbestand bietet keinerlei Anhaltspunkte, ihn als Fortschreibung und Auslegung des Jesajabuchs zu verstehen." I also regard such an explanation as too simple a solution, since the book is much more complex.

[9] There are more divisions in the book but the literary division is most obvious where 40:1 starts. Isa 56:1 also signals a new situation. For a fuller discussion of the substructures in the book of Isaiah, see for example Laato, *"About Zion I will not be Silent"*, 45–65. He divides the book into two major parts: 1–39; 40–66.

[10] For Isa 1, see Uwe Becker, *Jesaja – von der Botschaft zum Buch* (FRLANT vol. 178; Göttingen: Vandenhoeck und Ruprecht, 1997), and Kustár, *"Durch seine Wunden sind wir geheilt"*, 191–191. For Isa 6, see North, *The Suffering Servant*, 170, Williamson, *The Book Called Isaiah*, 30–56, and Kustár, *"Durch seine Wunden sind wir geheilt"*, 193–194. Odil Hannes Steck, *Bereitete Heimkehr: Jesaja 35 als redaktionelle Brücke zwischen dem Ersten und dem Zweiten Jesaja* (SBS vol. 121; Stuttgart: Katolisches Bibelwerk, 1985), understands Isa 35 as a redactional bridge between Isa 1–34 and Isa 40–62.

1. Isaiah 53 in Isaiah 40–55

Turning to Isa 40–55, we must first deal with the old assumption that Isa 53 belongs to a group of servant songs that are separate from the rest of the corpus. This means that the songs have to carry enough similarities to one another to be regarded as a group, and also that all of them can be separated from Isa 40–55 without disturbing the composition. There are several similarities between the servant songs. First, we have the presentations in Isa 42:1, הן עבדי, "Here is my servant", and Isa 52:13 הנה ישׂכיל עבדי, "See, my servant shall prosper". Both presentations are made by God in similar ways. We also have the term עבד, "servant", which is used in the first, the second, and the fourth song. The term עבד is, however, also used rather frequently in the rest of Isa 40–55. Nevertheless, one important foundation for most of the arguments in favour of a group of servant songs seems to be that the four texts occur inside Isa 40–55. However, the so-called servant songs are a rather heterogeneous group, especially with regard to the genre[11] but also with regard to the language, their length and their description of the servant.[12] Therefore, I claim that the tension that exists between the songs makes it less likely that only the four of them make a suitable starting-point and that they should be read together as a separate group. They are related to each other, but this relationship is partly based on their present position in Isa 40–55. Furthermore, it is not only the diversity between the songs which makes the assumption that they are a separate group questionable. There are also some positive arguments in favour of reading them as part of their present context. Mettinger has made a critical study of the foundations for Duhm's theory.[13] Mettinger spends much effort to show that the servant songs are well integrated into the composition of Isa 40–55. He emphasises the importance of the hymns in the composition and shows, first and foremost, how important the second servant song is in the overall composition of Isa 40–55. According to Mettinger, Isa 49:1–12 is set in relief by the two hymns that surround it. This section is also situated in one of the more important divisions of the

[11] Cf. Mettinger, *A Farewell*, 16–17.

[12] Janowski, "He Bore Our Sins," 59, argues that the servant in the fourth song must be differentiated from the first three songs. He concludes: "Both outside and inside the Servant Songs, then, various Servants appear – outside the Songs the Servant Jacob/Israel and the Servant 'Second Isaiah'; within the first three Songs a Servant who is identical with the prophetic Servant outside the Songs. The problem is different once again in the fourth Servant Song, which tells of this prophetic Servant's vicarious surrender of life, thus taking a position *post mortem servi Dei.*"

[13] Mettinger, *A Farewell.*

corpus.[14] Mettinger's investigation has received some criticism.[15] One important objection against his understanding of the composition of Isa 40–55 is that it does not pay due attention to the complicated growth of the corpus. Another problem is that Mettinger understand Isa 49:1–12 as a unit. Many scholars understand Isa 49:7–12 as a later extension of the original servant song.[16] Despite this criticism, Mettinger has shown that the second servant song cannot be removed without a significant gap in the composition, and Isa 49:1–12 is important in the composition of Isa 40–55. It is therefore likely that the text has been composed to fit this place in the book. This does, however, not rule out the possibility of a rather long process of growth of this book.[17]

Mettinger's compositional approach is, however, weaker with regard to the fourth servant song. In his examination of the hymns, Mettinger finds two other short sections that are bracketed in a similar way as Isa 49:1–12. These are Isa 44:24–45:7 and Isa 53.[18] At a first glance, it seems probable that also the fourth servant song has a similar position as Isa 49:1–12 does in the composition of the book. Mettinger points out that there is one section, which especially recalls the prologue, namely 52:7–12. The connections between the prologue, Isa 40:1–11, and 52:7–12 should be noted according to Mettinger, since this hymnic section immediately precedes the fourth servant song.[19] There are also some words that link Isa 53 to the preceding section. Isa 52:10 declares that:

---

[14] Mettinger, *A Farewell*, 20. See also his figure of the composition, Mettinger, *A Farewell*, 27. He discovers that the hymn of praise that precedes the section points forward and the hymn that succeeds it points backward.

[15] Especially from Hans-Jürgen Hermisson, "Voreiliger Abschied von den Gottesknechtsliedern," *TRu* 49, no. 3 (1984): 209–222, but also Roger Norman Whybray, "A Farewell to the Servant Songs," *JBL* 104, no. 4 (1985): 706–707. See Frank Matheus, *Singt dem Herrn ein neues Lied: die Hymnen Deuterojesajas* (SBS vol. 141; Stuttgart: Katholisches Bibelwerk, 1990), 104–112, and Werlitz, *Redaktion und Komposition*, 28–35, for an examination and elaboration of the critique.

[16] See Werlitz, *Redaktion und Komposition*, 36, as an example. It has also been suggested that even Isa 49:1–6 could be divided in a first written text with later expansions in v. 2a, 4a, and part of 5a, Rosario Pius Merendino, "Jes 49:1-6: Ein Gotteskenchtlied?" *ZAW* 92 (1980): 236–248. The proof of this is, however, rather weak since Isa 49:1–6 forms a rather coherent text.

[17] Cf. Albertz, *Israel in Exile*, 394: "Since Isa 49:1–13 is an important compositional element of the text, it was very likely created by the redactor of DtIE[1] (RE[1]), who took an existing Servant Song (49:1–6*) and furnished it with a commentary (49:8–12) linking it to its context and gave it special emphasis by bracketing it with hymns (48:20–21); 49:13). [...W]e must therefore insist that at least the Servant Song in 49:1–6* was an indispensable part of the very first edition of the book of Deutero-Isaiah."

[18] Mettinger, *A Farewell*, 20.

[19] Mettinger, *A Farewell*, 22–23.

YHWH has bared his holy arm (זרוע)
before the eyes of all nations;
and all the ends of the earth shall see (וראו)
the salvation of our God.

This is re-echoed in Isa 52:15–53:1:

for that which had not been told them they shall see (ראו) [...]
Who has believed what we have heard?
And to whom has the arm (וזרוע) of YHWH been revealed?

These are important links. However, the connections have probably been made at a later stage in order to incorporate Isa 53 into the preceding section. There are two further important arguments against the understanding advocated by Mettinger. First, it is questionable whether Isa 54:1–3 is an eschatological hymn.[20] This means that Isa 53 is not bracketed by hymns but only preceded by a hymn. Mettinger has also revised his position and later regarded Isa 51:9–52:12, and not Isa 53, as the counterpart of the Cyrus oracle.[21] Secondly, the connections between the prologue, Isa 40:1–11, and Isa 52:7–12 indicate that the latter text brings this section, Isa 40:1–52:12, to an end. The redaction-historical approach has often understood the literary connections between the prologue, Isa 40:1–11 and Isa 52:7–10 as an indication of the original end to the first edition of the book, with Isa 52:7–10 as the epilogue.[22] Following this, it is probable that Isa 53 is a later addition to an earlier edition of the book, of which the second song was already an integral part. This indicates that the second and fourth songs have different functions in the composition of Isa 40–55. This is also a further argument against simply reading the four songs as a separate group of texts.

Now I will turn to Isa 53 and its place in Isa 40–55. Since Isa 53 was probably incorporated at a rather later stage, it is important to determine how it is related to Isa 40:1–52:12. The connection to Isa 52:10, which was shown above, indicates that Isa 53 is placed here as a link to the preceding text and probably as a result of a special intention to interpret the preceding text. Furthermore, Isa 53 is not only related to the immediately preceding verses. In addition, I will examine the relationship to two other texts in Isa 40:1–52:12, namely Isa 40:27 and Isa 49:7.

---

[20] Cf. Albertz, *Israel in Exile*, 426.

[21] Tryggve N. D. Mettinger, "In Search of the Hidden Structure: YHWH as King in Isaiah 40–55," in *Writing and Reading the Scroll of Isaiah: Studies of an Interpretive Tradition* (ed. Craig A. Evans and Craig C. Broyles; vol. *VTsup*; Leiden: Brill, 1997), 154.

[22] E.g. among others Kiesow, *Exodustexte im Jesajabuch*, 165, Kratz, *Kyros im Deuterojesaja-Buch*, 217, and Reinhard Gregor Kratz, "Der Anfang des Zweiten Jesaja in Jes 40,1f. und seine literarischen Horizonte," *ZAW* 105 (1994): 400–419, 407–412.

First, I will examine Isa 40:27 and its relation to the confession in Isa 53:6. In Isa 40:27 we read:

My way (דרכי) is hidden from YHWH,
and my right (משׁפטי) is disregarded by my God.

The next time the receiver of the message speaks is in Isa 53:6. Now the tone is different:

All we like sheep have gone astray;
we have all turned to our own way (לדרכו).

The confession sounds as though it could be the people's own answer to their earlier complaint. Isa 40:27 is often understood to be an earlier text, which makes it likely that Isa 53:6 is a re-use or a reinterpretation of Isa 40:27.[23] Isa 40–55 often seems to quote the receiver of the message. However, Isa 40:27 and 53:6 are especially clear examples of when the receivers of the message come to speech in Isa 40–55. In Isa 40:27 their words are incorporated into the text by a clear quotation, and in Isa 53:6 the "we" are speaking.[24] The texts are similar, not only by consisting of quotations; but they both use the word דרך, "way", as a metaphor.[25] In Isa 53:6 the group who made the complaint in Isa 40:27, emphasise the new understanding that it is not YHWH who has done wrong, but it is they themselves, who have gone astray, and this is what they confess.[26] The confession in Isa 53 expresses a new insight compared to Isa 40:27. This is a re-use of the text, which is important for the interpretation of Isa 53, and it also gives a new meaning to Isa 40:27. Another link between Isa 40:27 and the servant songs is the use of the term משׁפט, "right". This term occurs in all of the servant songs.[27] There is a clear contrast between the complaint in Isa 40:27 and the servant, who brings fourth justice and who does not complain, even though he has suffered unjustly and has been taken away without justice. It is therefore likely that the servant songs, and especially Isa 53, are a response to Isa 40:27.

The second text to which I will turn is Isa 49:7. The first two servant songs are followed by interpretations.[28] Of these, the verse Isa 49:7 is particularly interesting:

---

[23] Cf. Oorschot, *Von Babel zum Zion*, 27–28.

[24] Cf. also Isa 42:24.

[25] See further Lund, *"Min vei er skjult for JHWH,"* 318.

[26] Cf. also Lund, *"Min vei er skjult for JHWH,"* 267–268.

[27] Isa 42:1, 3, 4; 49:4; 50:8; 53:8. The term also reoccurs in Is 54:17, the last time "servant" is mentioned in Isa 40–55.

[28] Isa 42:5–9 and 49:7–13. For further discussion of these texts see above.

Thus says YHWH,
  the Redeemer of Israel and his Holy One,
to one deeply despised (לבזה), abhorred by the nations,
  the slave (לעבד) of rulers,
"Kings shall see and stand up,
  princes, and they shall prostrate themselves,
because of YHWH, who is faithful,
  the Holy One of Israel, who has chosen you (ויבחרך)."

This verse bears a significant resemblance to Isa 53 in the general description as well as in some details. In both texts, we meet a "servant" (עבד). Furthermore, both servants are "despised" (בזה), and they astonish kings. Isa 49:7 is also linked to the other servant songs, and especially to the second, both through its place and its language. The despised servant is for example a "chosen" (בחר) servant, just like the servant in Isa 42:1.

Isa 49:7 is probably a secondary interpretation of Isa 49:1–6. It may also be secondary to Isa 49:8–12.[29] The verse has a rather closed form, starting with the message formula and ending with a conclusion, which states the reason for what is coming. In Isa 49:8 we have a new message formula, which indicates that this is a new section. This section, Isa 49:8–12, seems to be independent of Isa 49:7 and connects closer to Isa 49:1–6. According to Albertz, the interpretation made through Isa 49:7 is made in order to ensure that the fourth servant song is understood as a further commentary on the second song, Isa 49:1–6.[30] Here it is enough to conclude that we have one further example of how Isa 53 re-uses the preceding text, in this case, through a commentary-like addition to the text. To sum up, it seems as if Isa 53 is both connected to and separated from the preceding text. The section is separated as a later addition after an original ending in Isa 52:7–10. Isa 53 is also connected by several means, such as catchwords, to the immediately preceding verses through an interpretation of the text, as is the case with 40:27, and also by a later interpretation achieved by addition to the text, as is the case with 49:7.

Now I will leave the preceding text and turn to the following text. I will investigate the relationship and, as I understand it, the close relationship, between Isa 53 and Isa 54. There is probably a closer connection between these two texts than is generally acknowledged.[31] There are several words

---

[29] E.g. Albertz, *Israel in Exile*, 426. See Hermisson, *Deuterojesaja 45,8-49,13*, 324–327, for the understanding of Isa 49:7 as a closed verse.

[30] Albertz, *Israel in Exile*, 426. Cf. also Hermisson, *Deuterojesaja 45,8-49,13*, 338, who understands Isa 49:7 to anticipate the fourth servant song and to have been inserted later than Isa 49:8–12.

[31] To see a close connection between these two chapters and images is however not a new idea. See for example Leland Edward Wilshire, "The Servant-City: A New Interpretation of the 'Servant of the Lord' in the Servant Songs of Deutero-Isaiah," *JBL* 94 (1975): 356–367, John F. A. Sawyer, "Daughter of Zion and Servant of the Lord in

that link these two texts together: זרע, "offspring", (53:10 and 54:3), שָׁלוֹם, "peace", (53:5 and 54:10, 13) רבים, "many", (52:14–15, 53:11–12 and 54:1), and finally the root צדק, "righteousness", (53:11 and 54:10, 13).[32] There is more than simply a connection through these rather general words. Baltzer argues that:

> It is not only catchwords that link 52:13–53:12 with chap. 54; the way the language is used also shows that they belong together. In Isa 52:13–53:12 it is the sociomorpheme lord-servant that makes it possible to communicate the fate of the Servant of God. Here in chap. 54 it is the story of "the spouse of God." [...] The renewed bond is presented as a marriage.[33]

This means that in both corpuses, the heavenly and the earthly events are linked in a way that makes them comparable to each other.[34] Both the catchwords and the way that these two texts describe the fate of the servant/spouse link the two texts to each other.

There are important arguments in favour of reading Isa 53 and 54 together. Still, these rather general links do not help us very much in our interpretation of Isa 53. Therefore, I will now turn to a text in Jeremiah, which makes further connections between Isa 53 and 54 and, what is more important, also gives us an explanation for why Isa 53 and 54 should be interpreted together. In Jer 10:20–21 we see that the actual events described in Isa 53 and 54 could also be closely connected:

> My tent (אהלי) is destroyed, and all my cords (מיתרי) are broken;
> my children have gone from me, and they are no more;
> there is no one to spread my tent (אהלי) again,
> and to set up my curtains (יריעתי).
> For the shepherds are stupid,
> and do not inquire of YHWH;
> therefore they have not prospered (השׂכילו),
> and all their flock is scattered. (Jer 10:20–21)

Isaiah: A Comparison.," *JSOT* 44 (1989): 89–107, and Berges, *Das Buch Jesaja*, 406, who identifies the servant in Isa 53 with Zion. A close parallel without identification between the two is also argued by Knud Jeppesen, "Mother Zion, Father Servant: A Reading of Isaiah 49–55," in *Of Prophets' Visions and the Wisdom of Sages: Essays in Honour of R. Norman Whybray on His Seventieth Birthday* (ed. Heather A. McKay and David J. A. Clines; vol. *JSOTsup*; Sheffield: JSOT Press, 1993), Marjo C. A. Korpel, "The Female Servant of the Lord in Isaiah 54," in *On Reading Prophetic Texts: Gender-Specific and Related Studies in Memory of Fokkelien van Dijk-Hemmes* (ed. Bob Becking, et al.; vol. *Biblical interpretation series*; Leiden; New York; Köln: Brill, 1996), Richtsje Abma, *Bonds of Love: Methodic Studies of Prophetic Texts with Marriage Imagery: (Isaiah 50:1–3 and 54:1–10, Hosea 1–3, Jeremiah 2–3)* (SSN vol. 40; Assen: Van Gorcum, 1999), 105–107, and Baltzer, *Deutero-Isaiah*, 430.

[32] Cf. Beuken, *Jesaja*, 271–272, and Korpel, "The Female Servant," 164.

[33] Baltzer, *Deutero-Isaiah*, 430.

[34] See Baltzer, *Deutero-Isaiah*, 430.

Zion is described with the same images in both Isa 54 and Jer 10:20–21. However, Jer 10:20–21 describes the opposite event, compared to the sequences in Isa 53–54. The tent is destroyed as a consequence of the foolish shepherds, which leads to the scattering of the flock. In Isa 53–54 the tent will be re-established as a consequence of the embrace of the servant's suffering, i.e. of the servant, who will ”prosper” (שׂכל in *hip'il*, Isa 52:13). It is possible that Isa 53–54 use and reinterpret the actual text of Jer 10:20–21.[35]

Both texts are linked to one another through the use of similar words and images. In Jer 10:20–21, as well as in Isa 54, we read about "a tent" (אהל), "a cord" (מיתר), and "a curtain" (יריעה). Furthermore, which is more important, in both texts, these images refer to Zion. The text in Jeremiah describes the consequences of the Babylonian exile and the complaint about the broken tent. The tent is broken because the stupid shepherds did not inquire of YHWH and "therefore they have not prospered" (על־כן לא השׂכילו).[36]

Turning to Isaiah 53–54, we have no new human shepherd to lead the people. This is one of the new things in the whole of Isa 40–55. I have emphasised above that, in this corpus, it is YHWH himself who "will feed his flock like a shepherd" (Isa 40:11). In Isa 53–54, the tent will be enlarged, the children will become numerous, and Zion's maker will be her new husband (Isa 54:5). All this will happen following the suffering and prosperity (שׂכל, in *hip'il* "to prosper") of the servant.

We can conclude that there are important parallels between Isa 53–54 and Jer 10:20–21. Still, a literary dependence is almost impossible to prove, even though I believe it is plausible in this place. Both texts could, as an alternative, be dependent on similar traditions, since we encounter a similar sequence of events with reference to both the fall and the re-establishment of Jerusalem in other texts in both Isaiah and Jeremiah. First, we have texts, which give a similar sequence of events about the fall of Jerusalem. In Isa 3, it is declared about the people that boys will be their princes and babies shall rule over them. This will evidently lead to the fall of Jerusalem (Isa 3:1–12). In Jer 15, the destruction of Jerusalem is linked

---

[35] There is also a parallel between Isa 53:4 and Jer 10:19 in the description of חלי, "sickness". Cf. Georg Fischer, *Jeremia 1–25* (HTKAT Freiburg: Herder, 2005), 391. He states that: "Jes 53,4 ist die *nächste parallele* für das Tragen von "Krankheit" (חלי), doch mit gravierende Differenz, Dort trägt der Knecht Gottes die Leiden Anderen, hier die Stadt ihr eigenes (1. Sg. >meine<)." Maybe the differences should not be enforced too much since the difference is a part of bringing the texts together.

[36] Benjamin D. Sommer, *A Prophet Reads Scripture: Allusion in Isaiah 40–66* (Contraversions Stanford, Calif.: Stanford University Press, 1998), 36–40, remarks that the passage from Deutero-Isaiah seems to reverse the negative image in Jeremiah point by point.

to the exclusion of the prophet, and hence to his suffering. Secondly, we will turn to an important text, which shows the same sequence of events about the re-establishment of Jerusalem. The composition of Isa 48:20–49:21 has several similarities to Isa 52:7–54:17. There is the hymn that urges departure, followed by the obedient servant in the second servant song. After this follows the re-establishment of Zion. These later examples are radical readings of the final composition of texts – texts that have undergone several stages of redaction. However, these texts have probably been placed together deliberately. This indicates that the acts and fates of YHWH's servants have a significant impact on the destiny of Zion.

As we have seen, there are too many links between Jer 10:20–21 and Isa 53–54 in terms of both the language and the themes to be accidental. From this, I draw two conclusions: First, these connections link the two chapters together in describing a sequence of events. Therefore, secondly, the new song in Isa 54 is dependent on the embrace described in Isa 53. I will return to this in the interpretation of Isa 53.

To sum up, it is probable that a major part of the preceding Isa 40:1–52:10 (or 12) had emerged as a corpus when our text was incorporated. Therefore, Isa 53 belongs to a later addition to an existing corpus. However, Isa 53 is connected to the preceding corpus by several means. These links are not outstanding, but they do show that Isa 53 was probably composed with a special intention for its present position in the corpus. If Isa 53 is somewhat loosely connected to what precedes, it is certainly very closely connected to what follows, i.e. to Isa 54. Hence, I consider Isa 53 and 54 to be a unit, which is important in its present position in the book of Isa 40–55.[37] Therefore, I will not interpret Isa 53 on its own, and not as a text that solely belongs to the servant songs. I will try instead to interpret Isa 53 in relation to the preceding and the following contexts.

2. Isaiah 53 and Isaiah 1–39

Turning to the relationship between Isa 53 and Isa 1–39, I will investigate two metaphors, which are significant, both for the overall redaction of the book and for Isa 53. The first is the metaphor of the tree and the second is the metaphor of sickness or illness. Metaphors connected to trees are important, since they occur in the presentation of the servant, which we encounter in Isa 53:2a:

[37] I have not dealt with parts of the texts in Isa 40–55 that I believe has been inserted later than Isa 53 and 54.

For he grew up like a young plant by himself,
and like a root out of dry ground.

First, I will sum up some general conclusions regarding the metaphor of the tree. Nielsen has dealt exhaustively with this in her study of the tree as metaphor in Isa 1–39.[38] Her first conclusion is that the tree metaphor in Isa 1–39 has "the informative function of acting as theological interpretations of the political situation."[39] The use of the tree has many connotations for the hearers, and it was not a new invention by Isaiah; we meet it in several other texts in the Old Testament. The tree is something valuable and the hearers are interested to learn what will happen to the tree. Nielsen concludes:

> The main content of the *information* to be derived from the images employed is as follows: As the God of Israel, Yahweh is the master of the political events, both when they denote misfortune and when they denote success for his people; similarly, Yahweh can use foreign nations to accord with his plans. History is not therefore fortuitous; it has its own coherence. It has been possible in various ways to express this message by use of the vineyard image, the forest-felling image and the forest-fire image, or combinations of them. But a characteristic is that it was possible to use the tree images to *argue* that this coherence is *righteous*. [...] But tree images can inform not only about misfortune. The possibility of new life is part of Yahweh's plan.[40]

Both the misfortune and the future hope for the tree are clearly present in Isa 53. The image of the tree can also serve in many different situations and as a bearer of different messages. It can also describe sequences of events. Her second conclusion is that:

> The performative function of the tree metaphor in Isaiah 1–39 is to involve the hearers in such a way that they adopt the metaphor's interpretation of reality as their own.[41]

This is especially important when we return to the presentation of the servant. It is likely that there was, at the time, a discussion about which group or which person could represent the future hopes for Israel. The way in which the servant is presented is a mean to include the "we"-group in this understanding of the situation. Imagery does not only contain information, it can also influence the hearers. The third point in Nielsen's conclusion is that "[t]he use of metaphors has made continuous reinterpretation of the original message possible [.]"[42] As we will see, this is also true concerning the presentation of the servant. With this survey I turn to individual pas-

---

[38] The following is found in Kirsten Nielsen, *There is Hope for a Tree: The Tree as Metaphor in Isaiah* (JSOTSup vol. 65; Sheffield: JSOT Press, 1989), 223–239, conclusion.

[39] Nielsen, *There is Hope for a Tree*, 223.

[40] Nielsen, *There is Hope for a Tree*, 224–225.

[41] Nielsen, *There is Hope for a Tree*, 228.

[42] Nielsen, *There is Hope for a Tree*, 232.

sages in Isa 1–39, which make use of this metaphor and which are related to the presentation of the servant in Isa 53:2:

For he grew up like a young plant (יונק) by himself,
and like a root (שֹׁרשׁ) out of dry ground.

This presentation is seldom discussed at length. Still, it is a presentation of the servant, and as such it is both interesting and important. One important passage, in which similar images are used in the book, is found in Isa 11:1–9, 10, 11–16.[43] In that section, we have the promise of a Davidic dynasty. In Isa 11:1 we read:

A shoot shall come out from the stump of Jesse
and a branch shall grow out of his roots (משׁרשׁיו).

The same word שֹׁרשׁ, "root", is also used in Isa 11:10. The ptc. of the verb ינק ("suck", which as ptc. describes an infant) also occurs in this section (Isa 11:8). In that verse it has a different meaning compared to Isa 53:2. This is still interesting, since the whole section is linked to Isa 53:2. The description "a young plant" (יונק) is only used here in the entire Old Testament. The feminine noun of the same root is sometimes used to describe the future hope of Israel (Ezek 17:22; Hos 14:7). It is also used as a metaphor for the people of Israel (Ps 80:12). These examples are important indications that the servant represents Israel, or a part of Israel, but all these texts are found outside the book of Isaiah. The use of both the roots, שׁרשׁ and ינק, in Isa 53:2 makes it likely that Isa 53 wants to recall the hopeful text of Isa 11 in its description of the servant.[44] Isa 11:12 continues with a promise that:

He will raise a signal for the nations,
and assemble the outcasts of Israel,
and gather the dispersed of Israel
from the four corners of the earth.

This text indicates that the hope for the "root" in Isa 11:1, 10 could be interpreted as a hope for the exiled. It is likely that Isa 11:12 is part of a later

---

[43] Regarding this division see Willem André Maria Beuken, *Jesaja 1-12* (HTKAT Freiburg: Herder, 2003), 315–317.

[44] According to Baltzer, *Deutero-Isaiah*, 404–405, the words "shoot/branch" (יונק) and "root" (שֹׁרשׁ) associate this passage with Isa 11:1–9, 10. He does not develop this association with any length. Instead he finds the relevant parallel text in Exod 2. This connection is developed primary on the use of the root ינק that occurs in Exod 2:5–10 and Isa 53:2. This connection is, however, not very strong considering that the word has different uses in the texts, and the other important word, "root" (שֹׁרשׁ), does not occur in Exod 2.

edition.[45] This implies that the hope for the tree has changed from hope for Israel through the Davidic dynasty to hope through the assembling of the dispersed. This is also in line with Isa 53, since the only king who exists in Isa 53–54 is YHWH, not a new David.

There are further indications of such transference of the hope for the assembling of the dispersed in Isa 1–39. The word "root" (שׁרשׁ) occurs in another text that links Isa 1–39 to 40–55. In Isa 37:31–32 we read:

The surviving remnant of the house of Judah shall again take root (שׁרשׁ) downward, and bear fruit upward; for from Jerusalem a remnant shall go out, and from Mount Zion a band of survivors.

Isa 36–39 links the marvellous rescue during the Assyrian siege to the hope for the exiles when Cyrus arises on the scene.[46] Here, again, we find a text in which the hope is for the remnant, and not for a new David. This hope for the remnant could easily be transferred to a hope for the exiles. See also Isa 27:6:

In days to come Jacob shall take root (ישׁרשׁ), (!)[47]
Israel shall blossom and put forth shoots,
and fill the whole world with fruit.

It is possible that some of these texts that concern the future hope for the dispersed date from a later period than Isa 53. Still, whether individual texts have emerged before or after Isa 53 is not decisive for this particular interpretation. These examples still show that the presentation in Isa 53:2 stands in a tradition of a reinterpretation of the tree metaphor in the book of Isaiah.

The tree as metaphor does not only denote hope, it also denotes judgement. We have two important texts in this regard, namely Isa 1:29–31 and Isa 6:13:

---

[45] Hans Wildberger, *Jesaja 1-12* (BKAT vol. 10/1; Neukirchen-Vluyn: Neukirchener Verlag, 1980), 466, dates Isa 11:11–16 to sometime later than DI, Jeremiah, and Ezekiel but earlier than Deutero-Zechariah. Marvin A. Sweeney, *Isaiah 1–39: With an Introduction to Prophetic Literature* (FOTL vol. 16; Grand Rapids Mich.: Eerdmans, 1996), 204–205, on the other hand, dates the section to Josiah's attempt to rebuild the Davidic empire, this seems however less probable. Beuken, *Jesaja 1-12*, 306, regards a dating in relation to the second temple to be the most likely, since the section describes the people as dispersed among several nations and it expects a return from across the whole world.

[46] See Laato, *"About Zion I will not be Silent"*, 116–117. Cf. Joseph Blenkinsopp, *Isaiah 1–39: A New Translation with Introduction and Commentary* (AB vol. 19; New York: Doubleday, 2000), 47.

[47] With BHSapp. that proposes "In days to come", instead of "Those to come".

For you shall be ashamed of the oaks
in which you delighted;
and you shall blush for the gardens that you have chosen.
For you shall be like an oak
whose leaf withers,
and like a garden without water.
The strong shall become like tinder,
and their work like a spark;
they and their work shall burn together,
with no one to quench them. (Isa 1:29–31)

"Even if a tenth part remain in it,
it will be burned again,
like a terebinth or an oak
whose stump remains standing when it is felled (אשר בשלכת מצבת בם)."
The holy seed is its stump. (Isa 6:13)

These two texts are probably related to each other. The most decisive arguments in favour of this are the use of the rather unusual word אלה, "oak", and a similar use of the tree as metaphor. Regarding the relationship between them, I believe that Williamson is right in understanding 6:13 to be oldest, since it is a more general statement. It is more likely that a general statement is reused for a more specific reference, than the other way around.[48] Both texts are, however, probably rather late and neither of them can probably be dated to the eighth century B.C.E. The destruction referred to in Isa 6:13 is probably the experience of the exile.[49] What is most interesting here is the hope expressed in Isa 6:13, with the problematic word שׁלכת. There is a discussion if the word שׁלכת describes the felling of the tree or their loss of foliage.[50] The word is based on the verb שׁלך, "to throw". This verb is also used to express the exile.[51] It is probable that the unusual word שׁלכת has a double reference, both to the felling of the tree and to the dispersion through the exile. This means that the "stump" (מצבת) is the people in exile (Isa 6:13). Regarding the dating, it is likely that this last colon is secondary to the rest of the verse. It is not

---

[48] Hugh Godfrey Maturin Williamson, "Isaiah 6,13 and 1,29–31," in *Studies in the Book of Isaiah: Festschrift Willem A.M. Beuken* (ed. J. van Ruiten and Marc Vervenne; vol. *BETL*; Leuven; Paris: Leuven Univinersity Press; Peeters France, 1997). Cf. also Hugh Godfrey Maturin Williamson, *Isaiah 1–5: A Critical and Exegetical Commentary* (ICC London: T&T Clark, 2006), 151–155, for a post-exilic dating of Isa 1:29–31.

[49] Cf. Kustár, *"Durch seine Wunden sind wir geheilt"*, 55–56.

[50] For a full discussion of this problem, see J. A. Emerton, "The Translation and Interpretation of Isaiah VI. 13," in *Interpreting the Hebrew Bible: Essays in Honour of E.I.J. Rosenthal* (ed. J. A. Emerton and Stefan C. Reif; vol. *University of Cambridge Oriental Publications*; Cambridge: Cambridge University Press, 1982), and Williamson, "Studies in the Book of Isaiah," 120–123.

[51] E.g. Jer 22:28.

included in the Septuagint. It also changes the meaning of מצבת, "stump". by turning the negative description into a positive one.[52] Through this secondary insertion, the negative statement has been turned into one of hope and trust that those who return from the exile will be the "holy seed".[53]

I will now leave the metaphor of the tree and turn to the metaphor of sickness or illness. First I will turn to the sufferings described in Isa 1:5–9, since this section has several parallels to the suffering of the servant.[54] The noun חלי, "illness", occurs only in Isa 38:9 besides Isa 1:5 and Isa 53:3, 4 and possibly v. 10. The verb נכה, "to strike", occurs in Isa 1:5 and Isa 53:4 and these are the only occurrences of this word in *hopʿal* in the book of Isaiah. The noun הבורה, "wound", is used only in Isa 1:5 and Isa 53:4 in this book.[55] Isa 1:5–9 and Isa 53 form an antithetic parallel; the servant in Isa 53 is stricken, sick, and wounded just like the people in Isa 1:5–9. The difference is that people in Isa 1:5–9 are sinful and laden with iniquity (Isa 1:4), so they have to carry the consequences of their own guilt. By contrast, the servant in Isa 53 carries the guilt of the "we"-group. However, the image of a person who is beaten to death brings the two texts together. Furthermore, both texts are followed by a description of Zion. In Isa 1, Zion is left lonely like a shelter in a cucumber field. Contrary to this, Isa 53 is followed by the rejoicing of Zion. At the time described in Isa 1, Zion was marvellously rescued, from the Assyrian siege, but at the time of Isa 53–54 the situation is different, since the city lies in ruins. Isa 53–54 harks back to the picture in Isa 1:5–9. By embracing the suffering of the servant as the suffering that the "we"-group have deserved, and by the confession of the sins in Isa 53, the holy city can and will now be re-established.

Sickness and illness as a metaphor is also encountered in Isa 6. It is often argued that Isa 52:13 refers back on Isa 6:1.[56] Following this, it is also remarkable to see the parallel between the phrase נרפא לנו, "there was healing to us", in Isa 53:5 and רפא לו in Isa 6:10.

> Make the mind of this people dull,
> and stop their ears, and shut their eyes,
> so that they may not look with their eyes, and listen with their ears,
> and comprehend with their minds, and turn and be healed (רפא לו). (Isa 6:10)

In Isa 6 the prophet is commissioned to obdurate the heart of the people so that they will not be healed. They will die from their sins (Isa 6:10–11).

---

[52] Cf. Kustár, *"Durch seine Wunden sind wir geheilt"*, 56.

[53] Cf. Ezra 9:2. Cf. also Kustár, *"Durch seine Wunden sind wir geheilt"*, 56, and Beuken, *Jesaja 1-12*, 164.

[54] I follow the division proposed by Williamson, *Isaiah 1–5*, 54.

[55] Cf. Kustár, *"Durch seine Wunden sind wir geheilt"*, 191–193.

[56] E.g. North, *The Suffering Servant*, 170, Williamson, *The Book Called Isaiah*, 39–40, and Berges, *Das Buch Jesaja*, 404.

Against this, the fourth servant song lets us see the "we" who have escaped their just suffering, and who are healed through the suffering of the servant. As we have seen above, there is one more connection between Isa 6 and Isa 53. The gloss in Isa 6:13 turns the metaphor of the fallen tree into a promise. The original picture of total destruction is turned into hope through the ones who have been thrown away in exile. Isa 53:2 uses the same metaphor of the young plant that brings healing to the many through his own suffering.

Isa 53 is related to the preceding Isa 1–39 in several ways. The song is related to texts that are significant for the structure of the book, namely Isa 1, 6 and 11. These relationships further strengthen the impression that Isa 53 has been incorporated at a relatively late stage of the growth of the book. Both the tree as a metaphor, and sickness or illness as a metaphor, signal that the servant represents this new hope. The use of these metaphors also indicates that the servant is part of Israel. He is not a new king, which was the hope in Isa 11:1–9, 10. However, in Isa 11:12 we saw that the hope for the root is reinterpreted into a hope for the dispersed. This further strengthens the impression that the servant represents the exiled.

3. Isaiah 53 and Isaiah 56–66

Isa 40–55 and Isa 56–66 are inter-related in several ways. Here I will mainly discuss the most significant texts regarding Isa 53. These texts are Isa 57:17–21 and 59:16. First, I will examine Isa 57:17–21. We can observe that the beginning of the larger section Isa 57:14–21 refers back to Isa 40:3:

It shall be said, "Build up, build up, prepare the way,
remove every obstruction from my people's way."
(Isa 57:14)

A voice cries out:
"In the wilderness prepare the way of YHWH,
make straight in the desert a highway for our God."
(Isa 40:3)

However, Isa 57:14 does not only repeat what is previously stated, it also adjusts the message. The "way" that is prepared in Isa 57:14 is a spiritual way to salvation.[57] Furthermore, the section does not only refer back to Isa 40 but also to other texts. The descriptions in Isa 57:15 are clearly reminiscent of Isa 6:1–8.[58] It is in Isa 57:17–21 that we find parallels to Isa 53:

[57] See Westermann, *Isaiah 40–66*, 328.

[58] See Westermann, *Isaiah 40–66*, 328, and Brueggemann, *Isaiah 40–66*, 181.

Because of their wicked covetousness I was angry;
I struck them, I hid and was angry;
but they kept turning back to their own ways.
I have seen their ways, but I will heal them;
I will lead them and repay them with comfort,
creating for their mourners the fruit of the lips.
Peace, peace, to the far and the near, says YHWH;
and I will heal them.
But the wicked are like the tossing sea
that cannot keep still;
its waters toss up mire and mud.
There is no peace, says my God, for the wicked. (Isa 57:17–21)

In Isa 57:18 we find two words that link the section back to Isa 53, namely the verbs רפא, "to heal", and שׁלם, "to make/give peace". The roots of both these words occur in Isa 53:5. In Isa 53, it is the suffering of the servant that leads to peace and health. Here in Isa 57 that specific way seems to have vanished; now it is YHWH himself who heals and gives peace. It is also possible that Isa 57:17 alludes to 53:6. In 53:6 the "we"-group confess that they have gone astray, in 57:17 it is YHWH who complains that they have turned back to their own ways.

Isa 57:17–21 is also clearly differentiated from Isa 40–55. With the latter the salvation was clearly contoured, once for all event, when YHWH returns to Zion (Isa 40:10–11). The utterance in Isa 57:17–21 swings indeterminately between an announcement of an event and the description of a state.[59] A second difference is that, while the comfort in Isa 40:1 is directed to the whole people, here it does not apply to all alike, since the prophet directs his comfort to the mourners (Isa 57:18).

The second text that should receive attention for its connection to Isa 53 is Isa 59:16:

He saw that there was no one,
and was appalled that there was no one to intervene (מפגיע);
so his own arm brought him victory,
and his righteousness upheld him.

This text makes it even clearer that the suffering of the servant has lost its impact: "there was no one to intervene (מפגיע)".[60] This verb in *hip'il* only occurs three times in the book of Isaiah and five times in the whole of the Old Testament.[61] The two other occurrences in the book of Isaiah are in Isa 53:6, 12. This indicates that Isa 59:16 deliberately refers back to the servant in Isa 53. If we read the whole chapter 59 we see again, as in 57:14–21, that the problem is centred on the sins of the people. Again a

---

[59] Westermann, *Isaiah 40–66*, 330.
[60] Cf. Spieckermann, "Vicarious Suffering," 15.
[61] Isa 53:6; 53:12; 59:16; Jer 15:11; 36:25.

new possibility opens through YHWH, but here, in contrast to Isa 40–55, it is only for those who "turn away from transgression" (Isa 59:20).

Both Isa 57:17–21 and 59:16 are related to Isa 53 but, compared to Isa 53, they have a new meaning. Now the sins have come between YHWH and his people, and these sins can no longer be overtaken by any suffering of the servant. The suffering of the servant has vanished and it is only dimly referred to. Also, here it is YHWH who re-establishes the relationship. However, one significant difference seems to be that the promises do not apply to everyone without preconditions. Now it is up to each individual to take responsibility, there is no longer a whole group.

4. Conclusion

Isa 53 is related to the rest of the book of Isaiah in several ways. The presentation of the servant, with the help of the metaphor of the tree (Isa 53:2), links backwards to several texts in Isa 1–39, especially Isa 6, 11. This indicates that the servant represents the new hope, and also that the servant is part of Israel. Furthermore, the metaphors of sickness and illness link Isa 53 to Isa 1 and 6.

It seems likely Isa 40:1–52:10 (or 12) formed a consistent unit when Isa 53 was incorporated. Hence, Isa 53 is relatively loosely connected to what precedes it in Isa 40:1–52:10 (or 12). Isa 53 is linked to the preceding text through catchwords to Isa 52:7–10, through reuse of earlier texts (Isa 40:27), and through redaction in the preceding corpus (Isa 49:7). This indicates that Isa 53 probably was composed for its present position in the book. Furthermore, for the interpretation of Isa 53 it is important to notice that Isa 53 and 54 are more closely connected to each other than is generally acknowledged.

Even in the clearest links between Isa 53 and Isa 56–66 the work of the servant has disappeared and is only dimly referred to. This leads us to assume that there is a new problem that needs a new solution. In Isa 56–66, the sins have again come between YHWH and his people. Now it is not the embrace of the servant's suffering, which creates the new Zion. It is YHWH who re-establishes the relationship, but the promises do not appear to apply to everyone without preconditions.

Taken together, all this implies that both Isa 53 and 54 were intentionally created together for their present position; they are located in this position as a bridge between what precedes and what succeeds these chapters. Isa 53 and 54 are deliberately located between the glorious return described in 40–55 and the less glorious reality described in 56–66. Now, having established the position of Isa 53 in the book of Isaiah, I will attempt to determine the geographical domicile of Isa 40–55.

Chapter 12

The Geographical Domicile of Isaiah 40–55

The geographical domicile of Isa 40–55 is of great significance for the interpretation of Isa 53. Several interpretations of the text are based on a Babylonian domicile of the text. It is obvious that such a traumatic experience as the exile had a significant impact on the theologies and the texts produced during this time. The interpretation advocated in this work also depends on the experience of deportation, exile, and homecoming. I will, however, argue that the major part of Isa 40–55 has its origin in the land. Since there is only a minority of scholars who advocates this view, I will examine the question at some length.

1. The Traditional View

The traditional view is that Isa 40–55 has its domicile among the exiles in Babylon.[1] This view is partly based on the supposed familiarity with the

[1] E.g. Peter Runham Ackroyd, *Israel under Babylon and Persia* (The New Clarendon Bible. Old Testament vol. 4; London: Oxford University Press, 1970), 104–108. Thomas L. Leclerc, *Yahweh is Exalted in Justice: Solidarity and Conflict in Isaiah* (Minneapolis, Minn.: Fortress, 2001), 191, lists eight arguments which he believes are usually advanced for this position: "(1) specific mention of YHWH having delivered Israel over to destruction (42:24; 43:27–28; 47:6); (2) the description of Zion as destroyed and abandoned (49:14, 17, 19; 51:19); (3) frequent references to Babylon or Chaldea (43:14; 47:1, 5; 48:14) and, more specifically, the exhortation for the people to depart from Babylon (48:20; 55:12a); (4) the general and pervasive exodus imagery (for example, 43:16; 51:10), including especially the highway through the desert (40:3–5; 42:16; 43:19; 49:11) all of which presumes that the people are traveling or returning *to* Palestine; (5) the decisive action of YHWH's ingathering of the people from afar (49:22; 51:11); (6) the mention of Cyrus, the Persian conqueror, by name (44:28; 45:1); (7) detailed descriptions of Babylonian cultic practices (for example, 44:9–20; 46:1ff.); (8) the contrast between the "new things" of the present and the "former things," which presumes that those former things are truly in the past[.]" These arguments are rather diverse and some of them rather suggest that the text cannot be earlier than the exile. I regard the fourth and seventh argument as the most persuasive ones in favour of a geographical domicile in Babylonia. These arguments will be dealt with below.

Babylonian scene[2] and partly on the belief that Palestine was, following the Babylonian invasion, a land entirely in ruins. This latter belief, which Barstad calls *the myth of the empty land*, made a tremendous impact for the development of the belief in a Babylonian Deutero-Isaiah.[3] According to Barstad, the first argument, i.e. the supposed familiarity with the Babylonian scene, can "no longer be regarded valid."[4] I agree with Barstad. There are some parts of Isa 40–55 that seem to reflect familiarity with the conditions in Babylon,[5] but there are other parts that appear to have their origin closer to Jerusalem.[6] There are even sections that might indicate an ignorance of the condition in Babylon.[7] The second belief, the myth of the empty land, is no longer tenable. There is major agreement that life continued in the land after 586 B.C.E. There were a significant drop of population, but it is obvious that life continued.[8] Kapelrud has also questioned a Babylonian setting for Isa 40–55. His first objection is that Isa 46:1 shows that the prophet had incorrect conceptions of the Babylonian gods.[9] The second objection is that when the prophet urges the people to leave the exile, he uses "from there" (מִשָּׁם) and not "from here" (מִזֶּה) which would have been expected if it was uttered in Babylonia (Isa 52:11). The third objection is

[2] Roger Norman Whybray, *The Second Isaiah* (OTG Sheffield: Sheffield Academic Press, 1983), 8.

[3] Hans M. Barstad, *The Babylonian Captivity of the Book of Isaiah: "Exilic" Judah and the Provenance of Isaiah 40–55* (Instituttet for sammenlignende kulturforskning. Serie B, Skrifter, vol. 102; Oslo: Novus: Instituttet for sammenligende kulturforskning, 1997), 91. Vanderhooft argues that the evidence for the view that Second Isaiah spent part of his career in Babylon(ia) comes from his descriptions of Babylonian realia, from the expressed hope that the Judeans will return from Babylon, and from the similarities between the language of Second Isaiah and cuneiform inscriptions, David Stephen Vanderhooft, *The Neo-Babylonian Empire and Babylon in the Latter Prophets* (MSM vol. 59; Atlanta, Ga.: Scholars Press, 1999), 169–171. I am not arguing either for or against the possibility that the prophet spent part of his career in Babylon(ia). Vanderhooft, *The Neo-Babylonian Empire*, 208, does, however, mean that the prophet was present and active in Babylon during the final years of the Empire.

[4] Barstad, *The Babylonian Captivity*, 89.

[5] See for example Isa 44:24–28.

[6] See for example Isa 40:1–2, 9–11; 49:14–15; 51:17–19; 52:7–10, 11–12.

[7] Thus maybe Isa 46:1–2.

[8] See among others James Maxwell Miller and John Haralson Hayes, *A History of Ancient Israel and Judah* (OTL London: SCM Press, 1986), 426, Albertz, *Die Exilszeit*, 65–97, Oded Lipschits, "Demographic Changes in Judah Between the Seventh and the Fifth Centuries B.C.E.," in *Judah and the Judeans in the Neo-Babylonian Period* (ed. Oded Lipschits and Joseph Blenkinsopp; Winona Lake Ind.: Eisenbrauns, 2003), 364–366, and Jeffrey Zorn, "Tell en-Nasbeh and the Problem of the Material Culture of the Sixth Century," in *Judah and the Judeans in the Neo-Babylonian Period* (ed. Oded Lipschits and Joseph Blenkinsopp; Winona Lake Ind.: Eisenbrauns, 2003), 444–445.

[9] I will take a closer look at this question below.

that the prophet sees Cyrus coming from the north. This was a well-known expression in Israel, but not in Babylon. Kapelrud's last objection is that the prophet has a conception of the situation caused by the captivity, which does not correspond to the real situation.[10]

All these objections are important indicators that the prophet might have been active outside Babylon. However, the last objection is not altogether persuasive. It is likely that there was some contact between the two groups. We can see an example of their communication in Jer 29. Hence, if there was communication between the two groups, it would mean that even the ones at home would understand that this is not a correct description of the situation. However, Isa 40–55 is full of images. These words about the captivity, which do not correspond to the real situation, might be a way of using such metaphorical language. It makes sense to describe the life in exile by using the images of a prison and of dungeons if one wants to emphasise the suffering of others in order to evoke sympathies (cf. Isa 42:7).

Kapelrud has not only questioned a Babylonian setting, he also mentions two important arguments, which indicate that Deutero-Isaiah was active in Judah, close to Jerusalem. The first is that Deutero-Isaiah speaks to the personified Jerusalem in a way that indicates that this is the place where he is.[11] According to Kapelrud, it is even more important for a domicile in the land that the prophet sees the homecoming from the Jerusalem point of view.[12] I believe that these two arguments still are important indicators that that the background of the text is in the land itself and not in the exile.

There is no consensus about the geographical domicile of Isa 40–55. Several scholars favour the theory that some parts of the book have their domicile in Babylon and other parts in Jerusalem.[13] This view will be described in greater detail before I return to my own arguments regarding the geographical domicile. Baltzer holds the view that the work was composed in Jerusalem and performed as a drama in the Diaspora.[14] He dates the work to some times between 450 and 400 B.C.E.[15] There are also scholars who still favour what I have called the traditional view, namely that Isa 40–55 originates from among the exiled.[16] This diversity among

[10] Isa 42:7, 22; 49:9; 51:14; 52:2, Arvid S. Kapelrud, *Et folk på hjemferd: "Trøsteprofeten" - den annen Jesaja - og hans budskap* (Oslo: Universitetsforlaget, 1964), 32–33.

[11] Isa 40:9; 41:27; 44:26; 45:14; 49:14–26; 51:17–23; 52:1–10; 54.

[12] Isa 40:9–11; 52:7–10, Kapelrud, *Et folk på hjemferd*, 33.

[13] Albertz, *Die Exilszeit*, 299, Kratz, *Kyros im Deuterojesaja-Buch*, 186, and Oorschot, *Von Babel zum Zion*, 167.

[14] Baltzer, *Deutero-Isaiah*, 24.

[15] Baltzer, *Deutero-Isaiah*, 30.

[16] Brueggemann, *Isaiah 40–66*, 8–9, and Sarah J. Dille, *Mixing Metaphors: God as Mother and Father in Deutero-Isaiah* (JSOTSup vol. 398; London: T & T Clark, 2004),

scholars today makes it even more important to see how far we can come in our search for the geographical domicile of Isa 40–55.

2. A Contemporary View

There has emerged a view, especially among German scholars, that Isa 40–55 has a rather long growth. According to this view, only minor parts of Isa 40–55 belong to the time before 539 B.C.E. and only these parts have their geographical domicile in the exile. The very first edition of the book originated in the land among those who had left the exile.[17] This means that there is only a limited amount of texts that originates from the exile itself. These are mainly to be found in Isa 40:1–48:20; 52:7–10.[18]

This new view that has emerged means that the arguments from Kapelrud and Barstad have lost some of their importance. Most of the texts that they found in support of a domicile in the land now belong to later editions of Isa 40–55. In the following, I will not go into the discussion of the complicated growth of Isa 40–55, but I will argue that Isa 40–55 as a whole has its domicile in the land. This is important, since scholars often still assume or claim a Babylonian domicile.

3. Stages of Exile

We have seen that there are some important objections against the traditional view that Isa 40–55 has its domicile among the exiled. We have also seen that there is no longer any agreement about such an uncomplicated domicile. On the contrary, the view is rather turning in favour of an origin

31. Dille, *Mixing Metaphors*, 13, further notes that there are two main sections in Isa 40–55 that are distinguished from each other by various features. Therefore, she argues that chapter 49–55 might have been written after the fall of Babylon to Cyrus. Cf. Caroll. Stuhlmueller, "Deutero-Isaiah: Major Transitions in the Prophet's Theology and in Contemporary Scholarship," *CBQ* 42 (1980): 1–29, 4–5, for a similar view.

[17] See for example Rainer Albertz, "Darius in Place of Cyrus: The First Edition of Deutero-Isaiah (Isaiah 40.1–52.12) in 521 BCE," *JSOT* 27 (2003a): 371–383, 375–376.

[18] These texts are, according to Oorschot, *Von Babel zum Zion*, 93–97, Isa 40:12–31*; 41:1–4, 8*–13, 14–16, 17–20*, 21–29*; 42:14–16*, 43:1–3a, 8–13, 14–15, 16–21*, 44:2–4; 24–28*, 45:1–5a*, 8, 11–13*, 20–23*, 46:1–4, 9–11. The texts that originate from the exile can, according to Albertz, "Darius in Place of Cyrus," 376, be found especially in Isa 41*, 42:14–45:7*.[18] Kratz, *Kyros im Deuterojesaja-Buch*, 50–52, 216–217, is more reluctant to determine any exact division before the first literary composition, which consists of important parts of Isa 40:1–48:20; 52:7–10.[18]

in Jerusalem, at least for significant parts of the book.[19] I will present some recent research into the experience of forced migration, exile, and homecoming. Naturally, there is a significant difference between these more recent experiences and that of the Babylonian exile. Despite this difference, I think that the examples will help us to understand the experiences of such traumatic events and, therefore, they might also help us in the search for the geographical background of Isa 40–55.

To begin with, I will turn to a study made by two sociologists, Angela Xavier de Brito and Ana Vasquez.[20] They have studied the experiences of Latin-American women in exile, and they identify three stages that refugees go through. The first stage involves the departure from the home country and the arrival in the host country. This stage is characterized by the trauma caused by the violence of forced departure, the effects of sudden and unwilling transplantation, and the prohibition to return. The sufferings are heightened by a very complex feeling of culpability. This leads the refugees to employ all sorts of defence mechanisms; the most important is a refusal to live in the present, accompanied by an idealisation of their home country and of their past experience. This first stage is also characterised by a mourning process, which includes the loss of parents and friends as well as the loss of a lifestyle. The second stage is characterised by the transculturation process. This is a very painful process, permeated by the contradictions between the original culture and the new one. Xavier de Brito and Vasquez assert that refugees have the feeling that they are neglecting or even abandoning their cultural roots, which is not easily done. In the new context, they change their codes of social relationships little by little. This process, which begins as an instrumental practice, involves some profound changes, which call into question not only the cultural values and ways of being, but also the psychological structure of the individual. The third stage develops as time goes on as the enhancement of the transculturation process shakes the myths, around which the exiled group is constituted. In the case of Latin-American exiles, this crisis calls into question their own role, and whether a situation of political change will ever allow them to return to their home country. Xavier de Brito and Vasquez primary interest is in the differences in the way in which men and women experience these three stages.[21] Unfortunately, I believe that our information about the Babylonian exile is too meagre to examine

---

[19] Albertz, *Israel in Exile*, 399–404.

[20] Angela Xavier de Brito and Ana Vasques, "Circe or Penelope? Latin-American Women in Exile," in *Scapegoats and Social Actors: The Exclusion and Integration of Minorities in Western and Eastern Europe* (ed. Danièle Joly; Basingstoke: Macmillan, 1998).

[21] Xavier de Brito and Vasques, "Circe or Penelope?", 219–220.

such differences. However, these three stages are rather general; this makes them useful also in our context.[22]

The Babylonian captivity lasted for about fifty years. This is such a long time that it means that the second and third generation were growing up and the number of persons who had actually lived in the land was decreasing. Hence, it is important to pay regard to the changes that had taken place during this time. It was an acute crisis at the beginning, but it was also a crisis that had been subject to much reflection during this long time, and that reflection had led to a significant revision of the theology of the exiled.[23] It is also likely that they feared, or even that they had accepted, that they would never be allowed to return to their home country.

Amy Kaminsky has studied the literature of the Latin-American diaspora.[24] She adds a fourth stage which, is of great importance to our interpretation of Isa 40–55. This fourth stage marks the change that occurs when return is possible. This new situation she calls *desexilio*. It is the passage from exile to diaspora and, according to her, this is as well worth charting as the move from the exile to repatriation. She argues that the decision to stay or to return depends to a certain degree on what happens during the exile.[25] She also claims that the *desexilados*, the people in *desexilio*, must reconcile the different lives that they lived elsewhere with their life at home, not in the sense of making peace between the two, but by bringing them together and making sense of them as necessary parts of a whole. What the desexilados remembered as a mark of home has changed as a result of their leaving, and of the inevitable metamorphosis that any complex living organism, whether an individual or a nation, undergoes with the passage of time.[26]

The experience of desexilio is important for the present study, since it emphasises the new experience of the change from exile to diaspora, which is the change that we meet also in Isa 40–55. The question is whether we meet this new situation among the exiled or among those who remained in

---

[22] These stages have also been used by Aina Tollefsen Altamirano, *Seasons of Migrations to the North: A Study of Biographies and Narrative Identities in US-Mexican and Swedish-Chilean Return Movements* (GERUM Kulturgeografi vol. 2000:3; Umeå: Umeå Universitet, 2000), 120–121, in her study of biographies and narrative identities in US-Mexican and Swedish-Chilean return movements. Aina Tollefsen Altamirano has her main research interests in migration and development geography.

[23] Albertz, *Religionsgeschichte Israels*, 381.

[24] Amy Kaminsky is primarily known for her inter-disciplinary feminist approach to Latin American literature.

[25] Amy K. Kaminsky, *After Exile: Writing the Latin American Diaspora* (Minneapolis; London: University of Minnesota Press, 1999), 38.

[26] Kaminsky, *After Exile*, 37. The notions of home among refugees will be discussed further below.

the land. These are divergent points of view and, therefore, I believe that the experience of desexilio can help us in the search for the domicile of the text.

Hilary Pilkington has studied changing socio-cultural identities in contemporary Russia, especially youth culture, nationality identity, and migration processes. She analyses how contemporary Russia accepts the Russian-speakers who have been living outside the borders of Russia, in the former Soviet republics, when they move back to the Russian federation. She also analyses the push-and-pull factors that make the Russian-speakers migrate. She finds that the most important reasons for returning, according to their own subjective opinion, are the future of their children and the ethnic conflicts, even if they have not yet experienced harassment.[27] The returning Russians feel a cultural superiority over the titular nationality of the newly independent states, as well as over the locals in the areas of Russia, to which they migrate.[28] The migrants also claim that they are labelled as outsiders by the local community. Relatively few cases of direct conflict between the migrants and the locals are reported. All the same, there is a clear competition for housing and resources that creates tension.[29]

Nielsen draws interesting parallels between the novel *Jerusalem* by Selma Lagerlöf and what she believes are the urgings of Deutero-Isaiah to return to the land.[30] In *Jerusalem,* Lagerlöf tells the story of a Swedish rural community that is torn apart by a travelling evangelist, who convinces half the community that they should uproot themselves from their ancestral home and move to Jerusalem. In the novel, we meet both those who felt the call and went and those who stayed at home. Lagerlöf found much inspiration for this novel in a real event, namely in the emigration of several persons from the village Nås in 1896, which was led by a fanatic evangelist. In the novel, the community receives a letter from the evangelist Hellgum, in which he seeks to persuade the community to emigrate to Jerusalem.[31] The rhetoric of the letter from Hellgum is fascinating, since he confutes all the readers' arguments about staying in his eagerness to persuade them to go to Jerusalem. He clearly formulates what they will leave behind and he contrasts that by descriptions of what they will receive in Jerusalem.[32] Such rhetoric is absent from Isa 40–55 and that is one thing

[27] Hilary Pilkington, *Migration, Displacement and Identity in Post-Soviet Russia* (London; New York: Routledge, 1998), 131–138.

[28] Pilkington, *Migration*, 168.

[29] Pilkington, *Migration*, 172–180.

[30] Kirsten Nielsen, *Bilderna och ordet: Om Herrens tjänare och andra bilder i Gamla testamentet* (Örebro: Libris, 1998), 16.

[31] Selma Lagerlöf, *Jerusalem* (Westport, Conn.: Greenwood press, 1970), 134–144.

[32] "And at first we were glad at the thought that you would follow us, and lead a life in unity and joy together with us in Jerusalem. But afterwards we were filled with doubt,

I had expected to find if the text, had originated in the exile at the time when it was becoming possible to return.

It is possible that the people who lived in the Babylonian exile had similar agonies as those of the small parish had when they read the letter from Hellgum (and the same as the Russian-speakers had when they thought of returning to Russia).[33] In *Jerusalem,* as with the desexilados and the Russian speakers, there is a shift to a personal decision. During the exile, the collective is very important, but when the time comes to decide whether or not to return, the personal decision becomes more important.

We can also see such push-and-pull factors in the Genesis story about Jacob. In this story we meet the struggle that can take place inside a refugee, who is considering whether or not to return to his homeland. The push factors when Jacob decides to flee from Laban are, on the one hand, the conflict with the sons of Laban. They said that Jacob had gained all his wealth from what belonged to their father (Gen 31:1). On the other hand, Laban did not regard Jacob as favourably as he had done earlier on (Gen 31:1–2). The pull factor is that YHWH said to Jacob: "Return to the land of your ancestors and to your kindred, and I will be with you" (Gen 31:3). It is also Jacob's desire to see his father (Gen 31:18). We also know that he had longed to return earlier (see for example Gen 30:25) but it is now that the push-and-pull factors become strong enough to convince him to depart. One of the things that makes Jacob reluctant to return is the fear of meeting his brother, whom he had deceived (Gen 32–33). That fear was now weaker than the push-and-pull factors.

---

and said: 'Our brethren will never leave their big farms and their good fields, and their accustomed occupation.'

But the people from Jerusalem answered: 'We have no fields and no big farms to offer them; but we can show them the paths that Jesus trod, so that they can also walk in them.'

Still we were in doubt, and we said: 'Verily, our brothers and sisters will never go to a foreign land where no one understands their mother-tongue.'

The people from Jerusalem answered: 'They shall learn to understand what the stones in the Holy Land say to them about their Saviour.'

We said: 'They will never divide their property amongst strangers and become poor as beggars. They will never give up their influence and position, for they are the foremost men and women in their own town.'

The people from Jerusalem answered: 'We have no influence and no worldly goods to offer them, but we can offer them a share in the sufferings of their Saviour, Jesus Christ.'

When we heard that, we were again filled with a great joy, and thought that you would come. But now I tell you, dear brothers and sisters: 'Do not speak with each other when you have read this, but be still and listen; and what the voice of God bids you do, that do!'", Lagerlöf, *Jerusalem*, 141–142.

[33] Cf. Nielsen, *Bilderna och ordet*, 16, and Lagerlöf, *Jerusalem*, 142–144.

The traditional view is that Isa 40–55 has its domicile among the exiles in Babylon. If this is correct, it is likely that we should find convincing push-and-pull factors in the message, push-and-pull factors that could persuade the listeners to return. It is likely that the same kind of arguments as Pilkington sees among the Russian-speakers, i.e. the future of their children and the risk of harassment, would have been important to the exiled as well. It is also likely that the ones at home would have felt a similar reluctance to receive the returnees as the local Russian community felt according to Pilkington's research. Hence, I will now turn to the text Isa 40–55 in order to see in what way the text seeks to persuade the audience and what it is seeking to persuade them to believe or do.

4. The Complaint in Isaiah 40:27

The first echo from the receiver of the message is in Isa 40:27: "My way is hidden from YHWH, and my right is disregarded by my God." It is often assumed that Deutero-Isaiah here cites words from a lament in actual use by the exiled at the service at the time.[34] I believe that it is likely that this is a real quotation from the audience's complaint at the time. It is also possible that it belongs to the service at that time. I am, however, not convinced that the quotation is from the people in exile. Such words would have fitted better in the first, and maybe even in the second, stage of exile.[35] But we are now probably in the *desexilio*, the time when return is being/becoming possible. In this situation it is harder to understand such a complaint. Now the situation is changing and the change opens a new possibility to choose whether or not to return. It is possible that a service that was not bound to a specific place was a central element in the exilic service.[36] Even if the complaint belongs to such a service, it is unlikely that they would complain in the same way for fifty years. Furthermore, at the end of the exile, this kind of causal service was more important in the land than among the exiled.

The situation is quite different in the land. The rise of Cyrus (cf. Isa 41:1–4) makes the whole scene change for those at home as well. But they are not in the pleasant position to choose, the change might cause a new destabilisation in the land or in their lives. For them, it must have been a risk to have people coming back to the land, especially as the ones who were left in the land saw it as a gift from God.[37] In this situation it makes

[34] E.g. Westermann, *Isaiah 40–66*, 60.

[35] See Ps 44 for a lament during the early exile, Albertz, *Die Exilszeit*, 130.

[36] E.g. Albertz, *Religionsgeschichte Israels*, 385.

[37] Cf. Ezek 33:24.

perfect sense for the people to complain, and also for the prophet to answer the complaint by proving that Cyrus and the new things that are happening are the work of YHWH and not a threat.

Furthermore, in Isa 44:24–28, the prophet pronounces that Cyrus is YHWH's shepherd and this means that Jerusalem will be inhabited and the cities of Judah rebuilt. The perspective is not the agonies of the exiled and the question of whether or not to return if that would prove an option. The statement is rather an answer to the fear that the land will be devastated even more through Cyrus.[38] Furthermore, YHWH is talking directly to Jerusalem in the text. If this section belongs in the exile, YHWH would probably have been speaking about, and not to, Jerusalem.[39]

It is particularly interesting that we have a complaint outside Isa 40–55 that reflects the situation during the exile and probably even at a late stage, Ps 137.[40] This complaint has a rather different character compared to Isa 40:27. In this psalm we probably see problems and reflections that belong to the third phase of exile, when those who were growing old reflected on the possibility that they would never be able to return to Zion.[41] Ps 137 describes a longing for Zion and a remembrance of Zion. It is not an acute lament like Isa 40:27. We lack the question "Why" (למה), which is significant in the reproachful questions evoked by the divine promise and election on the one hand and by what God has done on the other.[42] Furthermore, the important question how the exiled would be able to sing in a *foreign* land (Ps 137:4) is not countered in Isa 40–55 with the natural promise that they will return to sing in their own land. In Isa 40–55 we read that YHWH will return to Zion (cf. Isa 52:8).

There is a discrepancy between the complaint in Ps 137 and the one in Isa 40:27. There is also a discrepancy between the complaint in Ps 137 and the answers given in Isa 40–55. An explanation would be that Ps 137 and Isa 40–55 reflects very different geographical conditions.

---

[38] Contra Elliger, *Deuterojesaja 40,1-45,7*, 466–467, and others.

[39] Contra Elliger, *Deuterojesaja 40,1-45,7*, 472, who translates Deutero-Isaiah's uses of the preposition "to" (ל) in connection with the verb "say" (אמר) to indicate an indirect object. This is contrary to the normal use when it is used to indicate a direct object.

[40] Albertz, *Die Exilszeit*, 130, dates it to 562–539 B.C.E. It is more probable that the psalm is post-exilic. Even so, it reflects the situation of the late exile.

[41] Contra Spieckermann, *Heilsgegenwart*, 115–122, who sees this psalm as reflecting the acute crisis caused by the deportation and the exile.

[42] Cf. Baltzer, *Deutero-Isaiah*, 82.

5. The Ruins

In Isa 40–55 "ruins" (חרבה) that will be rebuilt are mentioned frequently.[43] Both Jerusalem itself and its surroundings were thoroughly razed to the ground by the Babylonians, and there is no evidence of a settlement there until the Persian period.[44] Hence, it was no threat to the ones at home to say that these ruins would be rebuilt. It is likely that the word: "who says of Jerusalem, 'it shall be inhabited,' and of the cities of Judah, 'they shall be rebuilt, and I will raise up their ruins'" (Isa 44:26) is an answer to the question: "where shall they live?" This is a question that was probably asked by the ones in the land about the returnees.

To say that the ruins "shall be rebuilt" (Isa 44:26) makes perfect sense if the words are directed to the ones at home and if they mean that the exiled will rebuild them. (Even though God says that he will raise up the ruins, Isa 44:26, someone has to be God's hands and these hands are probably the people in exile). This could mean that the people in exile would come to live in the places not inhabited at the moment. To mention ruins is strange as a means of motivating the people in exile to go home. It does not sound very attractive to return to rebuild the ruins of the cities of Judah.

Furthermore, the departure from Babylon has frequently been called the new exodus, and there are some similarities to the original exodus.[45] There is, however, one important aspect missing if we compare Isa 40–55 to the original exodus, namely a clear motivation of why they should go out and return. One motivation for Moses to lead his people out of Egypt was that God had seen their suffering and promised a land "flowing with milk and honey" (Exod 3:8). Such description of the land is quite common in the story of Exodus and the same promise would have fitted perfectly to motivate a return.[46] Even though the exodus story has emerged over a long time, it is likely that such expressions were known by the people in the exile.

---

[43] Isa 44:26; 49:19; 51:3; 52:9, the noun also occurs in 48:21 with the meaning "deserts".

[44] Lipschits, "Demographic Changes," 364–365.

[45] See for example Westermann, *Isaiah 40–66*, 253. Barstad has forcefully criticized this view. He writes: "I have not succeeded in finding one single text that qualifies for the designation 'exodus text', in the accepted meaning of the phrase. What I have found, however, is that the prophet Second Isaiah, when expressing his particular message to the Judeans, used a rich variety of the different ancient Israelite traditions that were available to him, to some degree including also the exodus tradition", Hans M. Barstad, *A Way in the Wilderness: The "Second Exodus" in the Message of Second Isaiah* (JSS vol. 12; Manchester: University of Manchester, 1989), 108. I am not convinced that Barstad is right in every detail of his argumentation, but he is right that the exodus tradition is not as prominent in Isa 40–55 as has often been assumed. For a survey of the history of interpretation of this theme, see Lund, *"Min vei er skjult for JHWH"*, 18–40.

[46] Exod 3:8, 17; 13:5; 33:3; Lev 20:24; Num 13:27; 14:8; 16:13, 14; Deut 6:3; 11:9; 26:9, 15; 27:3; 31:20; Josh 5:6; Jer 11:5; 32:22; Ezek 20:6, 15.

It is hard to find arguments in Isa 40–55 which state why the people in exile should return home. There are some texts that could answer the question of why they should depart (the most important are: Isa 47 and 48:20–21), but this is not necessarily a reason to return home. And the argument for why they should break up from the place where they might have lived and rooted themselves for maybe fifty years is not particularly persuasive. If Isa 40–55 has its domicile among the people in the exile, I would have expected to find more arguments that made the listeners long for their land. It is that sort of argument that could attract the audience to return to the land. It is much easier to find arguments that the new things happening are the work of YHWH, but that is not the same as a motivation for why one should break up and return. To prove that the new thing was the work of YHWH was probably more important in the land than in the exile.

6. Isaiah 40–55 and the Idols

There is one text regarding the idols which is used as support for a Babylonian domicile of Isa 40–55. This is Isa 46:1–2.[47] This argumentation is based on the supposed familiarity with the religious conditions in Babylon. Bel, which is originally simply a designation for "lord" is a name for Marduk, and Nebo is the same as Nabu. Both these were important Babylonian gods. It is also likely that Isa 46:1–2 alludes to the Akitu festival.[48] According to Vanderhooft, this means that the polemic in the text, which

---

[47] See among others Vanderhooft, *The Neo-Babylonian Empire.*:171). Vanderhooft, *The Neo-Babylonian Empire*, 173, also tries to prove a Babylonian domicile of the text with the help of המסכן in Isa 40:20. He thinks that this is a special wood which "has not yet been discovered in the southern Levant." But he also says that the Neo-Babylonian texts do not show that the Babylonians used this wood specifically in the construction of divine statues. All the same, he concludes that it seems likely that this description derives from the prophet's knowledge of Neo-Babylonian practices or texts, Vanderhooft, *The Neo-Babylonian Empire*, 175. It is possible that המסכן refers to a specific kind of wood. See also Stephen Lee, *Creation and Redemption in Isaiah 40–55* (Jian Dao Dissertation Series. Bible and Literature vol. 2; Hong Kong: Alliance Bible Seminary, 1995), 34. Given the complexity of the text and the number of proposed interpretations, I think Vanderhooft has only weak arguments by which to prove a Babylonian domicile for this text. For an overview of the multitude of interpretations, see among others Tryggve N. D. Mettinger, "The Elimination of a Crux: A Syntactic and Semantic Study of Isaiah 40:18–20," in *Studies on Prophecy: A Collection of Twelve Papers* (vol. *VTSup*; Leiden: Brill, 1974), Elliger, *Deuterojesaja 40,1-45,7*, 60–62, and Baltzer, *Deutero-Isaiah*, 75. Baltzer, *Deutero-Isaiah*, 75, also concludes that: "this is a possible interpretation [a kind of ebonyliked wood], but surely the shallowest and most simplistic."

[48] E.g. Hermisson, *Deuterojesaja 45,8-49,13*, 103–104, and Vanderhooft, *The Neo-Babylonian Empire*, 178.

indicates the great hope that Isa 40–55 had placed in Cyrus, could not have been formulated before the final year of Nabonidus' reign. He also thinks that the prophet was present in Babylon at the end of Nabonidus' reign.[49]

If we keep to this dating (the end of Nabonidus' reign), it makes better sense if the text has emerged in the land. It is likely that the ones in the land also had some knowledge of the principal deities of the Babylonians, and even some knowledge of their cult.[50] But, as referred to above, Kapelrud argues that if the prophet was living in Babylon, it is likely that he would have known about the conflict between Nabonidus and the priests of Marduk.[51] Even Vanderhooft remarks that Nabonidus attempted to elevate Sin to the premier rank in the cult and thereby to demote Marduk.[52] However, the fact that this conflict is not reflected in the text of Isa 46:1–2 makes it more likely that it was formulated at a distance from Babylon.

Mark S. Smith has studied the polemic against idols and idolatry in Isa 40–55 in his search for the origins of biblical monotheism. He makes an important distinction when he says that the accusation and the satire in Isa 40–48 aims at the outsiders, that is at the adherents of neo-Babylonian polytheism. He continues: "On the other hand, the context is further rhetorical as it aims at persuading insiders, namely Judeans, about reality."[53] This distinction between the perspectives of the outsiders and insiders is important. According to Smith, these accusations were spoken at the end of the exile in Babylon.[54] The outside perspective with its polemic could very well belong in Babylon. The inside perspective could have had its domicile in Babylon during the two first stages of exile, when it was important for the people to keep their own identity. At the end of exile, and during the desexilio, the people in exile had reformed their traditional theology, and it was from this group that an important impulse to renewal of the Yahwism came.[55] This critique with its inside perspective, which was the most important one, seems to break into open doors in such an environment.[56]

---

[49] Vanderhooft, *The Neo-Babylonian Empire*, 180. Hermisson, *Deuterojesaja 45,8-49,13*, 96, on the other hand dates the text to about 480.

[50] Cf. Othmar Keel and Christoph Uehlinger, *Gods, Goddesses, and Images of God in Ancient Israel* (Minneapolis Minn.: Fortress Press, 1998), 374.

[51] Kapelrud, *Et folk på hjemferd*, 28.

[52] Vanderhooft, *The Neo-Babylonian Empire*, 52.

[53] Mark S. Smith, *The Origins of Biblical Monotheism: Israel's Polytheistic Background and the Ugaritic Texts* (Oxford: Oxford University Press, 2001), 180.

[54] Smith, *Biblical Monotheism*, 179.

[55] Cf. Albertz, *Religionsgeschichte Israels,* 381.

[56] I agree with Franke, *Isaiah 46, 47, and 48*, 236, when he argues that the charges of idolatry are directed at Jacob/Israel, since, it is the Israelites, not the Babylonians, who are criticized for making and worshiping idols.

Our information about the religion in the land is meagre. This makes it delicate to discuss the situation there. We know that Jerusalem and its environs were thoroughly razed to the ground by the Babylonians. But the settlement in Benjamin continued unabated throughout the sixth century B.C.E.[57] The cult also continued in some way. Mizpah and Bethel might have served as alternative sanctuaries after the destruction of the Jerusalem temple.[58] Hence, the critique of the former prophets against idolatry could still be valid.[59] The change in history at the end of the period of the exile may have caused this eagerness to persuade the people at home to believe that this change was good news from YHWH. It is more difficult to see the need for such persuasion in the exile, where Cyrus was more of a hope than a threat.

7. Conclusion

The traditional view is that Isa 40–55 originated among the people in exile in Babylon. This view has been based on the supposed familiarity with the Babylonian scene and on the belief that Palestine, following the Babylonian invasion, was a country entirely in ruins. Both of these assumptions have been put into question. Furthermore there are important arguments in favour of a domicile in the land, rather than in Babylon.

I believe that the two arguments put forward by Kapelrud remain important indicators that the background of the text is in the land. First, he argues that Deutero-Isaiah talks to the personified Jerusalem in a way that indicates that this is the place where he is. Secondly, he argues that the prophet sees the homecoming from the point of view of Jerusalem. The recent redaction-critical works on Isa 40–55 has changed the discussion somewhat. According to several scholars, it is only a small part of Isa 40–55, which originates from the exile. I agree that it is possible that some texts originate from the exile. Most of the individual sections lack any specific reference to the geographical environment, which makes it hard to determine the domicile for each individual section. Still, the perspective of Isa 40–55 is most probably from the land itself.

---

[57] About the situation in the land during exile, see B. Oded, "Where is the 'Myth of the Empty Land' to be Found? History versus Myth," in *Judah and the Judeans in the Neo-Babylonian Period* (ed. Oded Lipschits and Joseph Blenkinsopp; Winona Lake Ind.: Eisenbrauns, 2003), 71, and Lipschits, "Demographic Changes," 365.

[58] For further information, see Joseph Blenkinsopp, "Bethel in the Neo-Babylonian Period," in *Judah and the Judeans in the Neo-Babylonian Period* (ed. Oded Lipschits and Joseph Blenkinsopp; Winona Lake Ind.: Eisenbrauns, 2003), 93–105.

[59] See for example Isa 10:11 and Hos 8:4.

With the help of research among Latin-American women, we have seen some ways that the experience of exile changes over time. In the Old Testament, we have one text, which probably reflects the situation at the end of the exile and among the exiled, namely Ps 137. We have seen that there is a discrepancy between the complaint in Ps 137 and the complaint in Isa 40:27. Even more importantly, there is a difference between the issues raised in Ps 137:4 and the answers given in Isa 40–55. A possible explanation for these differences is that these texts reflect very different geographical conditions.

We have also seen that the change to *desexilio*, i.e. to the situation when return is being or becoming possible, is an important one. The personal decision becomes more important in such a situation. This is something we have seen with the help of Pilkington's research among Russian migrants and also in the novel *Jerusalem* by Lagerlöf.

It is hard to find arguments in Isa 40–55 that specifically show why the exiled should return home. There are some texts in Isa 40–55 that probably reflect the original exodus, even though scholars have questioned the thought of a second exodus. There is an important aspect missing in these texts, if we compare them to the original exodus, namely a clear motivation why the people in exile should return. The push factors, the motivations to depart, are meagre but the pull factors, the motivation to return, are absent. One motivation for Moses to lead his people out of Egypt was that God had seen their suffering and promised a land "flowing with milk and honey" (Exod 3:8). This, or similar arguments in favour of a return, is something that I had expected to find if Isa 40–55 had its domicile among the people in exile. It is easy to find arguments in favour of the claim that the new things that are happening are the work of YHWH, but such claims were just as important, or maybe even more important, in the land itself. This is not in itself a motivation to break up and return. The most important thing in exile, i.e. a clear motivation why they should return, is missing. It can also be positively asserted that Isa 40–55 generally stresses that there is no God comparable to YHWH. Therefore, the new things, which are about to take place, are not a threat but the work of YHWH.

In the next part I will try to show that the efforts that were put into convincing the people at home that these new things, which were happening, were the work of God, were based on a particular idea. The important thing was that the prophet urged the people at home to embrace and not exclude the returnees. Therefore, I will investigate the conflicts that emerged when the people in exile started to return.

Chapter 13

The Conflict

My theory is that Isa 53 is coloured by the conflict between the people returning from the exile and the ones left in the land. The relationship between these two groups has recently become an important area of research in the study of the Old Testament. Previously, research has been affected by *the myth of the empty land.* This myth reduced the interest in the relationship between these two groups, this since there was only one group left if the land was empty.[1] In the contemporary scholarly discussion, there are scholars who emphasise the conflict and also those who diminish the impact of such a conflict. Grabbe belongs to the latter group. According to him, the conflict should not be emphasised and he puts forth two arguments in favour of this view. First, he acknowledges that there probably were some tensions between these groups, but these have not left any impact on the archaeological findings. Secondly, he claims that it cannot have been too problematic to integrate the returnees, since they were only a small number.[2] Then he concludes that the two groups have been rather well integrated. Furthermore, according to Grabbe the real conflict arose almost a century later.[3] The other view is represented by Daniel Smith. He argues from another perspective, taking his starting point in recent refugee studies in order to analyse the occurrence of a conflict. According to him, we must first understand the importance of a crisis in order to proceed to an analysis of the kind of crisis that the exile represented.[4] He also argues that biblical exegesis must start with the assumption that social conflicts are likely to occur. He further claims that it is sociologically unrealistic to assume that the norm is that there was no conflict until the presence of a conflict has been undeniably proven. It was the social boundaries erected

---

[1] For a more extensive discussion see Hans M. Barstad, *The Myth of the Empty Land: A Study in the History and Archaeology of Judah During the "Exilic" Period* (SO vol. 28; Oslo; Stockholm: Scandinavian University Press, 1996), and Joseph Blenkinsopp, "The Bible, Archaeology and Politics; or The Empty Land Revisited," *JSOT* 27 (2002b): 169–187.

[2] Lester L. Grabbe, *A History of the Jews and Judaism in the Second Temple Period* (Library of Second Temple studies vol. 47; London: T&T Clark, 2004).

[3] Grabbe, *A History*.

[4] Daniel L. Smith, *The Religion of the Landless: A Sociology of the Babylonian Exile* (Bloomington Ind.: Meyer-Stone Books, 1986), 53.

as a mechanism for survival during the exile, which lead to a conflict after the return.[5]

In this example it is unnecessary to go into detail with the arguments. It is enough to establish the great difference between the arguments and the conclusions of Grabbe and Smith. Against Grabbe, it is worth noticing that such a conflict as described by Smith does not necessarily leave any archaeological traces, and such a conflict might survive for a long time and can flare up much later.

This survey has shown the importance of further examination of the occurrence of a conflict between the people who return from the exile and the ones left in the land, and of how such a conflict has made an impact on the Old Testament texts. I will start by analysing the conflict from recent experiences of returning refugees, and also from experiences of those remained at home while this was happening. Reports of these experiences can be found mainly in contemporary refugee studies. The next step will be to use the results about such tensions that I find in studies of contemporary circumstances, and to see if similar conflicts have made an impact on the Old Testament texts. After this I will narrow down to Isa 40–55 and see how such conflicts have coloured these texts. Finally I will turn to the conflict in Isa 56–66.

1. The Impossible Homecoming

The work of Daniel Smith is of particular interest, since he combines refugee studies with exegetical work in order better to understand how the exile has made an impact on the biblical stories. He draws important conclusions about the way in which the identities of minorities are shaped depending on their social conditions. He asserts that whether it is an individual or a group that is exiled makes a significant difference.[6] He further argues that the preservation of identity in the context of intercultural contact is an important focus for a sociological analysis of the Babylonian exile. There are two aspects, which he finds particularly important for the understanding of the preservation process for the Jews in exile. First, the Jews were a minority in a foreign environment. Secondly, they were forcibly settled in that foreign environment. He concludes:

> [T]he survival of a minority as a group depends on their success in creating a solid community with social boundaries. This solidarity in exile then creates separation from the population that did not endure exile. […] The final sociological element in the crisis of the Exile, then, would be a possible conflict between those who went into Exile and those

---

[5] Smith, *The Religion of the Landless*, 197.

[6] Smith, *The Religion of the Landless*, 53.

who did not. This conflict would not necessarily reflect the "degeneration" of religious faithfulness of those left in Palestine, but only that the crisis led to different social configurations.[7]

Our interest is not primarily in how a social identity is created by the experience of being a refugee. However, this is of indirect interest because such identity is an important factor in the conflicts that can emerge after the return.

Much research has been undertaken since Smith finished his study, both on how the images of home are created out of exilic experiences and on repatriation. This research has been correlated to a changing political view on repatriation. Chimni, in an article about a critical history of durable solutions to refugee problems, divides the research undertaken after 1945 into two main periods. The first period lasted roughly until 1985. During this period, resettlement was promoted in practice as the durable solution, even though voluntary repatriation was accepted in principle as the preferred solution. The second period is divided into three phases. In the first phase (1985–1993), voluntary repatriation was promoted as the durable solution. In 1993 the notion of safe return was introduced. In the continuum between voluntary and involuntary repatriation the idea of safe return aspired to occupy the middle ground. In 1996, the doctrine of imposed return was aired by the UNHCR. The growing emphasis on repatriation has turned the attention of the international community towards the problems of return.[8] The body of published work on the reintegration process has also grown considerably, especially since the end of 1990.[9]

What is particularly interesting for me, in the interpretation of Isa 53, is what happened after the return, and especially the way in which the people at home reacted and experienced the changes. Unfortunately, there is no direct research into the experiences of the people at home when others return after exile. Therefore, I will have to interpret their experience in an indirect way through the experiences of those who return. First, I will examine what is often called *the myth of return*. This so-called myth has a considerable effect on the actual return. Secondly, I will examine some experiences of the problems created by the actual return. Thirdly, I will turn to the experiences of those at home.

---

[7] Smith, *The Religion of the Landless*, 64–65.

[8] B. S. Chimni, "From Resettlement to Involuntary Repatriation: Towards a Critical History of Durable Solutions to Refugee Problems," *Refugee Survey Quarterly* 23, no. 3 (2004): 55–73.

[9] Cf. Johnathan Bascom, "The Long, 'Last Step'? Reintegration of Repatriates in Eritrea," *Journal of Refugee Studies* 18, no. 2 (2005): 165–180, 165–166. See also Lynellyn Long and Ellen Oxfeld, eds., *Coming home? Refugees, Migrants, and Those Who Stayed Behind* (Philadelphia Pa.: University of Pennsylvania Press, 2004).

The Myth of Return in Recent Refugee Studies

The *myth of return* is a concept which is used rather frequently in recent refugee studies. In this concept we find important components for an understanding of how ethnic groups are shaped by living in exile. The myth of return helps us to understand the way in which a group can shape and keep an identity without being assimilated into another environment. Furthermore, the concept is of interest, since it has been used as a background to understand the problems of return.[10]

Al Rasheed has studied the myth of return among Iraqi Arab and Assyrian refugees in London.[11] Frequent references are made to his article and I will therefore look at his definition of the myth. He argues that the distinctive element of refugee identity is an inherited, but exiled, past which is frequently reconstructed in an idealised form. In the myth of return, the concreteness of a family home or a "point fixed in space" is overlaid with an abstract or imagined realm. The concept, the myth of return, not only encapsulates the fictitious past, or at least one that is idealised and reinvented, but also a fictitious future when return is a remote aspiration. There are at least three important components. First, we have the concrete home which, by the distance, is overlaid with an abstract or imagined realm, secondly there is an idealised or reinvented past, and the third component is a fictitious future.

In their discussion of this concept, Cohen and Gold argue that the two words myth (usually a fantasy) and return (may be a reality) connote a wishful fantasy that the refugees will return to their homeland in the future.[12] The reference to the homeland is important, since the term is in some respects misconceived shorthand. What is mythologised is not the return *per se* but the home. What is being mythologised is what has been left behind, and what it is hoped that the return will accomplish.[13] Kaminsky also makes us aware that, what the Latin-American Diasporas remembered as marking home changed as a result of their leaving, of the dictatorships, and of the inevitable metamorphosis that any complex living organism

---

[10] E.g. Anders H. Stefansson, "Refugee Returns to Sarajevo and their Challenge to Contemporary Narratives of Mobility," in *Coming home? Refugees, Migrants, and Those Who Stayed Behind* (ed. Lynellyn Long and Ellen Oxfeld; Philadelphia, Pa.: University of Pennsylvania Press, 2004a), 170.

[11] Madawi Al-Rasheed, "The Myth of Return: Iraqi Arab and Assyrian Refugees in London," *Journal of Refugee Studies* 7, no. 2–3 (1994): 199–219.

[12] Rina Cohen and Gerald Gold, "Constructing Ethnicity: Myth of Return and Modes of Exclusion among Israelis in Toronto," *International Migration* 35, no. 3 (1997): 373–394, 375.

[13] Cf. Roger Zetter, "Reconceptualizing the Myth of Return: Contuity and Transition Amongst the Greek-Cypriot Refugees of 1974," *Journal of Refugee Studies* 12, no. 1 (1999): 1–22, 6, and Cohen and Gold, "Constructing Ethnicity."

undergoes with the passage of time.[14] She further argues that coming out of exile is not a singular and definite act but a long wound that might or might not heal.[15] Zarzosa remarks, from her own experience as a refugee, that there is a growing distance between the everyday life at home and life in the host country.[16] This distance cannot be measured while in exile, since exile and home evolve separately. The refugees experience changes and transformation outside home, while the compatriots at home do likewise at home. When she herself returned home, she experienced that the contrast between these changes was sharp.[17] Black, who has studied refugee repatriation in Bosnia-Herzegovina, asserts that the concept of home is not straightforward. It is intimately linked to concepts of identity and memory, as well as of territory and place:

> Home can be made, re-made, imagined, remembered or desired; it can refer as much to beliefs, customs or traditions as physical places or buildings. Most important, as a concept it is something that is subject to constant reinterpretation and flux, just as identities are renegotiated.[18]

Therefore, it is not only home and life at home that change over time. Also the refugees' interpretation of home changes and is idealised with distance of time and space. Zetter remarks, from the experience of the Greek-Cypriot refugees after 1974, that home is both physical and symbolical.[19] It has a spatial setting in the fields, orchards, farmland, and significantly in the cemeteries. Continuity is expressed, preserved, and reinforced by the culturally specific symbols of houses, built by preceding generations. Similarly, homage at the gravesides of ancestors is a critical cultural rite. Many refugees hypothesised that their second priority, after their return, would be to visit their family graves. Their first priority would be to visit their homes.[20]

There has also been important critique against a too simple view of the identity of refugees' view of their situation and how their concept of home

---

[14] Kaminsky, *After Exile*, 37.

[15] Kaminsky, *After Exile*, 115.

[16] Her research examines repatriation with respect to gender in the Chilean case.

[17] Helia Lopez Zarzosa, "Internal Exile, Exile and Return: A Gendered View," *Journal of Refugee Studies* 11, no. 2 (1998): 189–198.

[18] R. Black, "Conceptions of 'Home' and the Political Geography of Refugee Repatriation: Between Assumption and Contested Reality in Bosnia-Herzegovina," *Applied Geography* 22, no. 2 (2002): 123–138, 126.

[19] Zetter's main focus of his research has been the institutional and policy dimensions of forced migration, the impact of humanitarian assistance on refugees and asylum seekers, shelter and settlement policies for refugees, the experience of protracted exile, repatriation and post-conflict reconstruction.

[20] Zetter, "Reconceptualizing the Myth of Return," 11. Cf. also Neh 2:6 about the wish to return to the graves of the fathers.

has been shaped by the distance. Uehling argues that it is often described as if the refugees were either oriented towards the place that they come from (and hopefully will return to), or gradually reoriented to their new place of residence.[21] She argues against such a simple view with the help of Bakhtin's philosophy. She remarks that it is possible to have ambiguous attachments, dual loyalties, and alternative conceptions of home.[22] Ghorashi, who has experiences of being a refugee and who is also a scholar in this field, offers a different critique. She came to the Netherlands as an exile from Iran in 1988, 26 years old. She remarks that in the studies of migrants and refugees, the home is often equated with the past. She argues that to automatically consider the country of origin as home also assumes that refugees' attachment to their homeland and their desire to return are naturally given facts. Against this, she argues that, by adopting a deterritorialized notion of home, the feeling of belonging and foreignness do not need to be related to a fixed place, but to one's position in life.[23] The critique against a too simple view of the concepts of home and the myth of return is important. It warns us against having a too simple understanding of the experiences of refugees. Furthermore, the research of Uehling helps us understand how it is possible to have a strong myth of return during the exile and still not to return home when the opportunity is given. Even so, bearing this criticism in mind, I regard the myth of return as a useful concept.

To sum up, the myth of return has at least two important components. First, it contains a concept of home which is formed and idealised by the

---

[21] Greta Uehling, "Sitting on Suitcases: Ambivalence and Ambiguity in the Migration Intentions of Crimean Tatar Women," *Journal of Refugee Studies* 15, no. 4 (2002): 388–408, studies Crimean Tatar repatriation. Following 50 years in exile, some, but not all, Crimean Tatars have been repatriated to the Ukraine. Her article explores the ramifications of this for women, whose families are divided between the Ukraine and Uzbekistan.

[22] Uehling, "Sitting on Suitcases."

[23] Halleh Ghorashi, "When the Boundaries are Blurred: The Significance of Feminist Methods in Research," *European Journal of Women's Studies* 12, no. 3 (2005): 363–75. See also Takeyuki Tsuda, "When Home Is Not the Homeland: The Case of Japanese Brazilian Ethnic Return Migration," in *Homecomings: Unsettling Paths of Return* (ed. Fran Markowitz and Anders H. Stefansson; Lanham, Md.: Lexington Books, 2004), for the problem of equating home with the homeland, in her study of the return migration of second and third generation Japanese Brazilians from Brazil to Japan. Laura Hammond, "Tigrayan Returnees' Notion of Home: Five Variations on a Theme," in *Homecomings: Unsettling Paths of Return* (ed. Fran Markowitz and Anders H. Stefansson; Lanham, Md.: Lexington Books, 2004), argues that much of the academic and policy-oriented discourses on repatriation imply either that return is synonymous with homecoming or that true homecoming is not possible. Against both these views, her interview with a neighbour in Tigrayan highland, returning from a refugee camp in the Sudan, showed that the experience of repatriation was more a process of pragmatic homemaking than of a return to something familiar.

distance of time and space. In this aspect, the myth is oriented to the past. Secondly, the myth of return also contains a wish to return in the future. This is often linked to concrete places, houses, fields, cemeteries, and so forth. Furthermore, the myth of return is also an important component in the preservation of an ethnic community living in exile.

The Problematic Homecoming

In recent years there has been an increased amount of research into the return of refugees. At a concrete level, we see that the return of refugees creates conflicts between the returnees and the ones at home. Therefore, I will turn to some of these studies to see which conflicts that have emerged in various contexts.

First, I will turn to a study regarding the reintegration of returnees to Eritrea.[24] Here, it is argued, the reintegration has been rather smooth even though there have been some tensions. The solidarity among Eritreans in their struggle for freedom was one important component in the prevention of conflicts. It is claimed that, in other contexts, the population that stayed behind has been accused of collaborating with the enemy, or the ones that left could be accused of being cowards for leaving the country. Nevertheless, despite the lack of clearly articulated conflicts, there is a lack of contact between the two groups in Eritrea after the return. Farmland and rainfall are key issues that create tensions. In this study, conflicts about land were the principal problem reported. Many returnees had expected to return to the village of their birthplace and to be able to reclaim their farmland. This is, however, problematic and when the study was made, the returnee community was losing hope of ever being issued new farmland or of returning to their old farmsteads.

The next study is from Sarajevo and it is focused on refugees who returned after the war. Stefansson has examined what happens when the so-called myth of return becomes a reality.[25] He argues that in a justified revolt against understanding repatriation as a glorious return, much repatriation research has come to hold the equally untenable assumption of an impossible homecoming. In accordance with such a view, it is argued that refugees involved in voluntary repatriation are not returning home, but are merely returning to their country of origin and no more. Through his fieldwork, Stefansson wants to modify this view. He concludes that it is not possible either to maintain this view or the other view of repatriation as an unproblematic homecoming, which is maintained in the political debate. Against the latter, he argues that there are clear divisions between the returnees and the ones at home. In the concrete example studied by

[24] Bascom, "The Long, 'Last Step'?"
[25] Stefansson, "Refugee Returns."

Stefansson, refugees who return to Sarajevo feel structural discriminations and they are also accused of betraying Sarajevo by fleeing abroad. After their return they also find that those who stayed behind take no interest in hearing about their experience of being refugees, but merely want to preach about their own suffering during the war.[26] However, the social division also works the other way round. Some returnees feel superior because of their experience in Western countries. Despite these problems, Stefansson argues that the academic thought of an impossible homecoming must be questioned as well as the notion of an uncomplicated homecoming. He argues that:

> Despite the apparent differences between public policy repatriation discourse and its critics in the academic world, these two lines of thinking on repatriation seem to be united in a fundamentalist conceptualization of belonging and home, as an identification with a place and community frozen in time; from the former perspective this constructs return as natural, from the latter point of view dreams of going home becomes an illusion.[27]

For us it is enough at this point to see that the different notions of home among the refugees and those who stayed behind create a division when the return occurs.

To Be at Home

Since repatriation is seen as the durable solution to the refugee situation, the research in this field has increased radically since the 1990s up until now. This means that there is an extensive amount of research about the refugees' different experiences of return. Unfortunately, I have not found any direct research based on the experience of those who stayed at home, and how they experience the new changes when the return takes place. Therefore, I will leave the academic field and turn to a recent play, *War*, written by Lars Norén. This is a play that goes deeply into these issues.[28]

The play, *War*, deals with the story of a mother and her two teenage daughters, who have been left to fend for themselves during a war. When the husband finally returns unexpectedly, broken and blind after several years of soldiering, he is no longer the obvious father in the house. The

---

[26] See also Anders H. Stefansson, "Sarajevo Suffering: Homecoming and the Hierarchy of Homeland Hardship," in *Homecomings: Unsettling Paths of Return* (ed. Fran Markowitz and Anders H. Stefansson; Lanham, Md.: Lexington Books, 2004b), 56, where he claims that the relationship with those who stayed behind produced the strongest outbursts of frustration and anger after the return of the refugees. Cf. Éva V Huseby-Darvas, "*Extra Hungariam Non Est Vita?* The Relationships between Hungarian Immigrants and Their Homeland," in *Homecomings: Unsettling Paths of Return* (ed. Fran Markowitz and Anders H. Stefansson; Lanham, Md.: Lexington Books, 2004), 87, for a similar experience of the relationship among Hungarian-American immigrants.

[27] Stefansson, "Refugee Returns," 186.

[28] Lars Norén, *Krig* (Copy of an Unpublished Play at Dramaten Stockholm, 2004).

family has survived with the help of his brother and the older daughter, who has prostituted herself. The brother, who remained at home during the war, seems to have taken the father's place in more ways than one, and in the shadow of war, a relationship drama takes place

When the father returns, he is not met by his expected embrace of his daughter. Instead she only gives him her hand and she only does so at the mother's request. When the father tries to embrace the daughter, the embrace is too tight and she has to free herself. The father is not only physically blind, but he is also blind to everything that has taken place at home, and to the way in which they have experienced a war, from which he has been absent. They have been raped by their neighbours and they have seen their friends being taken away. In the play, we encounter the cleavage in the typical Norén, sure in aim and short in lines, exchange of words. No one is longer the same as before the war. In the house there is no place for a man who tries to take his place and his rights.

This play provides an image of what that can take place when a family is turned into strangers through the war, but maybe also through what has taken place before the war. We also understand that it is not necessarily most complicated for those who return. Those who were left at home have created their own life without the dead man. What place is the dead man supposed to receive when he returns, and when too much is beginning to change again?

Conclusion

Through *the myth of return* we have seen the ways in which the image of home is formed by the experiences of exile. It is an image shaped by the home that was left behind and the distance in time and place freezes and idealises the image. The hope of return evolves around the homes, the fields and so forth, which were actually left behind. Therefore, there can be a cleavage between the image of home and the reality, that the homes are occupied and the fields cultivated by others. This can easily create conflicts between those who return and those who have stayed behind. The persons at home have created a new life without the ones that have left. When they return and everything begins to change again, it is not clear whether they will be met by an embrace, a handshake or by exclusion.

The Conflict in the Old Testament

Now I will leave the contemporary refugee studies and return to the Old Testament. It is not possible simply to transfer contemporary experiences to Old Testament texts. We do not have any contemporary situation, which is directly comparable to the Babylonian exile. Even so, I believe that our knowledge of how people react to the experience of exile and homecoming today can help us to imagine how they might have reacted under those circumstances.

When people return after more than 50 years of exile it is natural that this creates some tension between those who return and those at home. After such a long time it is the second and third generations who meet one another. They are no longer brothers and sisters, but strangers who encounter one another. Most of the people who had first hand experience of the deportation were gone. As we have seen, in the contemporary refugee research, the cleavage in the image of home, between the refugees and those who stayed behind grows with the distance of time and place. This makes for a diversity of concepts about the world that may, or may not, be shared between these two groups. Therefore, it is not surprising that such a conflict might also have coloured some texts of the Old Testament. The conflict is most often implicit, but in a few examples it becomes explicit. It is for example obvious that the book of Jeremiah knows of two groups in Israel. In Jer 24, the prophet sees two baskets of figs, those in exile are the good figs and those at home are the bad ones. The tension between these two groups is also explicit in Ezek 11:14–21. Here it is the inhabitants of Jerusalem (ישׁבי ירושׁלם) who say about the whole house of Israel (וכל־בית ישׂראל כלה) that: "They have gone far from YHWH; to us this land is given for a possession" (Ezek 11:15). Against this statement, Ezekiel gives a promise from YHWH that he will gather them from the countries to which they have been scattered, and he will give them the land of Israel.

In this short text we see two sides of the conflict. First, those in the land are not described as a part of the people of Israel, they are only "the inhabitants of Jerusalem" (ישׁבי ירושׁלם). This is put in contrast to those in exile, who are described as "the whole house of Israel" (וכל בית ישׂראל כלה).[29] This is a clear example of exclusion through separation.[30] The second aspect of this conflict is that it is clearly a conflict about the land. Both these aspects also occur in other examples in the Old Testament.

In my examination of the conflict, I will first turn to texts where those left in the land are diminished in value and sometimes not even counted as a part of the people. Such descriptions occur in different ways and have an important function in excluding those who stayed behind in contrast to the people in the exile. According to 2 Kgs 24:14 and 25:12, only the poorest remained in the land after the deportation. And these poorest were left as vinedressers and tillers of the soil. By contrast, those taken in captivity were the elite of the nation. Finally, the land became totally empty, since: "all the people, high and low, and the captains of the forces set out and

[29] This description is however missing in LXX, see BHSapp. d–d.

[30] See further above.

went to Egypt" (2 Kgs 25:26). It is however not very likely that the land was totally emptied of all the people.[31] This is, nevertheless, a forceful instrument by which to exclude any people left in the land. In 2 Chr 36:20–21 we have another reason why the land is empty:

He took into exile in Babylon those who had escaped from the sword, and they became servants to him and to his sons until the establishment of the kingdom of Persia, to fulfill the word of YHWH by the mouth of Jeremiah, until the land had made up for its sabbaths. All the days that it lay desolate it kept sabbath, to fulfil seventy years.

This is just another way of excluding the people who were actually left in the land. Even though the land is described as empty in these texts, the people who were there do receive some attention in the letter of Jeremiah to the deported. Still, the description of those who were left in the land is very negative:

I will make them like rotten figs that are so bad they cannot be eaten. I will pursue them with the sword, with famine, and with pestilence, and will make them a horror to all the kingdoms of the earth, to be an object of cursing, and horror, and hissing, and a derision among all the nations where I have driven them. (Jer 29:17b–18)

In other examples in the book of Jeremiah, the land is described as desolate without human beings or animals.[32] At the same time there is hope that the land will flourish again.[33] These examples show that the myth of the empty land is a myth for those in exile, and it is a myth of return, which promises that the land will be given back to them at the end of exile, since the land is either empty or inhabited by the "wrong" kind of people.

The second form of the conflict is conflicts about land. These conflicts have a close connection to the former ones. In Ezek 11:17 the land is promised to those in exile and this is a promise, which was probably more popular among that group than among those left in the land. The important question of who that has the right to the land is also obvious in Ezek 47:13–23. When the land is divided, it is done by the people in exile. Only at the end are the "aliens" (גר) who reside among them mentioned. These people will have an inheritance among the tribes with whom they live, and this will be assigned to them as "native" (אזרח). At first this can seem like a generous policy and a just division.[34] However, if the text is read from the point of view of those who have lived in the land for more than fifty years and who were probably אזרח already, this text takes on another

[31] For a discussion of the situation in the land during the exile, see above.

[32] Jer 32:43 and 33:10–12.

[33] See for example Jer 33:12–13.

[34] E.g. Zimmerli, *Ezekiel 2*, 532, and Albertz, *Religionsgeschichte Israels*, 458. Cf. Thilo Alexander Rudnig, *Heilig und Profan: Redaktionskritische Studien zu Ez 40-48* (BZAW vol. 287; Berlin: de Gruyter, 2000), 179, 367, who understands Ezek 47:22–23 and this thought to be a later expansion.

value. This group is not mentioned at all, the land is divided as if it was a totally empty area. It is therefore probable that this text also reflects a real conflict about the right to land. We have seen two expressions of the conflict as we meet it in the Old Testament. Now I will turn to a more specific corpus, namely to Ezra-Nehemiah, which deals with the situation in the land after the exile.

While reading Ezra-Nehemiah it is obvious that there were significant tensions between different groups in the land. It is also clear that these tensions involve a conflict between those who stayed behind and those who returned.[35] The most obvious sign of such tensions is the way in which the identity of those who returned is articulated with respect of their experience of exile. They are frequently separated out as one group even after the return.[36] They are even counted and given separate lists.[37] Furthermore, they are described as the people of Israel[38] and as the remnant.[39] On the other hand, the people of the land are frequently equated with the foreigners. In Neh 1:2, Nehemiah asks about those who have escaped the captivity. He is told that:

> The survivors there in the province who escaped captivity are in great trouble and shame; the wall of Jerusalem is broken down, and its gates have been destroyed by fire. (Neh 1:3)

Even though this is a negative description of the people left in the land, it shows that Nehemiah knows of a group of the people who have escaped the exile. Such a group also exists in Ezra. However, in Ezra 4:1–5 "the people of the land" are self-confessed foreigners. The "adversaries" of Judah and Benjamin approach Zerubbabel in order to help rebuilding the temple:

> Let us build with you, for we worship your God as you do, and we have been sacrificing to him ever since the days of King Esar-haddon of Assyria who brought us here. (Ezra 4:2)

But Zerubbabel answers them that they shall have no part in rebuilding the temple. This short survey makes it clear that Ezra-Nehemiah emphasises a separation of the returnees from "the people of the land". It is, however, not obvious who were designated by the phrase עמי הארץ, "people of the land". In Ezra 9:1 they are defined as: "the Canaanites, the Hittites, the Perizzites, the Jebusites, the Ammonites, the Moabites, the Egyptians, and the Amorites." Therefore, only one Israelite community exists in the land,

---

[35] E.g. Peter R. Bedford, "Diaspora: Homeland Relations in Ezra-Nehemiah," *VT* 52, no. 2 (2002): 147–165, 149.

[36] Ezra 1:11; 2:1; 3:8; 4:1; 6:16, 19–21; 9:4; 10:6, 8; Neh 7:6; 8:17.

[37] Ezra 2:1–70 and Neh 7:5–72.

[38] Ezra 6:16, 21.

[39] Ezra 9:13–15.

and this is the returned exiles. This makes it probable that some portion of the עמי הארץ were actually descendants of the sons of Jacob.[40]

One issue frequently discussed among scholars is Ezra-Nehemiah's view on mixed marriages. There is an intense discussion, especially about Ezra 9–10. This discussion involves several important issues.[41] Here it is enough to see that the regulations against mixed marriages are a further step in separating the group of people who returned from the exile from the people in the land. For Ezra-Nehemiah, it is only the small group who returned from the exile that is the true Israel.[42]

There is also some conflict about land in the text of Ezra-Nehemiah. It is stated that the people returned to their own towns (Ezra 2:1, Neh 7:6).[43] There is no regard for the people who lived in those towns, nor for those who worked on the land. This must inevitably have led to problems regarding land ownership.[44] See also Neh 5:1–12, where the people and their wives cry out greatly against their Jewish kin. This is a clear conflict about land, but it is not necessarily between those who stayed behind and those who returned.

---

[40] Cf. Mary Douglas, *Jacob's Tears: The Priestly Work of Reconciliation* (Oxford: Oxford University Press, 2004), 71–72.

[41] One discussion regards the redaction of these two chapters. See Yonina Dor, "The Composition of the Episode of the Foreign Women in Ezra IX-X," *VT* 53, no. 1 (2003): 26–47, both for a survey and an interpretation of the composition of the episode. Another field of research regards the reason to the divorce of foreign women. Harold C. Washington, "Israels Holy Seed and the Foreign Women of Ezra-Nehemiah: A Kristevan Reading," *BibInt* 11, no. 3 (2003): 427–438, understands it as abjection of the female body. Douglas, *Jacob's Tears*, 64–87, focuses on purity and impurity. David Janzen, *Witch-hunts, Purity and Social Boundaries: The Expulsion of the Foreign Women in Ezra 9–10* (JSOTsup vol. 350; London: Sheffield Academic Press, 2002), 10, divides the scholarly discussion regarding the maintenance of the boundary in three categories: "(1) Ezra was simply enforcing the law in order to prevent apostasy; (2) there were issues of ethnic identity at stake that the divorces and bans were designed to address; or (3) the motivating factor behind the social boundary maintenance was really an economic or political issue." Janzen, *Witch-hunts*, 19, presents an alternative interpretation and argues that the reason to divorce was a ritualised act of purification, which is commonly called a witch-hunt. This he defines as: "the act of a social group to blame a sub-group for social dissension for which this sub-group is not responsible, occurring when there is no obvious candidate to blame for social dissension [...] They are blamed because of who they are, not because of what they have done".

[42] See Ezra 9:1, 11; 10:2, 11.

[43] Cf. Neh 11:1 where the people cast lots to determine who will live in Jerusalem and in the other towns.

[44] Douglas, *Jacob's Tears*, 67.

Conclusion

This survey makes it obvious that there were significant tensions between those who stayed and those who returned. The conflict is most often implicit, but it is still very clear. First, those who stayed have been robbed of their value and even of their existence. Secondly, in accordance with this view, the land was divided as if it had been empty. These tensions cannot be discovered through archaeological means. Still, it is probable that the conflict had some impact on a significant part of the community over a long period of time. We can note further that Ezra-Nehemiah differs from other Old Testament books. Both the conflicts and the view that those who returned are the true Israel are more clearly expressed in Ezra-Nehemiah.

The Conflict in Isaiah 40–55

There is a tension between those who stayed and those who returned also in Isa 40–55, even though that conflict is mostly implicit. The first time that the tension occurs is already in the prologue, Isa 40:1–11. This message is directed to Zion and to the people left in the land. The words of comfort are prominent. In Isa 40:11 we see how YHWH comes to Zion with his flock. If we read this verse remembering the conflict, it becomes a rather strong statement that YHWH has been away from the land together with the people in exile. Hence, it is also an exhortation to receive those who return as the flock of YHWH.

The second section I turn to is Isa 41:8–9. This text contains a similar division between the two groups. In Ezek 33:24 the people in the land claim their right to the land since they are connected to Abraham:

> Mortal, the inhabitants of these waste places in the land of Israel keep saying, "Abraham was only one man, yet he got possession of the land; but we are many; the land is surely given us to possess." (Ezek 33:24)

Regardless of this, the verdict in Ezekiel is that the land will be desolate and laid waste. In Isa 41:8–9 the parallel to Abraham shows that the offspring of Abraham are those who are taken from the ends of earth:

> But you, Israel, my servant,
> Jacob, whom I have chosen,
> the offspring of Abraham, my friend;
> whom I took from the ends of the earth,
> and called from its farthest corners
> saying to you, "You are my servant,
> I have chosen you and not cast you off ." (Isa 41:8–9)

In a situation where there is a conflict between those who stayed in the land during the exile and those who are at the ends of the earth, such a statement is a strong argument in support of YHWH's care of the latter group. It is only this group who are the offspring of Abraham. Those who were left in the land are not even mentioned.

An important conflict following the return arises from the problem about the right to land. This conflict occurs in some texts. Turning to Isa 49:8b–9a, we see that this is also central in Isa 40–55:

I have kept you and given you
as a covenant to the people,
to establish the land,
to apportion the desolate heritages;
saying to the prisoners, "Come out,"
to those who are in darkness, "Show yourselves."

Here it is settled that the land will be established and the heritages will be apportioned. This will happen in connection with the release of the prisoners. In v. 8 we have probably a reinterpretation of the servant as Cyrus.[45] For our concern, it is more important to observe the legislation about a division of the land. This legislation is based on the fact that it is YHWH who frees the prisoners. It is not Cyrus, nor any other servant, who acts in the first place. Cyrus is only a tool in the hand of YHWH. It is YHWH himself who acts and who directs the entire scene. It is reasonable to assume that it is the people who live in the land who have to be convinced that such apportion of the land is just and that it is the will of YHWH. Those in exile did probably not have the same problem in seeing both the positive aspects of returning and of receiving land.

As we have seen in other Old Testament texts, there is a tendency to diminish the value of the people in the land in favour of those in exile. This occurs also in Isa 40–55. In Isa 49:21 we hear these words put into the mouth of Zion:

Then you will say in your heart,
"Who has borne me these?
I was bereaved and barren,
exiled and put away –
so who has reared these?
I was left all alone –
where then have these come from?" (Isa 49:21)

In Isa 51:20 the people in the land do at least exist. However, the situation does not seem to be much better, either for those in the land or for Zion:

Your children have fainted,
they lie at the head of every street
like an antelope in a net;
they are full of the wrath of YHWH,
the rebuke of your God.

---

[45] Kratz, *Kyros im Deuterojesaja-Buch*, 128–147, and Hermisson, *Deuterojesaja 45,8-49,13*, 373.

It is obvious that there is a significant difference in the description of the people in the land and those in exile. The description of those in the land stands in considerable contrast to their own image of themselves (cf. Ezek 33:24). It is also obvious that Isa 40–55 takes the greatest interest in those excepted to return from the exile.

Maybe the conflict is most prominent in Isa 53, and that is also where we find a solution. As I have argued above, Isa 52:7–54:17 belongs together and describes a sequence of events. The liberation from captivity is connected to the exhortation of the servant. This continues with the "we", who embrace the servant's suffering as a suffering on behalf of their sins. This leads Zion to enlarge her tent in order to make room for all her children. In this reading the "we"-group receives the servant, i.e. the people who return from exile, with open arms by their confession of their part in the suffering of the exile.

The last time the word עבד, "servant", is used in Isa 40–55, occur in Isa 54:17.[46] This is also the only time עבד is used outside the servant songs in Isa 49–55:

> No weapon that is fashioned against you shall prosper,
>   and you shall confute every tongue that rises against you in judgment.
> This is the heritage of the servants (עבדי) of YHWH and their vindication from me,
>   says YHWH. (Isa 54:17)

Here the word עבד, "servant", is used about the people, but only about a part of the people. The plural indicates that that it is no longer the people as a group that is the servant. Rather, it is each individual who turns to YHWH. This leads us over to Isa 56–66 and to the description of the servant found there. In this section the word עבד is only used in plural.[47]

The conflict in Isaiah 56–66

In this section of the book there are clear tensions between different groups. The question is who can belong to the group of the servants of YHWH, not who has been a servant from his mother's womb.[48] Therefore, the conflict is no longer simply between those who have returned from the exile and those who stayed behind. It is not particularly important to determine here who exactly belongs to the group of servants.[49] Nevertheless,

---

[46] Knud Jeppesen, "Herrens tjener og Herrens tjenere: Om Jes 40-66," in *Studier i Jesajabogen* (ed. Bent Rosendal; Århus: Aarhus Universitetsforlag, 1989).

[47] Isa 56:6; 63:17; 65:8, 9, 13, 14, 15; 66:14. The verb is used in Isa 60:12. Cf. however BHSapp. regarding Isa 63:11.

[48] Jeppesen, "Herrens tjener."

[49] See Joseph Blenkinsopp, "The 'Servants of the Lord' in Third Isaiah: Profile of a Pietistic Group in the Persian Epoch," in *"The Place is Too Small for us": The Israelite Prophets in Recent Scholarship* (ed. Robert P. Gordon; vol. *Sources for Biblical and*

it is clear that this belonging is limited to a small group in the province. More importantly, to be servant is the result of an individual personal choice (Isa 65:12; 66:3). The question of belonging has therefore been individualised.

The use of עבד, "servant", in plural in Isa 54:17 is of special interest. The plural makes it likely that the word is related to its use in Isa 56–66. Therefore, already in the last verse of Isa 54, this belonging to YHWH has been individualised, so that it is no longer the servant as a group who is meant, but each single servant. In Isa 55 the individualisation has been taken one step further, compared to Isa 54:17.[50] Labahn argues that, as time went by and the promise from Deutero-Isaiah about liberation was still not fulfilled, an explanation was needed. This explanation to *the delay of salvation* was found in the guilt of the people.[51] In Isa 55:5–6 the rescue has been individualised and directed to the future.[52] The occurrence of עבד in plural further explains that Isa 53–54 is intended to be a bridge between the earlier expectations and the conflicts which took place. The explanation of this individualisation, given through Isa 53–54, is that those at home did not embrace those who returned and/or the returnees were not satisfied with being part of the flock, but wanted to be the shepherds again.

Conclusion

It is clear that there is a division between the people in the land and those who returned from the exile in Isa 40–55, even though the tension is only implicit in the text. Nevertheless, the division is apparent in Isa 40:1–11 where we have two groups, but it is only the flock who returned from exile that is pastured by YHWH. In Isa 40–55 there is also a tendency to diminish the value of those in the land compared to the other group. Finally, we have seen that the division of land is also important in Isa 40–55. It is worth noting that Isa 53 is the text which most clearly expresses the encounter of these two groups. In Isa 53 the conflict has been overcome by the confession of the "we".

Theological Studies; Winona Lake, Ind.: Eisenbrauns, 1995), for further discussion of which group that could be the servants.

[50] See especially Isa 55:6–7.

[51] Antje Labahn, "The Delay of Salvation within Deutero-Isaiah," *JSOT* 85 (1999): 71–84.

[52] Labahn, "The Delay of Salvation."

Part Four

Conclusion

Chapter 14

Conclusion

The variety and multitude of interpretations of Isa 53 could lead to despair and in some ways it does for me too. I do not think that we will ever reach a consensus regarding the interpretation of such an important and ambiguous poem. My hope is however that it will be possible to move the interpretation forward and to open up new possibilities previously unexplored.

In this study I have argued that the reconciliation between the "we" and the servant is more important than the atonement. Furthermore, it is by their confession that the "we"-group opens its arms to embrace the servant. The text has been analysed from two major points of view. First, the former and the present understandings of the servant's suffering of the "we" were discussed under the heading of *Exclusion and Embrace*. Secondly, three important contexts of Isa 53 were analysed, the literary, the geographical, and the social context. These two parts do of course overlap one another and the final interpretation is dependent on both of them. However, a purpose behind this division is to see that it is not necessary to agree with every single aspect of my work in order to find valuable pieces in the analytical parts.

My main aim in this study is to understand what problem Isa 53 addresses and seeks to answer. The question is asked as a historical question and I believe that Isa 53 addresses a specific historical problem, which lies in the conflicts created after the return of those in exile. Such conflicts are expressed in contemporary refugee studies, in other texts of the Old Testament, and also in Isa 40–55. I have primarily sought to show two expressions of this conflict in the Old Testament and in Isa 40–55. First, the people in the land were excluded by different means. Sometimes they are negatively described and sometimes the land is described as totally empty during the Babylonian exile. In Ezra-Nehemiah it is only those who returned from the exile who are seen as the true Israel. Secondly, there is a clear conflict about the rights to possession of land.

At the end of exile, there was a hope that the deported people would return to the land, that the land would be rebuilt, and that Jerusalem would flourish again. This hope is expressed most clearly in Isa 40:1–52:10. However, as time went by, there was a realisation that the glorious return was a rather limited return, and the joy of receiving those who returned was turned into conflicts, not least regarding possession of land and places to live. In this situation someone probably reflected on the message of Isa 40:1–52:10 and sought to understand what had gone wrong. Isa 53 was then inserted as an explanation of how the people in the land, i.e. the "we" should have received those who returned, i.e. the servant. If this embrace had taken place, Mother Zion would have rejoiced, as described in Isa 54. However, the situation turned out rather differently and the land became full of conflicts. Therefore, the idea that a special group represents the servant is dismissed. Already in Isa 54:17 we see that the basis for belonging to YHWH has been individualised, and this is taken a step further in Isa 55. Now it is up to each single person to seek YHWH.

In the analyses of exclusion and embrace in Isa 53, I have questioned the prominent view that the suffering of the servant is an atoning suffering. I have argued that it is merely vicarious. The servant is suffering instead of the "we" and instead of what the "we"-group had deserved. This interpretation was further strengthened by the analysis of some important concepts that describes the removal of guilt or impurity in other texts of the Old Testament. None of these are used in Isa 53. That analysis showed that there are important Old Testament concepts that describe how acts performed by various persons avert the wrath or the judgement of YHWH and makes him embrace the person or the people once again. Nevertheless, none of these concepts appear in Isa 53. This underlines my doubt that Isa 53 shows a totally new and unprecedented thought, namely that the suffering of an innocent person will make YHWH embrace another person, who is guilty.

Furthermore, if Isa 53 really does describe an atoning suffering, we could at least expect the removal of guilt to be a significant problem in the rest of Isa 40–55. However, the opposite is the case. In turning to the rest of Isa 40–55, we saw that it is "because you are precious in my sight" (Isa 43:4) that God turns again to his people. There is no cause outside God himself, which gives any reason for this new forgiveness. Even so, Isa 40–55 frequently mentions sins and iniquities. This is done in order to make the listeners recognise their own part in what has happened and to make them receive God, who turns to them. None of the sections studied mentions any need for expiation or atonement, even though the people are frequently described as guilty and absolutely undeserving of salvation. These passages emphasise that YHWH opens his arms to embrace his people, and there is nothing besides YHWH himself that has caused this embrace. The open arms of YHWH imply an expectation of a response, namely that the people should return to YHWH and that they should acknowledge their own guilt. Isa 53 contains such a response, since the "we", i.e. the receivers of the message, confess their responsibility for the suffering of the servant.

It is rather unlikely that only one single text in the entire book of Isaiah would contain the idea that one person's suffering atones for the guilt of others. And it is particularly unlikely that such text would occur in Isa 40–55, since the rest of this part of the book emphasises that the guilt has been blotted out because of Gods love and not because any atoning event. The relationship, which is in focus in Isa 53, is the relationship between the "we" and the servant and not their relationship to YHWH. By confessing their own guilt, the "we" open their arms to embrace the servant. For that embrace to happen, the servant must also open his arms. The servant and the "we" must meet on equal terms, since they are both described as "sheep". Neither of them is a "shepherd." The only shepherd in Isa 53 is YHWH himself.

We do not know exactly what happened. We only know that the embrace between these brothers did not take place in the way that Isa 53 had envisaged it, and the mother had to wait for her joy. Zion did not flourish as wonderfully as it is described in Isa 54. Rather than the pictures painted for us in Isa 53 and 54, we encounter the conflicts described in Isa 56–66.

Bibliography

Abma, Richtsje. Bonds of Love: Methodic Studies of Prophetic Texts with Marriage Imagery: (Isaiah 50:1-3 and 54:1-10, Hosea 1-3, Jeremiah 2-3). Vol 40, SSN. Assen: Van Gorcum, 1999.

Ackroyd, Peter Runham. *Israel under Babylon and Persia*. Vol 4, The New Clarendon Bible. Old Testament. London: Oxford University Press, 1970.

Al-Rasheed, Madawi. "The Myth of Return: Iraqi Arab and Assyrian Refugees in London." *Journal of Refugee Studies* 7, no. 2-3 (1994): 199-219.

Albertz, Rainer. "Darius in Place of Cyrus: The First Edition of Deutero-Isaiah (Isaiah 40.1-52.12) in 521 BCE." *JSOT* 27 (2003a): 371-83.

—. *Die Exilszeit: 6. Jahrhundert v. Chr.* Vol 7, Biblische Enzyklopädie. Stuttgart: Kohlhammer, 2001.

—. *Israel in Exile: The History and Literature of the Sixth Century B.C.E.* Vol 3, Studies in Biblical Literature. Atlanta: Society of Biblical Literature, 2003b.

—. Religionsgeschichte Israels in alttestamentlicher Zeit: Vom Exil bis zu den Makkabäern. 2 ed. Vol 8/2, GAT. Göttingen: Vandenhoeck & Ruprecht, 1997.

Ashley, Timothy R. *The Book of Numbers*, NICOT. Grand Rapids, Mich.: Eerdmans, 1993.

Asplund, Johan. *Rivaler och syndabockar*. Göteborg: Korpen, 1989.

Atkinson, James. "Atonement." Pages 18-24 in *A Dictionary of Christian Theology*. Edited by Alan Richardson. London: S.C.M. Press, 1969.

Aurelius, Erik. *Der Fürbitter Israels: Eine Studie zum Mosebild im Alten Testament*. Vol 27, ConBOT. Stockholm: Almqvist & Wiksell International, 1988.

Bailey, Daniel P. "Concepts of *Stellvertretung* in the Interpretation of Isaiah 53." Pages 223-50 in *Jesus and the Suffering Servant: Isaiah 53 and Christian Origins*. Edited by William R. Farmer and William H. Bellinger. Harrisburg, Pa.: Trinity Press, 1998.

Balentine, Samuel E. "The Prophet as Intercessor: A Reassessment." *JBL* 103, no. 2 (1984): 161-73.

Baltzer, Klaus. *Deutero-Isaiah: A Commentary on Isaiah 40-55*, Hermeneia. Minneapolis, Minn.: Fortress Press, 1999.

Barstad, Hans M. *The Babylonian Captivity of the Book of Isaiah: "Exilic" Judah and the Provenance of Isaiah 40-55*. Vol 102, Instituttet for sammenlignende kulturforskning. Serie B, Skrifter. Oslo: Novus: Instituttet for sammenligende kulturforskning, 1997.

—. The Myth of the Empty Land: A Study in the History and Archaeology of Judah During the "Exilic" Period. Vol 28, SO. Oslo; Stockholm: Scandinavian University Press, 1996.

—. A Way in the Wilderness: The "Second Exodus" in the Message of Second Isaiah. Vol 12, JSS. Manchester: University of Manchester, 1989.

—. "The Philological Expert: Jesaja 50–53. " Pages. Edited by The National Archives of Sweden: The Swedish Bible Commission's Deposit at the Regional Archives in Uppsala.

Bascom, Johnathan. "The Long, 'Last Step'? Reintegration of Repatriates in Eritrea." *Journal of Refugee Studies* 18, no. 2 (2005): 165–180.

Bauman, Zygmunt. *Postmodern Ethics*. Oxford: Blackwell, 1993.

Becker, Uwe. "Der Prophet als Fürbitter: Zum Literarhistorischen Ort der Amos-Visionen." *VT* 51, no. 2 (2001): 141–165.

—. *Jesaja - von der Botschaft zum Buch*. Vol 178, FRLANT. Göttingen: Vandenhoeck und Ruprecht, 1997.

Bedford, Peter R. "Diaspora: Homeland Relations in Ezra-Nehemiah." *VT* 52, no. 2 (2002): 147–165.

Begrich, Joachim. *Studien zu Deuterojesaja*. Vol 20, TB. München: Kaiser Verlag, 1963.

Bentzen, Aage. *Jesaja: Bind II Jes 40-66*. 2 vols. Kopenhagen: Gads forlag, 1944.

Berges, Ulrich. *Das Buch Jesaja: Komposition und Endgestalt*. Vol 16, Herders Biblische Studien. Freiburg: Herder, 1998.

Bergey, Ronald L. "The Rhetorical Role of Reiteration in the Suffering Servant Poem (Isa 52:13–53:12)." *JETS* 40, no. 2 (1997): 177–188.

Betz, Otto. "Jesus and Isaiah 53." Pages 70–87 in *Jesus and the Suffering Servant: Isaiah 53 and Christian Origins*. Edited by William R. Farmer and William H. Bellinger. Harrisburg, Pa.: Trinity Press, 1998.

Beuken, Willem André Maria. *Jesaja 1-12*, HTKAT. Freiburg: Herder, 2003.

—. *Jesaja: deel II B*, De Prediking van het Oude Testament. Nijkerk: Callenbach, 1983.

Bibelkommissionen. Bibelkommissionens komplement: Noter, uppslagsdel, parallellhänvisningar, textkritiska anmärkningar till Bibel 2000. Stockholm: Verbum, 2001.

Bjerg, Svend. Stedfortrædelse: Om Judas og Jesus, Gud og mennesket. Frederiksberg: Anis, 1991.

Black, R. "Conceptions of 'Home' and the Political Geography of Refugee Repatriation: Between Assumption and Contested Reality in Bosnia-Herzegovina." *Applied Geography* 22, no. 2 (2002): 123–138.

Blenkinsopp, Joseph. "The Bible, Archaeology and Politics; or The Empty Land Revisited." *JSOT* 27 (2002b): 169–187.

—. Isaiah 1–39: A New Translation with Introduction and Commentary. 1. ed. Vol 19, AB. New York: Doubleday, 2000.

—. Isaiah 40–55: A New Translation with Introduction and Commentary. Vol 19, AB. New York; London: Doubleday, 2002a.

—. "The 'Servants of the Lord' in Third Isaiah: Profile of a Pietistic Group in the Persian Epoch." Pages 392–412 in *"The Place is Too Small for us": The Israelite Prophets in Recent Scholarship*. Edited by Robert P. Gordon. *Sources for Biblical and Theological Studies*. Winona Lake, Ind.: Eisenbrauns, 1995.

—. "Bethel in the Neo-Babylonian Period." Pages 93–107 in *Judah and the Judeans in the Neo-Babylonian Period*. Edited by Oded Lipschits and Joseph Blenkinsopp. Winona Lake Ind.: Eisenbrauns, 2003.

Block, Daniel Isaac. *The Book of Ezekiel: Chapters 1–24*, NICOT. Grand Rapids, Mich.; Cambridge: Eerdmans, 1997.

Booij, Th. "Negation in Isaiah 43:22–24." *ZAW* 92 (1982): 390–400.

Branson. "יסר." Pages 127–134 in *TDOT 6*. Edited by G. Johannes Botterweck and Helmer Ringgren. Grand Rapids, Mich.: Eerdmans, 1990.

Brueggemann, Walter. *Isaiah 40–66*, Westminster Bible Companion. Louisville; London: John Knox Press, 1998.

Budde, Karl. "The So-Called 'Ebed-Yahweh Songs,' and the Meaning of the Term "Servant of Yahweh" in Isaiah, Chaps. 40–55." *AJT* 3, no. 3 (1899): 499–540.

Cassuto, Umberto. *A Commentary on the Book of Exodus*. Jerusalem: The Magnes Press, the Hebrew University, 1974.

Childs, Brevard S. *Exodus: A Commentary*, OTL. London: SCM Press, 1974.

—. *Isaiah*, OTL. Louisville, Ky.: Westminster John Knox Press, 2001.

Chimni, B. S. "From Resettlement to Involuntary Repatriation: Towards a Critical History of Durable Solutions to Refugee Problems." *Refugee Survey Quarterly* 23, no. 3 (2004): 55–73.

Clines, David J. A. *I, He, We and They: A Literary Approach to Isaiah 53*. Vol 1, JSOTSup. Sheffield: JSOT Press, 1976.

—, ed. *The Dictionary of Classical Hebrew*. Sheffield: Sheffield Academic Press, 1993.

Coggins, Richard. J. "Do We Still Need Deutero-Isaiah." *JSOT* 81 (1998): 77–92.

Cohen, Rina and Gerald Gold. "Constructing Ethnicity: Myth of Return and Modes of Exclusion among Israelis in Toronto." *International Migration* 35, no. 3 (1997): 373–94.

Collins, John Joseph. *Daniel: A Commentary on the Book of Daniel*, Hermeneia. Minneapolis, Minn.: Fortress Press, 1993.

Conroy, Charles. "The Four 'Four Servant Poems' in Second Isaiah in the Light of Recent Redaction-Historical Studies." Pages 80–94 in *Biblical and Near Eastern Essays: Studies in Honour of Kevin J. Cathcart*. Edited by Carmel McCarthy and John F. Healey. *JSOTSup*. London: T&T Clark, 2003.

Day, John. *Yahweh and the Gods and Goddesses of Canaan*. Vol 265, JSOTSup. Sheffield: Sheffield Academic Press, 2000.

Delitzsch, Franz. *Commentary on the Old Testament: Isaiah*. Vol VII. Grand Rapids, Mich., 1976.

Dille, Sarah J. *Mixing Metaphors: God as Mother and Father in Deutero-Isaiah*. Vol 398, JSOTSup. London: T & T Clark, 2004.

Dor, Yonina. "The Composition of the Episode of the Foreign Women in Ezra IX-X." *VT* 53, no. 1 (2003): 26–47.

Douglas, Mary. *Jacob's Tears: The Priestly Work of Reconciliation*. Oxford: Oxford University Press, 2004.

Duhm, Bernhard. *Das Buch Jesaja*. 4 ed. Göttingen, 1922.

Eagleton, Terry. *Literary Theory: An Introduction*. 2 ed. Oxford: Blackwell, 1996.

Elliger, Karl. *Deuterojesaja 40,1-45,7*. Vol 11/1, BKAT. Neukirchen-Vluyn: Neukirchener Verlag, 1978.

—. Deuterojesaja in seinem Verhältnis zu Tritojesaja. Vol 4, BWANT. Stuttgart: Kohlhammer, 1933.

Emerton, J. A. "The Translation and Interpretation of Isaiah VI. 13." Pages 85–118 in *Interpreting the Hebrew Bible: Essays in Honour of E.I.J. Rosenthal*. Edited by J. A. Emerton and Stefan C. Reif. *University of Cambridge Oriental Publications*. Cambridge: Cambridge University Press, 1982.

Fischer, Georg. *Jeremia 1-25*, HTKAT. Freiburg: Herder, 2005.

Franke, Chris. *Isaiah 46, 47, and 48: A New Literary-Critical Reading*. Vol 3, Biblical and Judaic studies from the University of California, San Diego. Winona Lake, Ind.: Eisenbrauns, 1994.

Friebel, Kelvin G. *Jeremiah's and Ezekiel's Sign-acts: Rhetorical Nonverbal Communication*. Vol 283, JSOTsup. Sheffield: Sheffield Academic Press, 1999.

Gestrich, Christof. Christentum und Stellvertretung: Religionsphilosophische Untersuchungen zum Heilsverständnis und zur Grundlegung der Theologie. Tübingen: Mohr Siebeck, 2001.

Ghorashi, Halleh. "When the Boundaries are Blurred: The Significance of Feminist Methods in Research." *European Journal of Women's Studies* 12, no. 3 (2005): 363–375.

Ginsberg, H. L. "Oldest Interpretation of the Suffering Servant." *VT* 3 (1953): 400–404.

Girard, René. *Things Hidden Since the Foundation of the World.* Stanford Calif.: Stanford University Press, 1987.

Goldingay, John. "Isaiah 43,22–28." *ZAW* 110 (1998): 191–203.

—. The Message of Isaiah 40–55: A Literary-Theological Commentary. London: T & T Clark, 2005.

Gottwald, N. K. "Social Class and Ideology in Isaiah 40–55: An Eagletonian Reading." *Semeia* 59 (1992): 43–57.

Grabbe, Lester L. *A History of the Jews and Judaism in the Second Temple Period.* Vol 47, Library of Second Temple studies. London: T&T Clark, 2004.

Gunton, Collin E. "Atonement: 3. Systematic Theology." Pages 156–157 in *The Encyclopedia of Christianity 1 A-D.* Edited by Erwin Fahlbusch. Grand Rapids Mich.; Leiden: Eerdmans; Brill, 1999.

Hammond, Laura. "Tigrayan Returnees' Notion of Home: Five Variations on a Theme." Pages 36–53 in *Homecomings: Unsettling Paths of Return.* Edited by Fran Markowitz and Anders H. Stefansson. Lanham, Md.: Lexington Books, 2004.

Hamp. "טבח." Pages 283–287 in *TDOT 5.* Edited by G. Johannes Botterweck and Helmer Ringgren. Grand Rapids, Mich.: Eerdmans, 1986.

Hengel, Martin. The Atonement: The Origins of the Doctrine in the New Testament. London: SCM Press, 1981.

—. "The Effective History of Isaiah 53 in the Pre-Christian Period." Pages 75–146 in *The Suffering Servant: Isaiah 53 in Jewish and Christian Sources.* Edited by Peter Stuhlmacher and Bernd Janowski. Grand Rapids, Mich.: Eerdmans, 2004.

Henning-Hess, Heike. "Bemerkungen zum ASCHAM-begriff in Jes 53,10." *ZAW* 109, no. 4 (1997): 618–626.

Hermisson, Hans-Jürgen. *Deuterojesaja 45,8-49,13.* Vol 11/2, BKAT. Neukirchen-Vluyn: Neukirchener Verlag, 2003.

—. Studien zur Prophetie und Weisheit: Gesammelte Aufsätze. Vol 23, FAT. Tubingen: Mohr Siebeck, 1998.

—. "Voreiliger Abschied von den Gottesknechtsliedern." *TRu* 49, no. 3 (1984): 209–222.

—. "The Fourth Servant Song in the Context of Second Isaiah." Pages 16–47 in *The Suffering Servant: Isaiah 53 in Jewish and Christian sources.* Edited by Peter Stuhlmacher and Bernd Janowski. Grand Rapids, Mich.: Eerdmans, 2004.

Hill, John. *Friend or Foe? The Figure of Babylon in the Book of Jeremiah MT.* Vol 40, Biblical Interpretation series. Leiden; Boston, Mass.; Köln: Brill, 1999.

Holladay, William Lee. A Concise Hebrew and Aramaic Lexicon of the Old Testament: Based upon the Lexical Work of Ludwig Koehler and Walter Baumgartner. Leiden: Brill, 1991.

Holt, Else Kragelund. *Prophesying the Past: The Use of Israel's History in the Book of Hosea.* Vol 194, JSOTSup. Sheffield: Sheffield Academic Press, 1995.

Holter, Knut. *Second Isaiah's Idol Fabrication Passages.* Vol 28, BBET. Frankfurt am Main: Peter Lang, 1995.

Hooker, Morna D. "Did the Use of Isaiah 53 to Interpret His Mission Begin with Jesus?" Pages 88–103 in *Jesus and the Suffering Servant: Isaiah 53 and Christian Origins.* Edited by William R. Farmer and William H. Bellinger. Harrisburg, Pa.: Trinity Press, 1998a.

—. "Response to Mikeal Parsons." Pages 120–124 in *Jesus and the Suffering Servant: Isaiah 53 and Christian Origins*. Edited by William R. Farmer and William H. Bellinger. Harrisburg, Pa.: Trinity Press, 1998b.

Houtman, Cornelis. *Exodus 20–40*. Vol 3, Historical Commentary on the Old Testamen. Kampen: Kok Pharos, 2000.

Huseby-Darvas, Éva V. "*Extra Hungariam Non Est Vita?* The Relationships between Hungarian Imigrants and Their Homeland." Pages 76–90 in *Homecomings: Unsettling Paths of Return*. Edited by Fran Markowitz and Anders H. Stefansson. Lanham, Md.: Lexington Books, 2004.

Janowski, Bernd. "Psalm CVI 28-31 und die Interzession des Pinchas." *VT* 33 (1983): 237–248.

—. Stellvertretung: Alttestamentliche Studien zu einem theologischen Grundbegriff. Vol 165, SBS. Stuttgart: Katholisches Bibelwerk, 1997.

—. Sühne als Heilsgeschehen: Traditions- und religionsgeschichtliche Studien zur Sühnetheologie der Priesterschrift. 2 ed. Vol 55, WMANT. Neukirchen-Vluyn: Neukirchener Verlag, 2000.

—. "Er trug unsere Sünden: Jesaja 53 und die Dramatik der Stellvertretung." Pages 27–48 in *Der leidende Gottesknecht: Jesaja 53 und seine Wirkungsgeschichte: Mit einer Bibliographie zu Jes 53*. Edited by Bernd Janowski and Peter Stuhlmacher. *FAT*. Tübingen: Mohr Siebeck, 1996.

—. "He Bore Our Sins: Isaiah 53 and the Drama of Taking Another's place." Pages 48–74 in *The Suffering Servant: Isaiah 53 in Jewish and Christian sources*. Edited by Peter Stuhlmacher and Bernd Janowski. Grand Rapids, Mich.: Eerdmans, 2004.

Janzen, David. Witch-hunts, Purity and Social Boundaries: The Expulsion of the Foreign Women in Ezra 9-10. Vol 350, JSOTsup. London: Sheffield Academic Press, 2002.

Jeppesen, Knud. "Mother Zion, Father Servant: A Reading of Isaiah 49–55." Pages 109–125 in *Of Prophets' Visions and the Wisdom of Sages: Essays in Honour of R. Norman Whybray on His Seventieth Birthday*. Edited by Heather A. McKay and David J. A. Clines. *JSOTsup*. Sheffield: JSOT Press, 1993.

—. "Herrens tjener og Herrens tjenere: Om Jes 40-66." Pages 68–93 in *Studier i Jesajabogen*. Edited by Bent Rosendal. Århus: Aarhus Universitetsforlag, 1989.

Johansson, Nils. Parakletoi: Vorstellungen von Fürsprechern für die Menschen vor Gott in der alttestamentlichen Religion, im Spätjudentum und Urchristentum. Lund: Gleerups, 1940.

Kaiser, Otto. Der Königliche Knecht: Eine traditionsgeschichtlich-exegetische Studie über die Ebed-Jahwe-Lieder bei Deuterojesaja. Vol 70, FRLANT. Göttingen: Vandenhoeck & Ruprecht, 1959.

Kaminsky, Amy K. *After Exile: Writing the Latin American Diaspora*. Minneapolis; London: University of Minnesota Press, 1999.

Kant, Immanuel. *Die Religion innerhalb der Grenzen der blossen Vernunft*, Philosophische Bibliothek, 545. Hamburg: Meiner, 2003.

Kapelrud, Arvid S. Et folk på hjemferd: "Trøsteprofeten" - den annen Jesaja - og hans budskap. Oslo: Universitetsforlaget, 1964.

Kaufmann, Yehezkel. History of the Religion of Israel: From the Babylonian Captivity to the End of Prophecy. Vol 4. New York: Ktav Publ. house, 1977.

Keel, Othmar and Christoph Uehlinger. *Gods, Goddesses, and Images of God in Ancient Israel*. Minneapolis Minn.: Fortress Press, 1998.

Kellermann. "אָשָׁם." Pages 429–437 in *TDOT 1*. Edited by G. Johannes Botterweck and Helmer Ringgren. Grand Rapids, Mich.: Eerdmans, 1974.

Kiesow, Klaus. *Exodustexte im Jesajabuch: Literarkritische und motivgeschichtliche Analysen*. Vol 24, OBO. Fribourg Suisse; Gottingen: Editions Universitaires; Vandenhoeck & Ruprecht, 1979.

Knierim, Rolf. "אשם." Pages 191–195 in *TLOT 1*. Edited by Ernst Jenni and Claus Westermann. Peabody, Mass.: Hendrickson Publishers, 1997.

Knöppler, Thomas. Sühne im Neuen Testament: Studien zum urchristlichen Verständnis der Heilsbedeutung des Todes Jesu. Vol 88, WMANT. Neukirchen-Vluyn: Neukirchener Verlag, 2001.

Koole, Jan L. *Isaiah 49–55*. Vol 3/2, Historical Commentary on the Old Testament. Kampen: Kok Pharos, 1997.

Korpel, Marjo C. A. "The Female Servant of the Lord in Isaiah 54." Pages 153–167 in *On Reading Prophetic Texts: Gender-Specific and Related Studies in Memory of Fokkelien van Dijk-Hemmes*. Edited by Bob Becking, Fokkelien van Dijk-Hemmes, and-Meindert Dijkstra. *Biblical interpretation series*. Leiden; New York; Köln: Brill, 1996.

Kratz, Reinhard Gregor. "Der Anfang des Zweiten Jesaja in Jes 40,1f. und das Jeremiabuch." *ZAW* 106 (1995): 243–261.

—. "Der Anfang des Zweiten Jesaja in Jes 40,1f. und seine literarischen Horizonte." *ZAW* 105 (1994): 400–419.

—. Kyros im Deuterojesaja-Buch: Redaktionsgeschichtliche Untersuchungen zu Entstehung und Theologie von Jes 40-55. Vol 1, FAT. Tübingen: Mohr Siebeck, 1991.

Kraus, Hans-Joachim. *Psalms 1–59*, CC. Minneapolis Minn.: Fortress Press, 1993.

—. *Psalms 60–150*, CC. Minneapolis Minn.: Fortress Press, 1993.

Kustár, Zoltán. "Durch seine Wunden sind wir geheilt": Eine Untersuchung zur Metaphorik von Israels Krankheit und Heilung im Jesajabuch. Vol 154, BWANT. Stuttgart: Kohlhammer, 2002.

Laato, Antti. *"About Zion I will not be Silent": The Book of Isaiah as an Ideological Unity*. Vol 44, ConBOT. Stockholm: Almqvist & Wiksell International, 1998.

—. The Servant of YHWH and Cyrus: A Reinterpretation of the Exilic Messianic Programme in Isaiah 40–55. Vol 35, ConBOT. Stockholm: Almqvist & Wiksell International, 1992.

Labahn, Antje. "The Delay of Salvation within Deutero-Isaiah." *JSOT* 85 (1999): 71–84.

Lacocque, André. *The Book of Daniel*. English ed. London: SPCK, 1979.

Lagerlöf, Selma. *Jerusalem*. Westport, Conn.: Greenwood press, 1970.

Lapsley, Jacqueline E. Can These Bones Live? The Problem of the Moral Self in the book of Ezekiel. Vol 301, BZAW. Berlin: de Gruyter, 2000.

Leclerc, Thomas L. Yahweh is Exalted in Justice: Solidarity and Conflict in Isaiah. Minneapolis, Minn.: Fortress, 2001.

Lee, Stephen. *Creation and Redemption in Isaiah 40–55*. Vol 2, Jian Dao Dissertation Series. Bible and Literature. Hong Kong: Alliance Bible Seminary, 1995.

Leene, Hendrik. "Auf der Suche nach einem redaktionskritischen Modell für Jesaja 40-55." *TLZ* 121 (1996): 803–818.

Lindblom, Johannes. *The Servant Songs in Deutero-Isaiah: A New Attempt to Solve an Old Problem*. Vol 47/5, Lunds Universitets årsskrift. Lund: Gleerup, 1951.

Lindström, Fredrik. God and the Origin of Evil: A Contextual Analysis of Alleged Monistic Evidence in the Old Testament. Vol 21, ConBOT. Lund: Liber/Gleerup, 1983.

—. "'Han bar de mångas skuld' Profetia och uppfyllelse utifrån Jes 53." *STK* 75, no. 3 (1999): 98–109.

—. Suffering and Sin: Interpretations of Illness in the Individual Complaint Psalms. Vol 37, ConBOT. Stockholm: Almquist & Wiksell International, 1994.

Lipinski, E. "שׂכל." Pages 781–801 in *ThWAT 7*. Edited by G. Johannes Botterweck and Helmer Ringgren. Stuttgart: Kohlhammer, 1993.

Lipschits, Oded. "Demographic Changes in Judah Between the Seventh and the Fifth Centuries B.C.E." Pages 323–376 in *Judah and the Judeans in the Neo-Babylonian Period*. Edited by Oded Lipschits and Joseph Blenkinsopp. Winona Lake Ind.: Eisenbrauns, 2003.

Long, Lynellyn and Ellen Oxfeld, eds. *Coming home? Refugees, Migrants, and Those Who Stayed Behind*. Philadelphia Pa.: University of Pennsylvania Press, 2004.

Lund, Øystein. "Min vei er skjult for JHWH." veimetaforikk og veitematikk i Jesaja 40–55. Oslo: Unipub AS, 2004.

Maiberger. "פגע." Pages 470–476 in *TDOT 11*. Edited by G. Johannes Botterweck and Helmer Ringgren. Grand Rapids, Mich.: Eerdmans, 2001.

Markschies, Christopher. "Jesus Christ as a Man before God: Two Interpretive Models for Isaiah 53 in the Patristic Literature and Theire Development." Pages 225–323 in *The Suffering Servant: Isaiah 53 in Jewish and Christian Sources*. Edited by Peter Stuhlmacher and Bernd Janowski. Grand Rapids, Mich.: Eerdmans, 2004.

Marti, Karl. *Das Buch Jesaja*. Edited by KHC. Vol 10. Tübingen: J. C. B. Mohr (Paul Siebeck), 1900.

Matheus, Frank. *Singt dem Herrn ein neues Lied: die Hymnen Deuterojesajas*. Vol 141, SBS. Stuttgart: Katholisches Bibelwerk, 1990.

McKenzie, John L. *Second Isaiah*. 1. ed, The Anchor Bible, 20. Garden City, N.Y.: Doubleday, 1968.

Melugin, Roy F. *The Formation of Isaiah 40–55*. Vol 141, BZAW. Berlin: de Gruyter, 1976.

—. "On Reading Isaiah 53 as Christina Scripture." Pages 55–69 in *Jesus and the Suffering Servant: Isaiah 53 and Christian Origins*. Edited by William R. Farmer and William H. Bellinger. Harrisburg, Pa.: Trinity Press, 1998.

Merendino, Rosario Pius. "Jes 49:1-6: Ein Gotteskenchtlied?" *ZAW* 92 (1980): 236–248.

Mettinger, Tryggve N. D. "The Elimination of a Crux: A Syntactic and Semantic Study of Isaiah 40:18–20." Pages 77–83 in *Studies on Prophecy: A Collection of Twelve Papers*. *VTSup*. Leiden: Brill, 1974.

—. *A Farewell to the Servant Songs: A Critical Examination of an Exegetical Axiom*. Vol 3, Scripta minora Regiae Societatis humaniorum litterarum Lundensis. Lund: Liber/Gleerup, 1983.

—. "In Search of the Hidden Structure: YHWH as King in Isaiah 40–55." Pages 143–154 in *Writing and Reading the Scroll of Isaiah: Studies of an Interpretive Tradition*. Edited by Craig A. Evans and Craig C. Broyles. *VTsup*. Leiden: Brill, 1997.

Milgrom, Jacob. Leviticus 1–16: A New Translation with Introduction and Commentary. 1. ed. Vol 3, AB. New York: Doubleday, 1991.

Miller, James Maxwell and John Haralson Hayes. *A History of Ancient Israel and Judah*, OTL. London: SCM Press, 1986.

Mowinckel, Sigmund. "Der Knecht Jahwäs." *Norsk Teologisk Tidsskrift* (1921): 1–69.

—. *He that cometh*. Oxford: Blackwell, 1956.

Nielsen, Kirsten. Bilderna och ordet: Om Herrens tjänare och andra bilder i Gamla testamentet. Örebro: Libris, 1998.

—. "'From Oracles to Canon'--and the Role of Metaphor." *SJOT* 17, no. 1 (2003): 22–33.

—. There is Hope for a Tree: The Tree as Metaphor in Isaiah. Vol 65, JSOTSup. Sheffield: JSOT Press, 1989.

Norén, Lars. *Krig*: Copy of an Unpublished Play at Dramaten Stockholm, 2004.

North, C. R. *Isaiah 40–55*. 2 ed, TBC. London: SCM Press, 1964.

North, Christopher R. The Suffering Servant in Deutero-Isaiah: An Historical and Critical Study. 2 ed. London: Oxford University Press, 1956.
Noth, Martin. *Exodus: A Commentary*, OTL. London: SCM Press, 1966.
Nyberg, H. S. "Smärtornas man: En studie till Jes. 52,13-53,12." *SEÅ* 7 (1942): 5–82.
O'Connell, Robert H. *Concentricity and Continuity: The Literary Structures of Isaiah.* Vol 188, JSOTsup. Sheffield: Sheffield Academic Press, 1994.
Oded, B. "Where is the 'Myth of the Empty Land' to be Found? History versus Myth." Pages 55–74 in *Judah and the Judeans in the Neo-Babylonian Period.* Edited by Oded Lipschits and Joseph Blenkinsopp. Winona Lake Ind.: Eisenbrauns, 2003.
Oorschot, Jürgen, van. Von Babel zum Zion: Eine literarkritische und redaktionsgeschichtliche Untersuchung. Vol 206, BZAW. Berlin: de Gruyter, 1993.
Orlinsky, Harry M. "The So-Called Servant of the Lord and Suffering Servant in Second Isaiah." in *Studies on the Second Part of the Book of Isaiah.* Edited by Harry M. Orlinsky and Norman H. Snaith. *VTsup*. Leiden: Brill, 1967.
Oswalt, John N. *The Book of Isaiah: Chapters 40–66*, NICOT. Grand Rapids, Mich.: Eerdman, 1998.
Pannenberg, Wolfhart. *Systematic Theology*. Vol 2. Edinburgh; Grand Rapids Mich.: T&T Clark; Eerdmans, 1994.
Parsons, Mikeal C. "Isaiah 53 and Acts 8: A Reply to Professor Morna Hooker." Pages 104–119 in *Jesus and the Suffering Servant: Isaiah 53 and Christian Origins*. Edited by William R. Farmer and William H. Bellinger. Harrisburg, Pa.: Trinity Press, 1998.
Phillips, Anthony. "'Double for all her Sins'." *ZAW* 94 (1982): 130–132.
Pilkington, Hilary. Migration, Displacement and Identity in Post-Soviet Russia. London; New York: Routledge, 1998.
Pohlmann, Karl-Friedrich. *Der Prophet Hesekiel (Ezechiel) Kapitel 20-48*. Vol 22,2, ATD. Göttingen: Vanderhoeck & Ruprecht, 2001.
—. Ezechielstudien: Zur Redaktionsgeschichte des Buches und zur Frage nach den ältesten Texten. Vol 202, BZAW. Berlin: de Gruyter, 1992.
Polliack, Meira. "Deutero-Isaiah's Typological use of Jacob in the Portrayal of Israel's National Renewal." Pages 72–110 in *Creation in Jewish and Christian Tradition*. Edited by Henning Graf Reventlow and Yair Hoffman. *JSOTsup*. London: Sheffield Academic Press, 2002.
Raabe, Paul R. "The Effect of Repetition in the Suffering Servant Song." *JBL* 103, no. 1 (1984): 77–81.
Rad, Gerhard von. "כפלים in jes 40:2 = Äquivalent." *ZAW* 79, no. 1 (1967): 80–82.
Rendtorff, Rolf. *Leviticus 1,1-10,20*. Vol 3/1, BKAT. Neukirchen-Vluyn: Neukirchener Verlag, 2004.
Reventlow, Henning Graf. *Gebet im Alten Testament*. Stuttgart: Kohlhammer, 1986.
Reventlow, Henning Graf. "Basic Issues in the Interpretation of Isaiah 53." Pages 23–38 in *Jesus and the Suffering Servant: Isaiah 53 and Christian Origins*. Edited by William R. Farmer and William H. Bellinger. Harrisburg, Pa.: Trinity Press, 1998.
Ricoeur, Paul. *The Rule of Metaphor: The Creation of Meaning in Language*, Routledge Classics. London: Routledge, 2003.
Rignell, Lars G. "Isa. LII 13-LIII 12." *VT* 3 (1953): 87–92.
Roth, W. M. "The Anonymity of the Suffering Servant." *JBL* 83, no. 2 (1964): 171–179.
Rudman, Dominic. "A Note on the Azazel-goat Ritual." *ZAW* 116, no. 3 (2004): 396–401.
Rudnig, Thilo Alexander. *Heilig und Profan: Redaktionskritische Studien zu Ez 40-48*. Vol 287, BZAW. Berlin: de Gruyter, 2000.
Sæbø, M. "עשׂר." Pages 446–452 in *ThWAT 6*. Edited by G. Johannes Botterweck and Helmer Ringgren. Stuttgart: Kohlhammer, 1989.

Sauter, Gerhard. "Reconciliation." Pages 504–506 in *The Encyclopedia of Christianity 4 P-Sh*. Edited by Erwin Fahlbusch. Grand Rapids, Mich.; Leiden: Eerdmans; Brill, 2005.

Sawyer, John F. A. "Daughter of Zion and Servant of the Lord in Isaiah: A Comparison." *JSOT* 44 (1989): 89–107.

Scharbert, Josef. *Heilsmittler im Alten Testament und im alten Orient*. Vol 23/24, QD. Freiburg im Breisgau: Herder, 1964.

Scheuer, Blazenka. *The Return of YHWH: The Tension between Deliverance and Repentance in Isaiah 40–55*. Lund: Centre for Theology and Religious Studies Lund University, 2005.

Schmidt, Ludwig. *Numeri 10,11-36,13*. Vol 7/2, ATD. Göttingen: Vandenhoeck & Ruprecht, 2004.

Schoors, Antoon. I am God your Saviour: A Form-Critical Study of the main Genres in Is. XL-LV. Vol 24, VTsup. Leiden: Brill, 1973.

Schwartz, Baruch J. "The Bearing of Sin in the Priestly Literature." Pages 3–21 in Pomegranates and Golden Bells: Studies in Biblical, Jewish, and Near Eastern Ritual, Law and Literature in Honor of Jacob Milgrom. Edited by David P. Wright, David Noel Freedman, andAvi Hurvitz. Winona Lake Ind.: Eisenbrauns, 1995.

Seebass, Horst. *Numeri 22,2-26,65*. Vol 4/3 2, BKAT. Neukirchen: Neukirchener Verlag, 2005.

Skinner, J. *The Book of the Prophet Isaiah: Chapters XL-LXVI*. Cambridge: Cambridge University Press, 1929.

Smith-Christopher, Daniel. *A Biblical Theology of Exile*, Overtures to Biblical Theology. Minneapolis, Minn.: Fortress Press, 2002.

Smith, Daniel L. The Religion of the Landless: A Sociology of the Babylonian Exile. Bloomington Ind.: Meyer-Stone Books, 1986.

Smith, Mark S. The Origins of Biblical Monotheism: Israel's Polytheistic Background and the Ugaritic Texts. Oxford: Oxford University Press, 2001.

Sommer, Benjamin D. *A Prophet Reads Scripture: Allusion in Isaiah 40–66*, Contraversions. Stanford, Calif.: Stanford University Press, 1998.

Spieckermann, Hermann. *Heilsgegenwart: Eine Theologie der Psalmen*. Vol 148, FRLANT. Göttingen: Vandenhoeck & Rupricht, 1989.

—. "The Conception and Prehistory of the Idea of Vicarious Suffering in the Old Testament." Pages 1–15 in *The Suffering Servant: Isaiah 53 in Jewish and Christian sources*. Edited by Bernd Janowski and Peter Stuhlmacher. Grand Rapids, Mich.; Cambridge: Eerdmans, 2004.

Starke, Christoph. Synopsis bibliothecae exegeticae in Vetus Testamentum Kurzgefasster Auszug der grundlichsten nutzbarsten Auslegungen uber alle Bucher Altes Testamentes. 2 ed. Vol 5. Leipzig, 1766.

Steck, Odil Hannes. Bereitete Heimkehr: Jesaja 35 als redaktionelle Brücke zwischen dem Ersten und dem Zweiten Jesaja. Vol 121, SBS. Stuttgart: Katolisches Bibelwerk, 1985.

—. Gottesknecht und Zion: Gesammelte Aufsätze zu Deuterojesaja. Vol 4, FAT. Tübingen: Mohr Siebeck, 1992.

—. *Old Testament Exegesis: A Guide to the Methodology*. 2. ed. Vol 39, Resources for Biblical Study. Atlanta, Ga.: Scholars Press, 1998.

Stefansson, Anders H. "Refugee Returns to Sarajevo and their Challenge to Contemporary Narratives of Mobility." Pages 170–186 in *Coming home? Refugees, Migrants, and Those Who Stayed Behind*. Edited by Lynellyn Long and Ellen Oxfeld. Philadelphia, Pa.: University of Pennsylvania Press, 2004a.

—. “Sarajevo Suffering: Homecoming and the Hierarchy of Homeland Hardship.” Pages 54–76 in *Homecomings: Unsettling Paths of Return*. Edited by Fran Markowitz and Anders H. Stefansson. Lanham, Md.: Lexington Books, 2004b.
Strömberg Krantz, Eva. "The Commentary of the Hebraist on Isaiah. pp. 142–151." Pages. Edited by The National Archives of Sweden: The Swedish Bible Commission's Deposit at the Regional Archives in Uppsala.
Stuhlmacher, Peter. “Isaiah 53 in the Gospels and Acts.” Pages 147–162 in *The Suffering Servant: Isaiah 53 in Jewish and Christian Sources*. Edited by Peter Stuhlmacher and Bernd Janowski. Grand Rapids, Mich.: Eerdmans, 2004.
Stuhlmueller, Caroll. “Deutero-Isaiah: Major Transitions in the Prophet’s Theology and in Contemporary Scholarship.” *CBQ* 42 (1980): 1–29.
Sweeney, Marvin A. *Isaiah 1–39: With an Introduction to Prophetic Literature*. Vol 16, FOTL. Grand Rapids Mich.: Eerdmans, 1996.
Tollefsen Altamirano, Aina. Seasons of Migrations to the North: A Study of Biographies and Narrative Identities in US-Mexican and Swedish-Chilean Return Movements. Vol 2000:3, GERUM Kulturgeografi. Umeå: Umeå Universitet, 2000.
Torrey, Charles Cutler. *The Second Isaiah: A New Interpretation*. Edingburgh: T&T Clark, 1928.
Tsuda, Takeyuki. “When Home Is Not the Homeland: The Case of Japanese Brazilian Ethnic Return Migration.” Pages 125–145 in *Homecomings: Unsettling Paths of Return*. Edited by Fran Markowitz and Anders H. Stefansson. Lanham, Md.: Lexington Books, 2004.
Uehling, Greta. “Sitting on Suitcases: Ambivalence and Ambiguity in the Migration Intentions of Crimean Tatar Women.” *Journal of Refugee Studies* 15, no. 4 (2002): 388–408.
Vanderhooft, David Stephen. *The Neo-Babylonian Empire and Babylon in the Latter Prophets*. Vol 59, MSM. Atlanta, Ga.: Scholars Press, 1999.
Washington, Harold C. “Israels Holy Seed and the Foreign Women of Ezra-Nehemiah: A Kristevan Reading.” *BibInt* 11, no. 3 (2003): 427–438.
Vattimo, Gianni. *Belief*. Stanford, Calif.: Stanford University Press, 1999.
Watts, Rikki E. “Jesus' Death, Isaiah 53, and Mark 10:45: A Crux Revisited.” Pages 125–151 in *Jesus and the Suffering Servant: Isaiah 53 and Christian Origins*. Edited by William R. Farmer and William H. Bellinger. Harrisburg, Pa.: Trinity Press, 1998.
Wellhausen, Julius. Prolegomena to the History of Ancient Israel: With a Reprint of the Article Israel from the Encyclopaedia Britannica. New York: Meridian, 1957.
Werlitz, Jürgen. Redaktion und Komposition: Zur Rückfrage hinter die Endgestalt von Jesaja 40-55. Vol 122, BBB. Berlin: Philo, 1999.
—. “Vom Knecht der Lieder zum Knecht des Buches: Ein versuch über die Ergänzungen zu den Gottesknechtstexten des Deuterojesajabuches.” *ZAW* 109 (1997): 30–43.
Westermann, Claus. *Isaiah 40–66: A Commentary*, OTL. Philadelphia Pa.: Westminster Press, 1969.
—. Sprache und Struktur der Prophetie Deuterojesajas. Stuttgart: Calwer, 1981.
Whybray, Roger Norman. “A Farewell to the Servant Songs.” *JBL* 104, no. 4 (1985): 706–707.
—. *Isaiah 40–66*, NCB. London: Oliphants, 1975.
—. *The Second Isaiah*, OTG. Sheffield: Sheffield Academic Press, 1983.
—. Thanksgiving for a Liberated Prophet: An Interpretation of Isaiah Chapter 53. Vol 4, JSOTsup. Sheffield: JSOT Press, 1978.
Vieweger, Dieter and Annette Böckler. “‘Ich gebe Ägypten als Lösegeld für dich’: Mk 10,45 und die Jüdische Tradition zu Jes 43b.4.” *ZAW* 108 (1996): 494–607.

Wilcox, Peter and David Paton-Williams. "The Servant Songs in Deutero-Isaiah." *JSOT* 42 (1988): 79–102.

Wildberger, Hans. *Jesaja 1-12*. Vol 10/1, BKAT. Neukirchen-Vluyn: Neukirchener Verlag, 1980.

Williamson, Hugh Godfrey Maturin. The Book Called Isaiah: Deutero-Isaiah's Role in Composition and Redaction. Oxford: Clarendon Press, 1994.

—. Isaiah 1–5: A Critical and Exegetical Commentary, ICC. London: T&T Clark, 2006.

—. "Isaiah 6,13 and 1,29–31." Pages 119–128 in *Studies in the Book of Isaiah: Festschrift Willem A.M. Beuken*. Edited by J. van Ruiten and Marc Vervenne. *BETL*. Leuven; Paris: Leuven Univinersity Press; Peeters France, 1997.

Wilshire, Leland Edward. "The Servant-City: A New Interpretation of the 'Servant of the Lord' in the Servant Songs of Deutero-Isaiah." *JBL* 94 (1975): 356–367.

Wilson, Andrew. *The Nations in Deutero-Isaiah: A Study on Composition and Structure*. Vol 1, Ancient Near Eastern Texts and Studies. Lewiston, N.Y.: Edwin Mellen Press, 1986.

Volf, Miroslav. Exclusion and Embrace: A Theological Exploration of Identity, Otherness, and Reconciliation. Nashville: Abingdon Press, 1996.

Wolff, Hans Walter. *Jesaja 53 im Urchristentum*. 3 ed. Berlin: Evangelische Verlagsanstalt, 1952.

Wright, David P. The Disposal of Impurity: Elimination Rites in the Bible and in Hittite and Mesopotamian Literature. Vol 101, SBLDS. Atlanta: Scholars Press, 1987.

Wright, David P. and Jacob Milgrom. "עצר." Pages 334–338 in *ThWAT 6*. Edited by G. Johannes Botterweck and Helmer Ringgren. Stuttgart: Kohlhammer, 1993.

Xavier de Brito, Angela and Ana Vasques. "Circe or Penelope? Latin-American Women in Exile." Pages 218–234 in *Scapegoats and Social Actors: The Exclusion and Integration of Minorities in Western and Eastern Europe*. Edited by Danièle Joly. Basingstoke: Macmillan, 1998.

Zarzosa, Helia Lopez. "Internal Exile, Exile and Return: A Gendered View." *Journal of Refugee Studies* 11, no. 2 (1998): 189–198.

Zetter, Roger. "Reconceptualizing the Myth of Return: Contuity and Transition Amongst the Greek-Cypriot Refugees of 1974." *Journal of Refugee Studies* 12, no. 1 (1999): 1–22.

Zimmerli, Walther. *Ezekiel 1: A Commentary on the Book of the Prophet Ezekiel, Chapters 1–24*, Hermeneia. Philadelphia Pa.: Fortress Press, 1979.

—. Ezekiel 2: A Commentary on the Book of the Prophet Ezekiel, Chapters 25–48, Hermeneia. Philadelphia Pa.: Fortress Press, 1983.

—. "Zur Vorgeschichte von Jes. LIII." Pages 236–244 in *Congress volume: Rome 1968*. Edited by John. A. Emerton. *VTSup*. Leiden: Brill, 1969.

Zorn, Jeffrey. "Tell en-Nasbeh and the Problem of the Material Culture of the Sixth Century." Pages 591–612 in *Judah and the Judeans in the Neo-Babylonian Period*. Edited by Oded Lipschits and Joseph Blenkinsopp. Winona Lake Ind.: Eisenbrauns, 2003.

Index of references

Author Index

Forschungen zum Alten Testament

Edited by Bernd Janowski, Mark S. Smith and Hermann Spieckermann

Alphabetical Index

Kagerer, Bernhard: see *Bodendorfer, Gerhard.*
Kakkanattu, Joy Philip: God's Enduring Love in the Book of Hosea. 2006. *Vol. II/14.*
Kiuchi, Nobuyoshi: A Study of Hata' and Hatta't in Leviticus 4–5. 2003. *Vol. II/2.*
Knierim, Rolf P.: Text and Concept in Leviticus 1:1–9. 1992. *Vol. 2.*
Köckert, Matthias: Leben in Gottes Gegenwart. 2004. *Vol. 43.*
Köhlmoos, Melanie: Das Auge Gottes. 1999. *Vol. 25.*
–: Bet-El – Erinnerungen an eine Stadt. 2006. *Vol. 49.*
Koenen, Klaus: see *Hermisson, Hans-Jürgen.*
Körting, Corinna: Zion in den Psalmen. 2006. *Vol. 48.*
Konkel, Michael: Sünde und Vergebung. 2008. *Vol. 58.*
Kratz, Reinhard Gregor: Das Judentum im Zeitalter des Zweiten Tempels. 2004. *Vol. 42.*
–: Kyros im Deuterojesaja-Buch. 1991. *Vol. 1.*
– und *Spieckermann, Hermann* (Ed.): Götterbilder – Gottesbilder – Weltbilder.
Vol. I: Ägypten, Mesopotamien, Kleinasien, Syrien, Palästina. 2006. *Vol. II/17.*
Vol. II: Griechenland und Rom, Judentum, Christentum und Islam. 2006. *Vol. II/18.*
Lange, Armin: Vom prophetischen Wort zur prophetischen Tradition. 2002. *Vol. 34.*
Levinson, Bernard M.: „The Right Chorale": Studies in Biblical Law and Interpretation. 2008. *Vol. 54.*
Liess, Kathrin: Der Weg des Lebens. 2004. *Vol. II/5.*
Lund, Øystein: Way Metaphors and Way Topics in Isaiah 40–55. 2007. *Vol. II/28.*
MacDonald, Nathan: Deuteronomy and the Meaning of ‚Monotheism'. 2003. *Vol. II/1.*
Marttila, Marko: Collective Reinterpretation in the Psalms. 2006. *Vol. II/13.*
Michel, Andreas: Gott und Gewalt gegen Kinder im Alten Testament. 2003. *Vol. 37.*
–: see *Groß, Walter.*
Millard, Matthias: Die Komposition des Psalters. 1994. *Vol. 9.*
–: see *Bodendorfer, Gerhard.*
Miller, Patrick D.: The Way of the Lord. 2004. *Vol. 39.*
Müller, Reinhard: Königtum und Gottesherrschaft. 2004. *Vol. II/3.*
Niemann, Hermann Michael: Herrschaft, Königtum und Staat. 1993. *Vol. 6.*
Nihan, Christophe: From Priestly Torah to Pentateuch. 2007. *Vol. II/25.*
Otto, Eckart: Das Deuteronomium im Pentateuch und Hexateuch. 2001. *Vol. 30.*
Perlitt, Lothar: Deuteronomium-Studien. 1994. *Vol. 8.*
Petry, Sven: Die Entgrenzung JHWHs. 2007. *Vol. II/27.*
Podella, Thomas: Das Lichtkleid JHWHs. 1996. *Vol. 15.*
Pola, Thomas: Das Priestertum bei Sacharja. 2003. *Vol. 35.*
Rösel, Martin: Adonaj – Warum Gott „Herr" genannt wird. 2000. *Vol. 29.*
Ruwe, Andreas: „Heiligkeitsgesetz" und „Priesterschrift". 1999. *Vol. 26.*
Sager, Dirk: Polyphonie des Elends. 2006. *Vol. II/21.*
Sals, Ulrike: Die Biographie der „Hure Babylon". 2004. *Vol. II/6.*
Schaper, Joachim: Priester und Leviten im achämenidischen Juda. 2000. *Vol. 31.*
Schenker, Adrian (Hrsg.): Studien zu Opfer und Kult im Alten Testament. 1992. *Vol. 3.*
Schmidt, Brian B.: Israel's Beneficent Dead. 1994. *Vol. 11.*
Schmitz, Barbara: Prophetie und Königtum. 2008. *Vol. 60.*
Schöpflin, Karin: Theologie als Biographie im Ezechielbuch. 2002. *Vol. 36.*
Seeligmann, Isac Leo: The Septuagint Version of Isaiah and Cognate Studies. Edited by Robert Hanhart and Hermann Spieckermann. 2004. *Vol. 40.*
–: Gesammelte Studien zur Hebräischen Bibel. Herausgegeben von Erhard Blum mit einem Beitrag von Rudolf Smend. 2004. *Vol. 41.*
Smith, Mark S.: God in Translation. 2008. *Vol. 57.*
Spieckermann, Hermann: Gottes Liebe zu Israel. *Vol. 33.*
–: see *Kratz, Reinhard Gregor.*

Stackert, Jeffrey: Rewriting the Torah. 2007. *Vol. 52.*
Steck, Odil Hannes: Gottesknecht und Zion. 1992. *Vol. 4.*
Stuhlmacher, Peter: see *Janowski, Bernd.*
Süssenbach, Claudia: Der elohistische Psalter. 2005. *Vol. II/7.*
Sweeney, Marvin A.: Form and Intertextuality in Prophetic and Apocalyptic Literature. 2005. *Vol. 45.*
Taschner, Johannes: Die Mosereden im Deuteronomium. 2008. *Vol. 59.*
Tiemeyer, Lena-Sofia: Priestly Rites and Prophetic Rage. 2006. *Vol. II/19.*
Turkanik, Andrzej S.: Of Kings and Reigns. 2008. *Vol. II/30.*
Vos, Christiane de: Klage als Gotteslob aus der Tiefe. 2005. *Vol. II/11.*
Weber, Cornelia: Altes Testament und völkische Frage. 2000. *Vol. 28.*
Weimar, Peter: Studien zur Priesterschrift. 2008. *Vol. 56.*
Weippert, Manfred: Jahwe und die anderen Götter. 1997. *Vol. 18.*
Weyde, Karl William: The Appointed Festivals of YHWH. 2004. Vol. II/4.
White, Marsha C.: see *Ehrlich, Carl S.*
Widmer, Michael: Moses, God, and the Dynamics of Intercessory Prayer. 2004. *Vol. II/8.*
Wilke, Alexa F.: Kronerben der Weisheit. 2006. *Vol. II/20.*
Willi, Thomas: Juda – Jehud – Israel. 1995. *Vol. 12.*
Williamson, Hugh: Studies in Persian Period History and Historiography. 2004. *Vol. 38.*
Wilson, Kevin A.: The Campaign of Pharaoh Shoshenq I into Palestine. 2005. *Vol. II/9.*
Young, Ian: Diversity in Pre-Exilic Hebrew. 1993. *Vol. 5.*
Zwickel, Wolfgang: Der Tempelkult in Kanaan und Israel. 1994. *Vol. 10.*

For a complete catalogue please write to the publisher
Mohr Siebeck • P.O. Box 2030 • D-72010 Tübingen/Germany
Up-to-date information on the internet at www.mohr.de